THE CANALS OF
NORTH WEST ENGLAND

VOLUME I

THE CANALS OF THE BRITISH ISLES

EDITED BY CHARLES HADFIELD

THE CANALS OF
NORTH WEST ENGLAND

by
Charles Hadfield
and Gordon Biddle

WITH PLATES AND MAPS

VOLUME I

DAVID & CHARLES: NEWTON ABBOT

ISBN 0 7153 4956 2

Printed in Great Britain by
Latimer Trend & Company Limited Plymouth
for David & Charles (Publishers) Limited
South Devon House   Newton Abbot   Devon

CONTENTS

Volume I

ILLUSTRATIONS

VOLUME I

PLATES

TEXT ILLUSTRATIONS AND MAPS

PREFACE

THIS has been a most interesting, though not an easy, book to write. Not easy, because of the absence of minute books for some important waterways: the Mersey & Irwell before 1779, the Bridgewater, the Sankey Brook and, except for one odd volume, the Ashton-under-Lyne Canal, However, we have been greatly helped by the work of Mr V. I. Tomlinson on the Bridgewater and Manchester, Bolton & Bury Canals, Mr Frank Mullineux on the Bridgewater, Professor T. S. Barker and Dr J. R. Harris on the Sankey Brook, and Professor T. S. Willan on the Weaver.

There is one major omission, the Manchester Ship Canal. It could not be included in a book whose balance is weighted towards the period of the Industrial Revolution without making it both top-heavy and inordinately long. The Ship Canal has, however, a chapter in *British Canals*, the introductory volume of this series, and for the rest must await an historian who will bring Sir Bosdin Leech's great work up to date.

We have collaborated happily: Gordon Biddle has written Chapters III, VII, VIII, XVI and XVII, Charles Hadfield the remainder.

Because of coming decimalization, figures have been rounded up to the nearest pound when the shillings and pence element is unimportant. In other cases, except within a quotation, the decimal equivalent of 6d, and of sums of 1s and over, is given in brackets.

To write such a book as this is both a labour and a pleasure. The labour has been lightened by the help and forbearance of our wives and families and the efficiency of Charles Hadfield's secretaries, Mrs Whittaker and later Mrs Tomlinson, who have typed and retyped successive drafts. The pleasure comes from the help we have so generously received, from old friendships renewed and new ones made.

CHARLES HADFIELD
GORDON BIDDLE

PART ONE—TO 1790

CHAPTER I

Old Quay and New Canal

++++++++++++++++++++++++++++++++++ ✦ ++++++++++++++++++++++++++++++++++

THE waterway history of the north-west begins with Thomas
Steers, engineer and businessman. Steers,[1] born in 1672, started
in the army, probably learned engineering from George Sorocold,[2]
in 1715 completed Liverpool's first dock, was appointed dock-
master in 1716, and by 1718 had reclaimed land round it for
building. He was concerned with three early river navigations in
the area, the Mersey & Irwell, the Weaver and the Douglas.

Upwards from Liverpool the Mersey estuary broadens past
Ellesmere Port, narrows sharply at Runcorn Gap, then widens a
little before contracting to a recognizably small river past Warrington until it loses itself in the ship canal to near Irlam, whence that
great work follows the line of its tributary the Irwell into Manchester. A Bill to make the Mersey and Irwell navigable to
Manchester had been introduced in the 1660s, but failed to pass.[3]
Late in the seventeenth century Thomas Patten, merchant of
Warrington, cleared fish-weirs[4] from the Mersey to that town, after
which, he said in 1698, 'there have been sent to Liverpool and
from Liverpool 2,000 tons of Goods a year'. He wanted to continue the good work, 'for the River to Manchester is very capable
of being made Navigable at a very small charge. And this would
encourage all tradesmen . . . to come to Liverpool and buy their
goods, instead of going to Chester, Bristol, or London'.[5]

Cheaper local transport was needed. John Moss, giving evidence
on the Bill of 1721, said that 'the Land-carriage betwixt Manchester
and Liverpool doth amount to about Fifteen hundred Pounds per
Annum'[6] with consequent heavy road repair bills. But this journey
was also part of the route to Hull. In 1701 Patten himself was send-
ing tobacco by cart from Bank Quay, Warrington, the navigation
limit, to Stockport, thence by packhorse to Doncaster, and so by
water to Hull;[7] in 1712 Steers wrote that such a work 'might . . . be
of the greatest importance in time of War, in Joyning a communica-

15

tion of the East and West Seas . . . with only 28 Miles of Land Cariage';[8] and while the Bill was in Parliament, supporters argued that it would open a communication to Wakefield and Leeds and shorten the present land carriage by half, and were backed by Wakefield traders.

In 1712 Steers' proposals to make the Mersey and Irwell navigable by building eight locks and making a cut at Butchersfield were published in map form, but action had to wait for a favourable financial climate and also, we may think, for the result of another of Steers' enterprises. The Douglas Navigation, intended to carry coal from the Wigan area to the Ribble estuary for coasting flats,* which he had also surveyed in 1712, was authorized in 1720 (see Chapter III) with Steers as a principal promoter.

Once the Douglas Act was through, Bills were introduced for the Weaver and the Mersey & Irwell. Coal was essential to the former scheme, for it was needed to make salt, and it is not surprising therefore that Steers was called to give evidence. Coal and cannel† were also the first two commodities mentioned in the preamble to the Mersey & Irwell Bill. This named 38 promoters; two were justices, 33 Manchester men from most of the leading business families, and three, including Thomas Steers once more, from Liverpool.[9] The drive had come from Manchester, but we may think that Steers provided the skill and the Douglas Act an important incentive.

The Mersey & Irwell Act[10] was passed on 17 June 1721, authorizing the promoters to make the rivers navigable with locks, cuts and a towpath from Bank Quay, Warrington, to Hunt's Bank, where the town of Manchester stood above the Irwell's high rocky bank to the south-east, and Salford on the lower and inner side of the curve to the north-west. A toll of 3s 4d (16½p) a ton was granted for the use of the whole or any part of the navigation (a charge that was to remain unaltered for a century and a half), except on dung, marl and manure to be used on lands within five miles of the rivers.

Perhaps because the Act had been passed in the aftermath of the South Sea Bubble, and because little had happened on the Douglas, a start was not made until February 1724, when seven managers were appointed to get the work done, and share certificates issued.[11] In 1728 it was said that the enterprise 'hath gained a considerable

---

* The local name for the sailing vessels of the time, afterwards extensively used on the Mersey & Irwell and the Weaver.

† A particularly rich coal (hence 'candle' or cannel coal) found near Wigan. The word is often thought to be derived from 'canal', but this is not so.

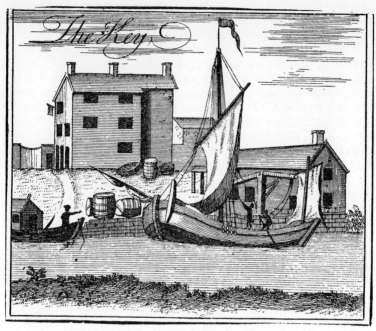

The Key,

1. Manchester Quay, from Casson & Berry's map, 1741

progress',[12] and by 1734 the navigation was open after a fashion, for two small landing places had been made on the Manchester side of the Irwell, John Moss's* small open wharf leading up to Black-friars, and the Rock House, with a warehouse into which goods could be taken directly from the boats.[13] They were followed in 1736 by a wharf and warehouses at Bank Quay, run by a group of Mersey & Irwell men, and wharves also at Atherton's Quay (below Bank Quay) and Great Sankey Quay, probably that at Sankey Bridges[14] (see p. 43). The work was probably completed in 1736. A deed of 7 August 1736[15] concerning Bank Quay says: 'whereas the said navigation is entirely or very nearly perfected'. Later, about 1739, an unknown author wrote: 'the work is now finished and boats pass and repass upon the river with large quantities of goods from Warrington and Liverpool, but the profits are as yet but small'.[16] By 1740 the company had built a big open quay and ware-

---

* He was one of the managers.

B

houses at the end of Quay Street, Manchester, ¾-mile below Hunt's
Bank and outside the town as it was then. This became until 1840
the upper limit of the navigation.

When the work was almost done, probably in 1736, the company,
despairing of action on the Douglas, with the consent of Scroop,
first Duke of Bridgewater, proposed to make the Worsley Brook
navigable from the Irwell up a 40-ft rise to Worsley with a canal
onwards to Booth's Bank, in order that coal could be carried to
Manchester.[17] Thomas Steers did the survey, and an Act[18] was
passed in 1737. It enabled the Brook to be made navigable for two
miles to the Irwell and granted the undertakers a toll of 9d a ton,
but no action resulted, perhaps because the re-starting of work on
the Douglas in 1738 promised a cheaper alternative, probably
because the main concern was not doing well and had been
diminished by the deaths of two of its leaders.[19] Confirmation that
action on the Worsley Brook was taken by the Mersey & Irwell
company itself comes from a minute of 1783, made when they sold
the lease of a stone quarry at Tyldesley: 'the Reason of obtaining it
(which was in prospect of making Worsley Brook navigable)
having now ceased . . .'.[20]

Eight locks had been built: from Manchester, at Throstle Nest,
Mode Wheel, Barton, Stickings, Holmes Bridge, Calamanco,
Hollins Ferry (Partington), and Howley, a little above Warrington;
and before 1761 two substantial cuts had been made, the old
Woolston, with Woolston (Powder Mill) lock at its lower end, and
Howley. Hugh Oldham's map of that year[21] shows these, and
marks Butchersfield as 'Intended to be cut. The land is agreed for'.
Flats were sailed when possible, and otherwise seem to have been
bow-hauled by men, at any rate to 1760.[22] By about the same date
£41 had been called on each of the 500 shares, though some had
been forfeited, so that actual expenditure had been about £18,000.
Trade, which had to be carried on mainly when spring tides gave
enough water between Runcorn and Warrington, was slow to
grow, and later the proprietors were to say that they had made no
profit between 1724 and 1749.[23]

Industrial, and especially colliery, growth north of the Mersey
led to an Act[24] of 1753 to improve roads in the Salford-St Helens-
Warrington and Worsley-Wigan-Chorley-Bolton areas. The
guardians of the third Duke of Bridgewater, who had been born in
1736 and succeeded to the title in 1748, included two business-like
men, Lord Trentham (who in 1754 became the second Earl Gower),
and the Duke of Bedford. They approved of the road Bill, pre-

sumably seeing a better road to Salford as useful to the Duke's Worsley mines, but there were other reactions to its passing.

The Mersey & Irwell was at last succeeding, and a newspaper note of 1753 gives an impression of solidity:

'On Friday last was launch'd at our Key, a new vessel called the *Smith*. Tis said, the Proprietors intend to build some more, as the Navigation is considerably increased within these late Years'.[25]

But they foresaw greater competition from improved roads, and in the same year advertised their carrying charges, inclusive of tolls, as: Manchester to Bank Quay, 6s 8d (33½p) a ton; Bank Quay to Manchester, 10s (50p) in summer and 11s 8d (58½p) in winter.[26]

The road Act also caused colliery owners to encourage canal building. Further west the Sankey Brook Navigation (see Chapter II) was begun, and in the Worsley-Wigan area a move was made by a Manchester-based group, almost certainly supported by the Mersey & Irwell, to promote a level canal from Salford by Eccles, Worsley and Leigh to within half a mile of Wigan, which at that time had water transport only by the Douglas to the sea. It was surveyed by William Taylor, who was soon to work with Henry Berry on the Sankey Brook. Water was to be taken from the Irwell, but returned to the navigable part.

The promoters' petition said that Manchester consumed great quantities of coal and fuel, which were brought 'several Miles, by Land Carriage, at great Expence'. Samuel Horridge, supporting, told the Commons committee that 'no Coals are used in Manchester, but what must be brought Four Miles, and some 10 Miles; the Carriage whereof is a greater Expence than the prime Cost of the Coals'. Wigan, Leigh, the Duke's guardians, and groups of business men in Manchester and Salford supported the Bill, but it was intemperately opposed by other Manchester interests, as well as by landowners and road trustees, and failed.[27] When the Duke was promoting his 1759 Bill, he showed how closely he had studied its predecessor of 1753-4 when he said it had been lost because water was to be taken from the Irwell above Manchester, which

'would have impaired the Stream of the River flowing between the Towns of Manchester and Salford whereby the Health and Conveniency of the Town might have been materially affected. That the Powers in the Act for making Mills, Warehouses and Conveniences gave an alarm to the Traders that it might be a Means of diverting the Trade out of its present Chanel and give the Undertakers some Advantages tho' desirable to themselves yet injurious to the General Good of the Town. And that it was not stipulated or ascertained at what Prices the Town should be supplyed with Coals nor what Quantities would be brought up and delivered'.[28]

Fear of monopoly may have been a motive in the establishment of a Liverpool-based carrying and warehousing concern, the Salford Quay Company. It was based on land bought where the towpath ended, about 200 yd above the Mersey & Irwell's Manchester Quay on the opposite side of the river. Here a wharf, warehouse and street were built, more land being added in 1760. From about this time the Mersey & Irwell was known as the Old Quay Company.

John Gilbert was the Duke's agent at Worsley, his brother Thomas agent of the Duke's guardian, Earl Gower. John had introduced James Brindley, millwright and engineer, to the Earl, who in 1758 employed him to survey for a canal from Wilden Ferry on the Trent to Stoke.[29] Lord Gower and the Gilberts were businessmen, concerned with industrial development not only round Worsley but in Staffordshire and Shropshire, and it is not surprising that their enthusiasm should have rubbed off on the unhappily brought up young Duke,[30] or that they should have been dissatisfied with road charges of 9s (45p) to 10s (50p) a ton for coal carried to the growing towns of Manchester[31] and Salford, with their combined populations of about 20,000.

The story of the Duke sounding the Mersey & Irwell company upon what tolls they would charge were he to revive something like the 1737 Worsley Brook scheme, and being told that they would want their full toll of 3s 4d (16½p), comes from an uncorroborated and hostile source,[32] and seems unlikely. He was conversant with Earl Gower's Staffordshire canal ideas, the progress of the Sankey Brook Canal, part of which had been opened in November 1757, and the old canal scheme of 1753–4. It therefore seems more likely that he contemplated an all-canal route to Manchester from the start, and with John Gilbert's help prepared for it.

In 1758 Francis Reynolds of Strangeways wrote to Edward Chetham:

'The Duke of Bridgewater is come into the Country to visit his Estate of Worsley, and does me the honor to take up his quarters with me . . . his Grace has found so large a Mine of Coal, for which he has so small a consumption, that he is inclinable to make a Water road from Worsley mill to Salford, at his own expence, by which means he will be able to supply Manchester with any quantity at a much cheaper rate'.[33]

His plan was for a level canal from Worsley by Patricroft to a point above and near Salford quay. In 1759 he bought 14 acres of land between what is now Irwell Street and Ordsall Lane, which may have been intended as a terminus, with access by road to the town, and with the possibility of joining the river through two locks, though there is no evidence that this was intended.

The Duke prepared a Bill and sought landowners' consents. Mrs Chetham's land would be badly cut up, but her solicitor wrote early in 1759:

'The Land owners who are willing to join Mrs Chetham in an opposition to the ... Navigacon Bill are now so few and terrified with the prospect of Expence & hazard of Success that I foresee she will be left almost alone therein. But she is unwilling to stand in that Light, & I don't find that the Navigators* or any others will come in as auxiliaries'. A little later he wrote that 'the bill is pushed on with unusual speed', and mentioned that printed copies were only available after second reading.[34]

In the circular letter the Duke sent round to those interested, he met the criticisms that had been made of the 1753–4 scheme: he said that he would make the canal at his own cost within three years, supply it with water from Worsley Brook, and deliver coal at Manchester throughout the year 'on much easier Terms than the same are or can be done by Land Carriage', and promised to state terms and prices for coal before going to Parliament. He went on to agree that his canal would carry goods and merchandise at reasonable tolls, and 'Lime, Muck and Manure' free.[35] It was clear that the Duke was determined that his Bill should not fail, as had that of six years before.

Here we face two puzzles: the inclusion in the Bill and subsequent Act of powers to build a second canal from Worsley to Hollins Ferry on the Mersey & Irwell Navigation about six miles below Barton; and the lack of opposition from the Mersey & Irwell company. The canal was inherently improbable, because it would carry coal towards the Warrington-Weaver area already being supplied from the much more accessible collieries on the Sankey Brook, and because its success would depend upon the Mersey & Irwell's agreement to specially low tolls. One might guess that an understanding had been reached between the Duke and the Mersey & Irwell, who had long sought for a source of coal

* The Mersey & Irwell Company.

supply to their navigation, whereby the latter would not oppose the Bill in expectation of benefits to come from participating in a coal trade at Hollins Ferry. If such an agreement indeed existed, we may wonder whether the Duke had had reservations when making it.

For whatever reason, there was no Parliamentary opposition, and the Act[36] was passed on 23 March 1759. Like those for the Mersey & Irwell and the Sankey Brook, it authorized a maximum toll only, in this case 2s 6d (12½p), proportionately much higher than either of the others, and also wharfage charges for goods left more than 24 hours, a right which was later considerably to help the Duke's finances, and a maximum retail price for coal sold to local inhabitants of Manchester of 4d* against the alleged current price of 5½d a cwt, to be maintained for forty years. A week later the Duke gave a ball, perhaps to celebrate the Act or perhaps to say farewell to Elizabeth Gunning,† and then left London to concern himself with canal building, and to buy more land in and around Worsley.

Construction now began, with John Gilbert in charge and James Brindley brought in on 1 July. By the year's end nearly two miles of canal had been built from Worsley towards Patricroft, and rather over two miles of the Hollins Ferry route,‡ as well as some 150 yd of the underground colliery canal the Duke was at the same time driving into the hill north of Worsley. But about October 1759 the Duke decided to change the canal line onwards from Patricroft so that, instead of keeping north of the Irwell to his proposed terminus at Salford, it would cross the river on an aqueduct at Barton and then turn north at Stretford to end at Dolefield, a destination later changed to Castlefield. From Stretford a branch would run south-west for half a mile to Longford bridge.

Mr Tomlinson[38] discusses fully the Duke's probable motives for the change. Maybe he realized that his coal was not going to compete successfully with that from the Sankey, and therefore the Hollins Ferry line was a mistake. Instead, he now saw fresh markets

* According to Mally,[37] he raised this to 4½d in 1793, six years before he was legally entitled to do so.

† The widowed Duchess of Hamilton, to whom he had been engaged.

‡ As far as Botany Bay wood east of Eccles. This remained in use into the nineteenth century to boat waste from the mines for land improvement. Light tramroads were laid to help distribute this, after which the land was farmed or afforested. A branch from it, 1,614 yd long, was cut between 1799 and 1803. A separate short branch, also served by tramroads, to carry moss from Chat Moss, is shown on a map of 1785.

in Cheshire,* to reach which, as well as supply Manchester, his canal must cross the Irwell and run by Stretford. Maybe also he thought that it would be a first step which, once safely taken, would help him later to reach Liverpool independent of the Mersey & Irwell and develop a market there.

It is also possible to surmise, with Mr Tomlinson, that the Duke had never intended to carry out the 1759 Act, but had used it as a blind to avoid opposition and to conceal from the Mersey & Irwell his intention to by-pass the whole river line and seek a Liverpool as well as a Cheshire trade. Perhaps, again, the possibility worked in his mind that if he extended his canal, he could link up later with that projected by Earl Gower in 1758 from the Trent to Stoke, on which Brindley was working at the time he was building the line to Patricroft, and which had obvious possibilities of extension to the Mersey. Certainly his motives must have been strong, for the engineering problems of the changed route were formidable: the embankment north of the Irwell, the aqueduct across it, the canal over Trafford Moss, and the basin in Manchester.

Probably the Mersey & Irwell company now realized their danger, and made their offer of access to their navigation for 6d (2½p) a ton 'as an inducement to him to communicate his canal with their river',[40] but again this offer is unconfirmed from a neutral source.

The Act[41] was passed on 24 March 1760, and though it altered the line, it transferred the Duke's powers, privileges and penalties from that of 1759. Mr Tomlinson submits evidence[42] that the Duke then tried to get rid of copies of the earlier Act so that people would not know what these really were. An interesting pair of clauses[43] halve turnpike tolls on the Stretford–Manchester road on carts carrying coal off the canal, abolish them completely for carts having 9-in wheels, and enable the Duke to compound for all road tolls for coal carts.

Work then continued on the line to Manchester and the canal into the mines at Worsley, while the Duke planned his next move towards Liverpool. Great interest was taken in his activities. Writing on 29 December 1760, the *Annual Register's* correspondent said of the canal that it

'will be the most extraordinary thing in the kingdom. . . . The boats in some places are to go under ground, and in another

* This hope shows in evidence given for the Longford bridge branch in 1760: 'which will be a Means of supplying . . . a considerable part of the County of Chester, with Coals.'[39]

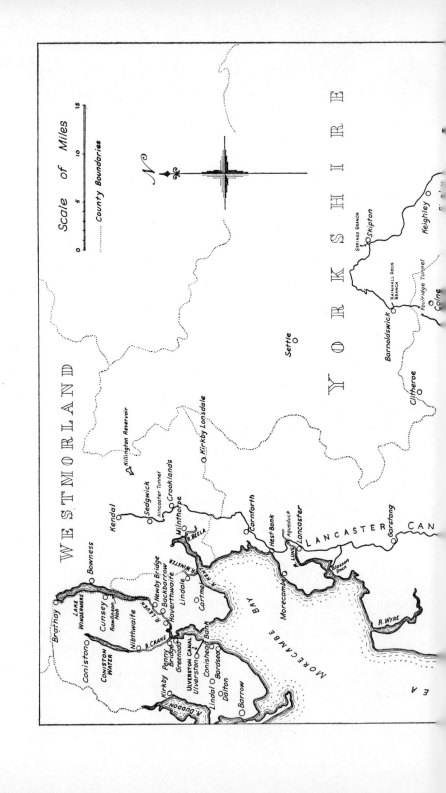

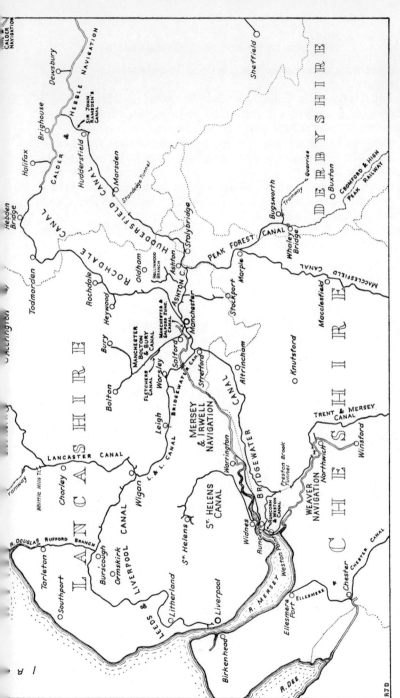

2. The waterways of the north-west as they were in 1845, with their connections. For the Carlisle Canal, see Fig 24

place over a navigable river, without communicating with its waters'.[44]

Brindley's Barton aqueduct over the Mersey & Irwell Navigation's channel and towpath was opened on 17 July 1761, when the Duke came with a party to see water admitted to it.

'As soon as the water had risen to the level of the Canal a large boat carrying upwards of 50 tons was towed . . . over arches over the River Irwell which were so firm, secure and compact that not a single drop of water could be perceived to ouze thro' any of them, although the surface of the Canal is 38 feet above the navigable river under it'.[45]

With this headroom, and 63 ft width of arch, flats could sail beneath it. It was a local wonder, and inspired poetry:

> *Cotton** may boast, in his descriptive song,
> Of wonders in the Peak, admir'd so long;
> These words no less a prodigy can boast,
> Where admiration, where description's lost!
> Seen and acknowledg'd by astonish'd crowds,
> From underground emerging to the clouds;
> Vessels o'er vessels, water under water,
> *Bridgwater* triumphs—art has conquered nature'.[46]

By about the end of 1761 the canal had been built to Stretford, together with the Longford bridge branch, and also a short way towards Manchester. Coal supplies for Manchester were taken to Longford on the main road from Chester, and transferred there to carts. By September 1763 the Manchester line was open to Cornbrook, 1¾ miles from Stretford junction. About now the Duke and Brindley must have chosen Castlefield instead of Dolefield as the terminus, as having fewer engineering difficulties.[47]

An inland port was to be built here, using part of the river Medlock, and the first wharf was in use by 1 August 1765. As the years went by, lay-bys were excavated, and stables, boat repair facilities and kilns constructed. Two warehouses were soon built, the Duke's (later the Bridgewater, or Old), and that shared by Hugh Henshall & Co† and Gilbert, Worthington & Co‡ (later the Grocers'). The first was burnt in 1789 (it was uninsured, and £30,000 worth of damage was done), rebuilt, and finally burnt

* Charles Cotton (1630–87) wrote *Wonders of the Peake*, 1681.
† The carrying department of the Trent & Mersey Canal company.
‡ John Gilbert was the son of the Duke's agent—he and his father, as Gilbert & Son, had been carrying in the salt trade as early as 1784; Jonathan Worthington was a carrier on the Bristol route.

down in 1914. The second was demolished in 1960. The nine-storey Staffordshire warehouse was built in 1794, and probably soon taken over by Henshall's: it was destroyed by enemy action in World War II.[48] Others followed. A letter-writer of 1766 wrote of Manchester: 'this Place . . . is become a sort of Maratime Town, or Dutch Seaport: for by the . . . Canal . . . we have Coal Barges, Timber Barges and Corn Barges, and we have Pleasure Barges too.'[49]

The small boats from the Worsley mines, each carrying twelve iron containers holding 8 cwt of coal, were taken into a tunnel driven into the hill behind what was later to be called Henshall & Gilbert's warehouse, above which was a shaft. Each boat in turn was manoeuvred under this, and a swivel crane, powered by a waterwheel, then lifted each container. This was emptied at street level and returned to the boat. The tunnel and shaft probably started work late in 1765,[50] and Earl Gower thought well enough of the idea to use it on the Donnington Wood Canal,[51] from which it was later copied by the Coalbrookdale company.[52] Coal was also brought to the open quay in 50-ton craft.

The underground canal into the Worsley mine, an integral part of the Duke's 1759 project, probably originated with John Gilbert. Small-sized narrow boats, 47 ft × 4½ ft, with a loaded draught of about 2 ft 6 in, were to be used. Their containers could be filled in the mine, and five boats, towed by a horse or two mules, could then be taken in a gang to be unloaded at Manchester.

The surface line of the canal was therefore continued into the vertical rock face at Worsley Delph. The average size of the underground tunnels was 10 ft width, 3 ft 6 in to 4 ft depth, and 8 ft headroom above water level.[53] Loading-places were built at intervals, to which the coal was dragged on basket-sledges holding about 2 cwt for loading into the containers. Boat passing places were cut, and side-tunnels wherever a thick seam of coal intersected the level. Two other canals were built, one at 56 yd, the other at 83 yd, below the main level, but without physical connection to it. Containers of coal were boated on these levels to vertical shafts, up which they could be winched to the main level and loaded into boats there.

North from Worsley mine lay Walkden, and beyond that Dixon Green and Morris Green. From Walkden onwards a third canal was cut, this time 35 yd above the main level and also connected to it by shafts. In 1795 John Gilbert started to link this higher canal to the main level by an underground inclined plane, 151 yd long with a slope of 1 in 4. Twin locks were built at its head, into which a laden boat was run. The water was let out, and the boat settled on an iron cradle running on rails. When the brake was released, cradle and boat descended the plane, hauling up an empty boat on another cradle running on parallel rails. It was ready for for use in October 1797, and worked until 1822, when the higher canal seems to have been abandoned.

The main level was about 4 miles long to Dixon Green, but the total length of the system was some 46 miles including branches. A quite separate underground canal was in use from 1822, running from Boothstown beyond Worsley on the Leigh branch of the Bridgewater Canal for 1½ miles to Mosley Common. From 1850 the main system slowly ceased to be used, and the last working boat moved in 1887. Since then the main level has served as a drain.

Full boats were moved with the help of a slight current downwards, created by raising sluice gates; empty ones in trains of about 20 by two or three men using canvas belts fitted with shoulder slings to which were attached 6-ft lengths of rope with hooks on the end. A man stood at the front of the train, placed his hook through an iron ring in the tunnel roof, and then pushed the boats along under him with his feet. Boats were pulled round corners into side arms by means of fixed ropes.

From Gilbert's day the tunnels became a tourist attraction. On such occasions our ancestors were apt to burst into verse:

'To Worsley's pits the channel forward goes,
And thro' the sever'd rock the water flows.
Now we ascend the barge, and onward move,
The subterraneous joys of life to prove.

    .   .   .

At length arriv'd, the destin'd port we gain,
And the wish'd object of our voyage attain.
In yon recess the coal spreads all around
A gloom most horrid; darkness most profound:
All things are hid in universal night,
Save where yon candle gives a glimm'ring light
To those poor wretches, in this dismal bed
Who pant and toil, yet hardly earn their bread.'[54]

The old tradition was briefly revived in 1961, on the 200th anniversary of the canal's opening, when parties were taken for a boat trip on the main level and a visit to the inclined plane.

In September 1761 Brindley was surveying for a further extension from Longford bridge to the Hempstones a little above Run-

corn, with a branch from Sale Moor to Stockport. He continued
to do so until January 1762, when he went to London to give evidence on the Bill.* About now a pamphlet appeared, clearly inspired by the Duke, which called the Mersey & Irwell's route 'very
imperfect, expensive and precarious', and pointed out that the
Duke's line would be 9 miles shorter. It said that the Duke would
take no more toll than his present 2s 6d (12½p), so that goods might
be carried between Manchester and Runcorn for 6s (30p) freight
and toll, a figure that was included in the Act and applied to all
carriers on the Bridgewater Canal.† The Old Quay rate was quoted
as 12s (60p) Liverpool to Manchester, and 10s (50p) Bank Quay to
Manchester, but as we have seen, the actual Bank Quay–Manchester rate varied from 6s 8d (33½p) to 11s 8d (58½p). The Duke
promised not to abstract any of the Mersey & Irwell's water, saying
that there was enough at Worsley 'to fill upwards of 18 Locks in
24 Hours, being many more than is requisite to answer all the Trade
that the Country can possibly supply on both Navigations', and
ended with an encomium on canals: 'This Mode of Navigation is
new in its Kind: which, from the Experiments already made, carries
the most promising Appearance of Success.'[55]

The Mersey & Irwell company now strongly opposed the Bill,
but failed to prevent it passing. The Duke seems to have offered
them £30 a share or about £15,000 for their business,[56] but they
declined. Only a week after the Act, they issued a belligerent
advertisement offering to carry, toll included, to and from Bank
Quay and Manchester at 2s 6d (12½p) per truss of Irish or Scottish
linen yarn,‡ and 6s 8d (33½p) for everything else; through rates
Liverpool to Manchester or return, 3s (15p) a truss, 10s (50p) for
cotton and wool, 6s 8d (33½p) for everything else.[57] In other words,
they were offering a rate from Liverpool only 8d more than the
Duke's legal rate from Runcorn after he had built his canal.

The Duke, who must now have wished that he had offered more
for the navigation, replied by joining the Salford Quay company,
which a month later promised to carry at the same rates as the
Mersey & Irwell.[58] A few years later, the Duke owned two-thirds
of the Salford Quay shares.[59] It looks therefore as if the competition in carrying became too hot for the Mersey & Irwell, who by
1765 had leased their tolls, and also somewhat raised their rates.

---

* The Stockport branch was not included, but was the subject of another, in 1766.
† In addition, the Duke could levy wharfage, and was to add porterage and ware-
housing charges. The effective rates were therefore usually higher than the nominal.
‡ Not exceeding 7½ cwt per truss.

The Salford Quay company probably ceased to carry in 1774, when its land was used for building: the Duke became the sole owner in 1779.

The Duke's Act[60] authorized him to extend his canal from Longford bridge over the Mersey and Sale Moor to Altrincham, then over the Bollin, past Lymm, and so the estuary at the Hempstones, about 1½ miles short of Runcorn. It was to be level with his existing line except for a terminal flight of locks into the river. Brindley had assured the Lords committee of

> 'the great Use it will be in assuring a Trafick to Liverpool and Manchester, and if it is carried into Execution will reduce ye price of ye Carriage of Goods full one Half'.[61]

However, that was before the Old Quay's price-cutting, and meanwhile the Duke was busy developing and paying for Castlefield, extending his mines, and buying or leasing new coal-bearing and agricultural land, and was in no hurry to start the new line.

One guesses, indeed, that it did not look a very economic proposition until early in 1765 Josiah Wedgwood and his friends began to promote what became the Trent & Mersey Canal, from the Trent at Wilden Ferry above Nottingham by way of the Potteries to the Mersey.[62] Their obvious course was to join the Weaver, and this was indeed their first plan. But in mid-April they met John Gilbert, who suggested a link to the Duke's projected canal instead, and offered to approach the great man. Although construction had begun earlier, it is probable that it was only now pushed ahead in order to convince the Trent & Mersey's backers that the Runcorn line would indeed be made.

In the course of his negotiations with the canal promoters, the Duke had the idea of extending his own proposed waterway past Runcorn and then by an aqueduct over the Mersey and so to Liverpool, so eliminating the tidal river passage from his own trade and that for which he hoped from the Trent & Mersey. However, he did not press it. For the rest, he played his cards well, and the Trent & Mersey's Act of 14 May 1766[63] recorded his agreement that his canal should, instead of ending in the river at the Hempstones, join theirs at Preston Brook, and that he should build the rest of their intended line to Runcorn at his own expense. He was not empowered to alter the tolls on his own traffic, but he could now charge 1d per ton per mile on that between the Trent & Mersey and Runcorn.* The agreement benefited both parties: the Trent &

* Vessels using all the Runcorn locks paid another 6d, i.e. the same toll as from Runcorn to Preston Brook.

Mersey company saved several miles of construction cost and got canal access to Manchester; the Duke got control of the Runcorn entrance, and an approach to the Midlands.

In May 1765 a group originating in Macclesfield and headed by Charles Roe[64] proposed a canal to link their town with the Weaver at Witton bridge by way of Knutsford, Mottram St Andrew and Stockport, and later changed to a line from Macclesfield to Stockport and Manchester, though it was 'to have no communication with the Duke's, which makes his Grace oppose it'.[65] He must then have negotiated with the promoters, and agreed that he himself would build a branch from his canal at Sale Moor to Stockport, and they a continuation to Macclesfield. The former was authorized on 18 March 1766,[66] 7½ miles long with a rise of 60 ft to Stockport, but the latter failed in the Lords after having passed the Commons in January 1766.[67] Having safeguarded his position, the Duke felt no need to act. However, it seems possible that the Stockport line was begun. A newspaper report of 1772 says that the Duke 'has already broke ground the length of two miles, from Sale Moor towards Stockport',[68] and another of 1776 says that he intended in the following year to 'finish his Navigation to Stockport, by which he will ingross the Carriage of Salt, Iron, Lime-Stone, Deal-Baux and Grocery to that Town, whence most of the Articles will be conveyed to Macclesfield and the Peak of Derbyshire'.[69] But it was never built, and Stockport had to wait until the 1790s for water communication, and Macclesfield much longer than that.

A major work on the first part of the new line forward from Longford bridge was the mile-long embankment across the Mersey valley, and the single-arched aqueduct over the river.[70] On 6 June 1766 the first tolls were taken on the new line to Altrincham, in October the canal was cutting through Dunham, in September 1767 the Bollin had been crossed and at Altrincham coal prices had already been reduced by about half. By 1769 the canal had reached Lymm.

It seems that up to the end of 1768 the Duke had not decided upon the width of Runcorn locks, nor the Trent & Mersey company whether to build the lower part of their canal to barge rather than narrow boat width. About this time, encouraged by a Liverpool group, Brindley had been reconsidering the Duke's earlier idea of an aqueduct over the Mersey. According to S. R. Harris,[71] Brindley had intended a narrow boat aqueduct, and lost interest in it when the Duke and the Trent & Mersey company decided upon a barge canal.

When the canal had reached Lumbrook in 1770 and Stockton Heath in 1771, the Duke had goods transhipped from barges to road and then again to river craft at Warrington for Liverpool. In 1773 fifteen river craft were working for him. By 1770, however, he had run into serious trouble with Sir Richard Brooke of Norton Priory, between Preston Brook and Runcorn. His difficulty was that whereas his Act prohibited him from taking his line within 360 yd of the house, his engineers now advised him that this was necessary. Held up by Sir Richard's refusal to sell land on an altered course, and his own reluctance to risk what might happen if he applied for a special Act, he went on to complete his canal on each side of the Norton Priory land.

The building of Runcorn locks in 1772 created much local excitement. By June he had bought 200 bedsteads and chaff mattresses, and put them in his house and in three old hulks brought from Liverpool, partly as living quarters for about a third of his labour force there, and partly to act as a breakwater to work at the lower locks.[72] Construction went on night and day 'with no stoppage except for Sunday Prayers'; a letter-writer tells his readers, 'you will have no Cheese from this part of Cheshire, for the Duke's men, like Locusts, devour the Fruits of the Earth'.[73]

The ten barge locks were built in staircase pairs. Each fell 7 ft, but the lowermost had a fall of 22½ ft at low water, to enable craft to enter and leave at any tide. The great flight was opened on 1 January 1773. The first flat through was the *Heart of Oak*, of 50 tons, one of the Duke's, from Liverpool. Afterwards over 600 of the workmen were entertained beside the locks 'with an ox roasted whole, and plenty of liquor', the beef being supplemented with the Duke's bread and potatoes. One hopes the two barrels of ale he provided kept the cold out.[74] Brindley did not live to be there: he had died on 27 September 1772.

By 1774 the Runcorn line extended to Astmoor, and the rest to Norton. Land carriage at the Duke's expense covered the uncut mile at Norton Priory, and in June and July the canal is said to have brought 43,000 bushels of corn from Liverpool to Manchester.[75] Preston Brook tunnel was opened in February 1775 and his canal joined to the end of the Trent & Mersey, only then navigable to Acton, by a short branch. With the approaching completion of that great enterprise, and conscious that public opinion was now in his favour, the Duke decided towards the end of 1775 to move in Parliament against Sir Richard. Brooke gave way, helped by a payment of £1,900, the necessary land was bought, and in the two months from 22 January 1776, during which there were twenty-one days of hard frost, the last mile was cut and four bridges built.[76] The whole line was opened on Thursday, 21 March 1776; craft went through to Manchester on Friday and Saturday, and some returned to Liverpool on Sunday evening.[77] 'The greatest rejoicings were made on this occasion by all ranks of people, and a grand entertainment was given by the gentlemen and merchants in Manchester,'[78] then, we must remember, a town of some 24,000 people.[79]

The Duke's efforts to find money to build the Runcorn line while financing developments at Castlefield and his collieries have been well, almost too well, told.[80] Phillips[81] says that the Worsley to Manchester canal cost about a thousand guineas a mile. This would be cheap, and probably does not include the Duke's own staff costs. On the other hand, about £2,500–£3,000 a mile for the Longford bridge–Runcorn section would be fair,[82] and would give us between £63,000 and £76,000 spread over eleven years. The figure of some £220,000 often quoted must include a great deal of mining and agricultural land purchase costs. Nor can we altogether believe Smiles's stories of the Duke's financial difficulties when we relate them to the comparatively small sums he actually borrowed and the extent of his countrywide estates. We may reflect that ready cash is often short even when plenty of resources are available, and that an impression of penury did no harm to the impression the Duke was making on public opinion.

The Bridgewater canals were supplied with water from the Worsley mines and springs there, the Trent & Mersey, the Bank Top tunnel, which led water from Shooter's Bank into the Medlock,* and later from the waste water of the Rochdale and Ashton canals. The Medlock itself entered Castlefield basins at one end, and to maintain a constant level, Brindley led it out again through a huge clover-leaf weir.† This tended to choke up; a writer of 1783 says:

'the ... curious weir ... was much admired at its first construction, but the mud which has been deposited by floods has greatly disfigured it, although the work seems thereby to have acquired more stability'.[85]

In 1773[86] the Duke had made a cut across the marshy spit of land

---

* This 'Navigable Sough Level', 649 yd long, was begun in April 1787 and finished two years later[83] when: 'The first coal from Worsley arrived at Bank Top, consisting of three boat loads'.[84] Bank Top was near the present Piccadilly station; We assume that navigation along the level ceased about 1800, when the Ashton Canal was opened to Piccadilly basin, and the Rochdale's line thence to Castlefield.

† The curious shape was to get the largest circumference, in this case 366 yd.

C

just upriver from Runcorn locks. This ended in a basin, with a warehouse, at the far end of which was the bottom lock of the flight, with the line of sunken hulks still acting as a breakwater. From the lowest pound of the flight a basin ran eastwards, dividing into three. The bottom-most of these had a lock at each end, and was an alternative way of reaching the river via another small basin. These two locks and their basin seem to have been begun in October 1790 and opened on 21 November 1791,[87] after which the other basins were extended.

As early as January 1768 the Duke had obtained land at Liverpool near Salthouse dock by purchase and corporation lease, and in October 1776 a newspaper reported him as preparing to build a dock 'to contain his own Vessels and . . . afterwards erect Wharehouses in the Manner of those he has built at Manchester'.[88] The Duke's dock adjoining Salthouse dock with its great eight-storey warehouse was completed between 1780 and 1783,[89] and extended in the 1790s.

Fourteen months after the Bridgewater Canal was finished, the Trent & Mersey was also completed, and the Duke's fortune was made. For the ten years 1770–9 the Duke took £21,472 in freight between Manchester and Liverpool; in the two years 1780 and 1781 he took £7,381, while in the eighteen months from 4 July 1777, Hugh Henshall & Co paid him £2,479. In May 1784 he agreed to give them reduced tolls in return for reductions on his coal to Middlewich. By 1785 clay* sheds, a warehouse and a salt office had been built at Preston Brook for the Chester, Frodsham and Potteries transhipment trade.

The Duke also worked hard to sell his coal, about three-quarters to four-fifths of his mines' output being sold off the canal, the rest direct from the pits. At Liverpool in January 1774 he was said to be selling at Liverpool

> 'a single Penny-worth of Coals to everyone who chuses to purchase, at the same Rate as by the Cart-load . . . he sells twenty-four pounds of Coal for One Penny, and if it were not for the unfortunate Obstruction in Cheshire† he would sell them to the poor even cheaper than that'.[90]

But he does not seem long to have been able to withstand the competition in Liverpool of the Sankey Brook Navigation and the Leeds & Liverpool Canal. Judging by the day-books, less and less coal seems to have gone down the extension line, until by 1786 little

---

* Clay to be carried to the Potteries.
† At Norton Priory.

moved beyond Altrincham. But the Manchester demand boomed, and the Runcorn line was busy with the Liverpool and Manchester merchandise trade and traffic exchanged with the Trent & Mersey.

Passenger carrying also contributed to revenue. This began in October 1767[91] between Broadheath (Altrincham) and Manchester, in early 1769 was extended to Lymm, and later to Stockton (for Warrington), using converted barges. On 1 September 1774 the Duke was reported just to have built two packet-boats for the same run, one carrying 120 passengers and the other 80. Each had a

> 'Coffee-room at the Head, from whence Wines &c are sold out by the Captain's Wife. Next to this is the first Cabbin, which is 2s 6d, the second Cabbin 1s 6d, and the third Cabbin 1s for the Passage'.[92]

They were successful, if sometimes overcrowded: a letter of 4 July 1784 notes that on that day the boat from Manchester carried 152 passengers.[93]

In 1788 two boats were working a Monday to Friday service through to Runcorn: Manchester 08.00, Altrincham 10.00, Lymm 11.30, Stockton Quay 13.00, Preston Brook, 14.30, Runcorn, 16.00. On Saturday the boat left at 16.00. The down boats were met at London bridge (Stockton) by a connecting coach to take passengers on to Liverpool, and at Preston Brook by another for Chester. The up boat left Runcorn between 08.00 and 09.00, picking up Liverpool and Chester passengers on its way. On board, 'tea and cakes elegantly served for breakfast, and in the afternoon, in each boat'.[94] Another passenger boat had begun to work between Manchester and Worsley at about the beginning of 1775. The Duke's passenger station was near Henshall & Gilbert's warehouse at Castlefield, where there were waiting-rooms and a ticket office. The boats were popular, and average takings rose as follows:

Years	Takings £	Years	Takings £
1776–78	1,303	1785–87	2,425
1779–81	1,395	1788–90	2,905
1782–84	1,771		

Total receipts also showed a very satisfactory trend, as did profits, though these are shown before charging interest on capital. The coal tonnages carried on the canal in its early days are, however, lower than the expectations aroused by the canal's reputation might have justified. Here are averaged figures:

Years	Coal tonnages tons	Receipts £	Profits £
1773–75	37,168	14,832	
1776–78	45,695	19,876	9,738*
1779–81	45,778	21,017	
1782–84	52,157	27,138	
1785–87	52,251	41,633	22,713†
1788–90	64,220	51,306	29,494

* 1778 only.
† 1785 and 1787 only.

By the year 1791, total tonnage carried had reach 267,536, and the revenue from tolls, freight, warehousing and porterage was £61,143. Of the tonnage, 83,835 was carried from Liverpool: 53,935 tons to Manchester, 10,594 to places up the line from Runcorn to Worsley, and 19,306 to Preston Brook for transfer to the Trent & Mersey. To Liverpool the tonnage was much less: 33,370, of which 26,695 tons came off the Trent & Mersey (12,213 tons being rock salt), 5,804 from Manchester and 871 from the rest of the line. Of the balance, 25,858 tons came off the Trent & Mersey towards Manchester, and 10,598 in the opposite direction; 60,461 was the Duke's own coal and 15,831 his own limestone.[95]

Except for the trade between the Trent & Mersey and the canal towards and from Manchester and Worsley, all the carrying was by the Duke's own craft, including that off the Trent & Mersey towards Runcorn and Liverpool, which was transhipped at Preston Brook. Over half the revenue came from the direct trade between Manchester and Liverpool—£31,162 out of £62,143. Of the balance, £12,051 was earned from the Trent & Mersey trade, £7,326 on notional tolls on the coal traffic, and £3,782 from passenger boats. Against the total revenue of £61,143, the accounts show expenditure of £40,118 attributable to the canal and its related carrying and warehousing businesses.

The opening of the Duke's canal weakened the Mersey & Irwell's position so much that in January 1779 'the whole Estate, Benefit and Interest of the Company', including wharves, warehouses and vessels, were offered for sale by auction on 2 March.[96] It is unlikely that it was actually auctioned. Instead, it was probably bought privately by a group of Liverpool and Manchester men, who paid £10,000 or £20 a share for it.

In May they announced 'that the utmost Dispatch Care will be used, and they flatter themselves that the State of the Works and their Attention to the Vessels, will enable them to do Justice to

their Employers'. They went on to say that they would be glad
to contract with independent owners 'at a reasonable Tonnage' and
that 'All Goods from Manchester by this Navigation for Warrington, Liverpool, Chester, Preston, Lancaster, and all Parts of the
North, likewise all Goods coming up to Manchester, by this
Navigation, will be forwarded to Stockport, Macclesfield, Rochdale, Halifax, Leeds, Wakefield, Sheffield, and all Places adjacent,
with the utmost Care and Dispatch'.[97] The second part of this
announcement, offering to forward goods over the Pennines, may
have been connected with a Calder & Hebble Navigation announcement a month earlier, advertising a twice weekly barge service from
Sowerby Bridge to Hull, 'and goods sent by the carriers from
Manchester on Mondays and Thursdays about noon, will reach
Sowerby Bridge the next day soon enough to be sent by the said
Vessells without loss of time'.[98]

The new company began briskly, compelling the owners of
Throstle Nest mills to make their section of towpath, building craft
and warehousing, and buying land that might prove useful later.
By 1783 they were considering whether their Act enabled them to
make a cut from Woolston to Runcorn to by-pass the river, but had
doubts and laid the idea aside. In 1784, to improve their accommodation at Liverpool, they asked the corporation for 'the exclusive
Use of the Quay adjoining to the Bank where the Flats usually lie
for loading and unloading';[99] this* they got, but they had to wait
until December 1789 for the 'Sheds, Cranes and other Conveniences . . . for the accommodation of the Merchants, Dealers
and others in the loading and unloading of Goods from Flats'.[100] In
1787 Hugh Henshall and two other engineers, investigating flooding, noted that the navigable depth had improved at Hollins Ferry
from 20 inches sixteen years before to between 2 ft and 2 ft 9 in.

In 1788 an alternative to the Woolston–Runcorn cut was suggested, one from Woolston to Bewsey below Winwick, on the
Sankey Brook Navigation, which would then be extended from
Fiddler's Ferry to opposite Runcorn. It was decided to seek an Act,
and raise the money from existing resources and calls on shares, but
after a year's negotiation it was reported that the two companies
had been unable to agree on terms for the use of the Sankey by
Mersey & Irwell craft.

A directory for 1788 lists twenty vessels working between
Liverpool and Manchester, and says that some leave the Old Quay
at 4 pm on three days a week with cargoes, 'and seldom fail deliver-

* It became their Manchester basin or dock.

ing them at Liverpool the second day'. Another four craft traded between Manchester and Warrington.[101]

From the time of the take-over, the Mersey & Irwell's minute books show no sign of worry at competition from the Bridgewater Canal: indeed, before 1790 it is not mentioned. One now gets the impression of a securely-based concern, with their own trade, paying a steady 5 per cent on their £10,000 capital, financing improvements and the building of new craft out of income, their £20 shares already standing at £37[102] and confident of ability not only to hold their own, but to progress. And, as we shall see, they did. (*To continue the history of the Mersey & Irwell Navigation and the Bridgewater Canal, turn to Chapter IV.*)

CHAPTER II

The Weaver and the Sankey

++++++++++++++++++++++++++++++++++++ ✦ ++++++++++++++++++++++++++++++++++++

THE river Weaver runs, wholly in Cheshire, past Nantwich, Winsford and Northwich and, before the ship canal was built, entered
the Mersey estuary at Frodsham. It had always been navigated to
the tidal limit at Pickerings when there was enough water; here it
was joined by the pack-horse track through Acton Cliff. There had
been no general navigation above Pickerings, though two rather
half-hearted attempts were made in 1663 and 1670 to get navigation
Acts.[1] But it flowed through the salt district, and two developments in that industry caused renewed demands for the river to be
made navigable. In the seventeenth century, coal had replaced
wood for heating the salt pans. Most of this came at first by land
from Staffordshire, but later it was replaced by that from Lancashire by pack-horse to Hale, then across the Mersey by boat to
Frodsham bridge, and then by pack-horse or cart: in both cases
expensively. As a ton of coal was needed to make $1\frac{1}{2}$ tons of salt,
costs could be reduced if Lancashire coal could be brought by water
to the salt district. Again, from 1670 onwards rock salt began to be
produced. This was exported unrefined,* and therefore needed a
lower rate of carriage than the refined white salt made from brine.
Such a lower rate might be found on a river navigation, while the
brine men, who had to pay an upwards transport charge for coal as
well as one down for refined salt, desperately needed lower coal
charges.

These were the motives of those who supported improvement.
On the other side were the interests of the land carriers, who in
this case were often small farmers also. They were supported by
the bigger landowners, who feared a lowering of farming rents
and the flooding of their riverside lands alike. With them were
some of the brine producers, whose competitive position against

---

* The main refineries were established at Liverpool, Dungeon almost opposite
the mouth of the Weaver, and Frodsham.

those who produced rock salt was threatened. This opposition was enough to defeat Bills of 1711, 1715, 1718 and 1720. But each time it weakened, until on 23 March 1721 an Act[2] was passed to make the Weaver navigable to Winsford and the Witton Brook to Witton bridge. The Act to make the Douglas navigable had been passed a year before, and it seems likely that coal supplies from it were in mind: certainly its two chief promoters, Thomas Steers and William Squire, were among those examined by the parliamentary committee on the Bill; William Marsh also appeared before it in support of both schemes. Yet the carriage of coal was not mentioned in their preliminary petition; the emphasis was all on salt.

Those concerned with brine workings near Middlewich wanted the Dane made navigable also, considering that otherwise they would be put at a disadvantage, and on 7 June 1721 a separate Act was passed for this purpose. It named five undertakers, James, Earl of Barrymore, Sir Richard Grosvenor, Sir Thomas Brooke, Charles Cholmondeley, and Roger Wilbraham, but these took no action, and the Dane remained unnavigable.

The Act for the Weaver also named undertakers, John Egerton of Oulton, John Amson of Leese, and Richard Vernon of Middlewich, and empowered them to charge 1s 3d (6p) a ton in tolls until all their expenses had been repaid, and then 1s (5p). The undertakers were to build one of their locks at Pickerings, below which point the river was already navigable to Frodsham bridge when there was enough water. They could therefore only levy tolls over this stretch at times when, if it had not been for their lock, the river would have been unnavigable. Commissioners were appointed to mediate in land purchase disputes, but they were given power also to appoint new undertakers if necessary (though not to remove them), and to authorize the issue to them of £9,000 which various people had agreed to subscribe, this being repayable out of profits and meanwhile carrying 6 per cent interest. Finally, the Act stated that after the undertakers' costs had been repaid, and those of maintenance met, the balance should be handed to the county of Cheshire to maintain the public bridges, for repairing roads near the river, then other roads, and lastly for general county charges.

Of the three undertakers named, only Richard Vernon was active, but he and the commissioners could not agree on his costs in connection with getting the Act, or the other undertakers with him, and deadlock followed until Vernon died in 1726. Then the surviving undertakers joined with others to seek a new Bill to make the Weaver navigable to Northwich only, and to improve the Dane. It was defeated.

After further manoeuvres, three new undertakers were appointed in 1730 and 1731, Thomas Eyre of Stockport, Thomas Patten of Warrington and John Dickenson of Manchester, who were supported by Jonathan Patten. The commissioners agreed that they should spend up to £12,000, on which they were to get 6 per cent, and in addition £1,000 for their trouble, and another £1,000 if they completed the work by 25 March 1732, decreasing by £200 a year for delay. The commissioners (not the undertakers) now began to appoint staff, and work began, with Thomas Robinson as surveyor-general. On 1 January 1732 tolls began to be taken on the Northwich section, and on 18 April to Winsford. Records show that a craft carrying 45 tons could then reach Northwich, and 38 tons Winsford. To help get trade started, the commissioners reduced most tolls to 10d in June 1732, but in 1740 started to raise them again.

The undertakers seem to have spent £15,885, having built mainly timber locks and weirs at Pickerings, Dutton Bottoms, Acton Bridge, Saltersford, Winnington, Northwich, Hunts, Hartford, Vale Royal, Newbridge and Butty Meadow, and built a towing path for men, not horses. Nothing had yet been done to Witton Brook. They became entitled to £1,800 also, and in September 1733 were owed a total of £18,022.

From 1 January 1732 to 29 September 1740 the average yield of tolls was £1,521 10s p.a. This did not cover expenses and interest charges by about £280 p.a., and deficits were added to the debt, which by September 1740 had reached £19,649. In the next ten years the annual revenue rose to an average of £2,179, which showed a yearly profit of about £350, and debt was reduced. By September 1750 it was down to £16,207; seven years later it was £9,809. Trade was predominantly in salt carried downwards and coal upwards, the latter in rough proportion to the former, with a certain amount of clay upwards to the Potteries and cratesware (packages of pottery) downwards, and, for the rest, miscellaneous merchants' goods and a little agricultural produce. Here are the toll figures, averaged over three years, for the first quarter century of the navigation:

Years to 29 September	*Average toll receipts*
	£
1732–34*	1,098
1735–37	1,596
1738–40	1,616
1741–43	2,147
1744–46	1,897
1747–49	2,338
1750–52	2,601
1753–55	2,575
1756–58	3,281

* From 1 January 1732. Therefore some three months short; for Winsford trade, some six months short.

Most salt-works had their own carrying craft. When the Bye-flat works at Anderton were offered for sale in 1757, the property included two quays on the Weaver and two flats.[3]

By the early 1750s the increasing demand of the salt-manufac-turers along the Weaver for coal was paralleled by that from Liverpool. Here it was needed for salt refining, sugar baking, pottery-making, glass-making and brewing, as well as for domestic use: in addition, it was needed for shipment along the coast and to Ireland. It was said in 1754:

'Liverpool and Northwich have generally been supplied with coal from the coal pits and coal works at or near Prescot and Whiston . . . such coal hath of late years become scarce and difficult to be got, and, as well from the advanced price thereof at the pits, as of the rate of carriage from the same, is become very dear to the great discouragement of the trade and manu-factories of the said places.'[4]

An Act to turnpike the road from Liverpool to Prescot had been passed in 1726, and this had been extended to St Helens by another of 1746 and again to Warrington from Prescot and to Ashton-in-Makerfield from St Helens by another of 1753. To build the 1753 extensions, road tolls, which had been reduced in 1746, were raised again to the 1726 level, while at the same time the pit-head price of coal at Prescot was also increased.[5] Results were riots in December 1753, toll concessions the following month, and on 5 June 1754 a resolution of the Common Council of Liverpool that 'two able and skillful surveyors' be employed at their expense to survey the Sankey Brook* which led upwards from the Mersey to the coal areas round Parr and St Helens, and

* They called it the 'Dalham Brooke which Emptys itself near Sankey Bridges'.

which was already navigable for $1\frac{1}{4}$ miles from the river to the quay at Sankey Bridges.[6] This lower section was probably a free navigation, at the head of which goods were landed at private wharves. These were established by 1745, and in 1756 warehouses, a coalyard and a public house are recorded at Sankey Bridges. Two years later a 60-ton sloop worked from there.[7]

There was a double need: to tap a plentiful supply of coal, and carry it cheaply to the Mersey. The work was done by Henry Berry, dock engineer at Liverpool since 1751, helped by William Taylor. Berry, now 34 years old, had been a pupil of Thomas Steers. It is likely, too, that he had been brought up in Parr, and knew the area well. He reported to the corporation, who on 25 October, agreed to lend £300 towards the cost of a Bill, and inserted a press advertisement that subscriptions for 120 shares would be received at the Mayor's office, in spite of a panic halving of coal tolls made by the turnpike trustees in September. In doing so, the corporation gave the chief object of the proposed navigation as:

'the better Supplying this Town with Coals which of late Years are become scarce and dear and the measure greatly lessened, to the great imposition and Oppression of the Traders, manufacturers and Inhabitants of this Corporation'.[8]

The two leading promoters were John Ashton and John Blackburne jun. Ashton, who took up 51 of the 120 shares, was a Liverpool merchant who owned the Dungeon salt-works and had been town bailiff in 1749, Blackburne owned the Liverpool salt-works, where rock-salt was dissolved and evaporated to produce a higher-grade product, and also had considerable interests in Northwich rock-salt mines. Between Michaelmas 1741 and 1742 he had paid £324 in Weaver tolls at Northwich out of a total of £1,704.[9] Three other Liverpool merchant supporters who appear as undertakers were James Crosbie, the mayor, Charles Goore, who was to succeed him, and Richard Trafford. The Bill was introduced, was supported among others by the principal landowners and colliery proprietors on the upper part of the Sankey Brook, who wanted craft to come up its tributary branches to them, was not petitioned against, and passed on 20 March 1755.[10] It authorized the making navigable the Sankey Brook, and 'Three several Branches thereof; videlicet, to Boardman's Stone Bridge on the South Branch thereof, to Gerard's Bridge on the Middle Branch thereof, and to Penny Bridge on the North Branch thereof'.

Here we must remember that in the previous year, 1754, a Bill for a canal from Salford to Worsley and Wigan, which had been surveyed by Henry Berry's colleague William Taylor, had foundered on opposition from landowners and others. With this warning of opposition to canals before him, there is no reason to doubt what Professor Barker suggests, that Berry, who must have known perfectly well that the Sankey Brook was too small for a practical navigation, with Ashton's connivance went forward for a Bill to make it navigable, relying on a clause similar to that in the Mersey & Irwell's Act, in this case:

'to make such new Cuts, Canals, Trenches or Passages for Water, in, upon or through the Lands or Grounds adjoining or near unto the same River, or the Three several Branches aforesaid . . . as they shall think proper and requisite',

though the Act's preamble clearly read:

'the River or Brook called Sankey Brook . . . from the Place where it empties itself into and communicates with the River Mersey, below Sankey Bridges, is capable of being made navigable up the Stream or Current of the said River or Brook, and of the three several Branches thereof'.

The Act of 1755 was not generous. As with the Mersey & Irwell, and later with the Duke, it granted a maximum and not a mileage toll, in this case 10d a ton, and went on to define a ton in terms of coal* and timber, and also a bushel of coal, and to order the use of standard bushel measures. An extensive free list appeared:

'Lime Stones for all Purposes, Paving Stones, Granet, Sand, and all other Materials, for making and repairing of Roads, Keys and Wharfs, to and upon the said intended Navigation, and for the private use of the persons whose Lands shall be cut or made use of for the same, Soapers Waste, Dung, and all sorts of Manure for Land respectively.'

It protected the proprietors of Sankey Quays from competition by new wharves, gave powers to extend branches to 800 yd beyond the named limits, and laid down that work must begin before 29 September 1755 and end before the same date in 1766.† No limit was set to the company's capital powers.

In April 1755 Liverpool corporation gave Berry two days' a week leave to make the navigation on condition that he provided

---

* The coal definition of 63 cu. ft to a ton was later found to allow about 27 cwt to the ton; this must be borne in mind in interpreting both tonnage statistics and the level of tolls.

† Extended to 29 September 1768 under the 1762 Act.

a substitute at the dock, on 5 September work began, and, seemingly without protest from landowners or anyone else, he proceeded to cut a canal. Some years later, in Gloucestershire, those behind the Stroudwater Navigation also tried to cut a canal under river powers; but they were opposed, and had to obtain a fresh Act to authorize their work.[11] Water supply was from the streams that entered the upper stretches of the Brook—Blackbrook, Ramford Brook, Windle Brook, and later, Thatto Heath Brook.

An advertisement of November 1757 announced that the
'Sankey Brook Navigation is now opened for the passage of flatts to the Haydock* & Parr collieries. And there is a very considerable quantity of coal laid near the said Navigation ready for sale & three collieries already opened'.[12]

Six weeks later, another advertisement said that
'the collieries belonging to Mrs Clayton in Parr adjacent to the Sankey Brook Navigation are opened ... Mrs Clayton proposes to put the new raised coal on board the flatts in the navigation at four shillings and tenpence a ton. The waggon road and other conveniences are fixed in such a manner that flatts may be laden in a few hours'.[13]

Calls of £90 per share were made in 1756 and 1757, and in all, £155 per share was raised, giving a total expenditure of £18,600. The canal, 5 ft deep, began a little below Sankey Bridges, at Sankey lock. This, and seven more single locks,† took it to a staircase pair, the Old Double lock, 8 miles up, at the head of which the north (Penny Bridge or Blackbrook) branch (⅝ mile), and the west (Gerard's Bridge) branch (1½ miles) led off. By spring 1759 the line had been built as far as Gerard's Bridge, and the Blackbrook branch partly so.[14] The latter was probably navigable by 1762 and was later extended about 1770. By 1772 the canal had also been extended from a point just over a mile above the Old Double lock past another staircase pair, the New Double lock or Pocket Nook locks, to Boardman's Bridge to complete the original plan.[15] Later, this branch was further extended over Hardshaw Brook and past the edge of St Helens to the Ravenhead Copper Works and St Helens Crown Glass Works, with a short branch from near the brook towards Sutton colliery.

Nothing is certainly known of the small waterway marked as

* Haydock colliery was on the Blackbrook or Penny Bridge branch.
† Bewsey, Hulme, Winwick, Hey, Bradley, Newton Common and Engine or Haydock. Assuming that they were not later enlarged, their ruling dimensions were 72 ft 4in. × 16 ft 9 in.

'Old Canal' on the 1848 O.S. map which runs for about ½ mile
from Thatto Heath to the Ravenhead British Plate Glass Works.
It is likely that it was built by John Mackay to carry coal from his
Thatto Heath collieries to the Plate Glass Works, which were
opened in 1773.[16] It is shown on maps of 1793 and 1795. It was
not connected to the Sankey Brook Navigation.

There was also a small private canal between the Stanley copper
mill at Blackbrook, at the head of an arm of the Sankey Navigation, and the mills at Carr Pool higher up the Blackbrook. It is
described in 1784 as 'a navigable canal, with a boat upon it, from
the works at Carr, to those at Stanley, suitable for conveying
goods between the two places, distant about half a mile'.[17]

By February 1758 Sankey coal was being advertized in Liverpool;

'New Navigation Coals, both wholesale and retail. At the Coal
Yard near the Salt-house in Liverpool. Kept by Edward Woods
and Company, who will supply ships, merchants, Pot-houses,
Sugar-houses, Brewers and Housekeepers, at the lowest terms'.[18]

and in April Parr coals were being offered delivered

'to such vessels, at Liverpool, as the flat can lye along side to
discharge into after the rates of 7s for 30 sealed bushels, weigh-
ing about a ton. And to all house keepers and places in Liverpool after the rate of 7s 6d for the same quantity'.

Haydock coal was 7s 4d (36½p) and 8s (40p) respectively. The
Haydock flat would 'take freight for either the Bank Quay, or the
Navigation, at the lowest prices'.[19] This triangular trade of loading coal in the navigation and taking it to Liverpool, loading
there for Bank Quay, and then running empty thence to the Sankey, seems to have grown. In April 1761, to encourage trade and
meet Liverpool complaints of high coal prices, the authorized
toll of 10d was reduced to 7d a ton,[20] a very cheap rate given the
actual content of a ton.

For a time, towing on the canal may have been by men. Otherwise flats were horse-hauled or sailed, swing and not overhead
bridges having been built. Craft using the canal in 1760 had
burthens of 35, 45 and 50 tons,[21] and did not get much larger, for
though in 1778 a newly-built boat of 100 tons was being offered
for sale from a boat-building yard at St Helens, toll-sheets of 1826
show cargoes varying from 40 to 48 tons, in craft drawing up to
5 ft 4 in.

The company soon found that at neap tides there was not
enough water for flats in the tidal Sankey Brook below Sankey

Bridges. John Eyes therefore surveyed for an extension of the canal downwards to the Mersey itself. This was authorized in 1762[22] from a point 250 yd above Sankey lock to Fiddler's Ferry, where a new entrance lock was built. An extra toll of 2d was chargeable on craft using the new cut. Thenceforward, according to Aikin,[23] empty vessels could pass at any time, but those loaded were still neaped for three days in each month. Afterwards the old lock was still sometimes used 'when a number of vessels are about entering from the Mersey at once, in which case some of the hindmost sail for the Sankey brook in order to get in before the others'.[24] There is an implication in the 1830 Act that it was then still open, and that craft could use it to avoid paying the supplementary 2d toll. It is interesting to note that a letter to the press by an opponent in 1771 says that the Sankey proprietors, then seeking their Act to extend to Fiddler's Ferry, had the 'intention of still further powers to continue their canal to Bower's Pool near Runcorn Gap' to avoid the most difficult section of the Mersey.[25]

The opening of the first part of the Sankey Brook in November 1757 had immediate repercussions upon the Weaver, where the undertakers had contented themselves with maintaining, in some cases inadequately, what they had first built. Some locks and weirs were in bad condition, more were run down, and a good deal of money needed to be spent. In September, Liverpool corporation received a petition from merchants of the town complaining of the river's management. They offered to

'bear the Expenses of any Gentleman who shall take the trouble to go and order a survey of the said River and to meet any Gentlemen concerned in the said Navigation in order to have the Inconveniences and mismanagement of the said River redressed'.[26]

In October and again in January merchants' representatives met the Weaver commissioners, two of the three from Liverpool at the January meeting being Ashton and Blackburne of the Sankey. This meeting agreed that Henry Berry would survey the river, and at some time the merchants even offered to take over the navigation. Instead, the commissioners decided that they would themselves buy out the undertakers for £17,000, being the £8,809 owed them and the balance for giving up the rights. The transfer took place on 11 October 1758.

The merchants and Sankey interests wanted the Weaver locks a little wider than those on the Sankey Brook, to take craft drawing

5 ft instead of the current 4 ft, and more canalization, while the commissioners had less ambitious ideas. Berry did his survey with both alternatives in mind, but having had it, the commissioners, perhaps disliking outside interference, preferred their own scheme, and in October appointed a committee from among themselves to carry it out. They compromised on locks just over 17 ft wide, roughly the same as on the Sankey, and a depth of $4\frac{1}{2}$ ft.

In this same year of 1758 the commissioners began work on a new lock-cut, lock and weir at Pickerings; they had decided also to rebuild Saltersford, when in early 1759 they were faced with the collapse of Northwich lock after a rock-salt pit had given way and divided the navigation into two parts. Goods had to be moved round the obstruction by land. In this state the commissioners found that they had no power to sue those who damaged the navigation, and that the Act of 1721 was no longer relevant to the situation in which they found themselves, as a body directly responsible for the navigation, and not merely supervising undertakers. So they sought a new Act, the text of which reflected further pressure from the Liverpool merchants.

It was passed in May 1760,[27] and named 105 trustees to assume the powers of the old undertakers, new ones to be elected as vacancies occurred. These could sue, own or rent land, and appoint a managing committee. Such a committee of nine, later increased, was at once appointed and thereafter managed the waterway. All new locks were to be as wide as the new Pickerings, which was 17 ft $3\frac{1}{2}$ in., and there was to be a depth of $4\frac{1}{2}$ ft to Winsford. The trustees could build wharves and warehouses above Pickerings (but not thence to Frodsham bridge), and borrow money without limit for the purposes of the navigation. There were also toll reductions: coal and some other commodities went to 1s at once, another list to 10d, but salt remained at 1s 3d until 1775, when it too had to be reduced to 1s.

The river already had a debt of £20,500, and now the trustees raised more. They needed it, for the new weir at Pickerings failed, followed by the lock, and had to be rebuilt. A new lock at Northwich was finished at the end of 1761, and a cut and lock at Saltersford a year later. In 1756 the previous commissioners had started to make the Witton Brook navigable with $3\frac{1}{2}$ ft depth, and to build a lock. Now, in 1764, Pownall, the trustees' engineer, was told to produce a plan to give a $4\frac{1}{2}$ ft depth in the Brook. He did so, it was checked by Brindley, and the work was carried out in 1765.

The trustees had been made nervous by the Duke of Bridge-

Page 49   Mersey & Irwell Navigation: (*above*) the pair of locks at Butchersfield; (*below*) Latchford lock, at the entrance of the Runcorn & Latchford Canal

Vuë du Canal du Duc de Bridgewater près du Pont de Worsley.
Par J.J. Rouleau.

Page 50 Bridgewater Canal: (*above*) an impression of Worsley in its early days, showing a packet boat, two 'starvationers' and early cranes; (*below*) a pair of Mersey Weaver narrow boats at Runcorn in 1950

water's Bill to extend his canal to the Mersey at Hempstones, but
had not opposed his Act of 1762. The Trent & Mersey Canal,
first seriously proposed in 1765, was much more dangerous. As
soon as they learned of it, they tried hard to persuade its promoters to join their river, while the Duke tried equally hard to get
them to link with his canal instead. The trustees suggested possible
routes, and offered toll concessions. In May 1765 they asked
Robert Pownall and Hugh Henshall to survey routes between
Winsford and Lawton (Kidsgrove) via either Middlewich or
Nantwich, while the canal promoters were considering a line to
Northwich. By December they were supporting rival schemes,
one for a canal from Witton Bridge to Stockport and Manchester
which had not originated with them, but which would conveniently cut off the Trent & Mersey from the Duke's canal; the
other to build a canal themselves from Winsford to Wrinehill,
whence it would be continued by others to the Trent, the Severn,
or both. These schemes were probably meant only to bring about
negotiations with the Trent & Mersey promoters, but they failed,
for these were determined to have an all-canal route. A Bill for
the first did pass the Commons; the second only got to petition
stage. And in May 1766 the Trent & Mersey Bill passed, authorizing a junction with the Duke's canal; it would pass through
Middlewich and so affect the land carriage trade to Winsford, and
pass very near the Weaver at Anderton.

The trustees followed a sensible policy of improving the river
to safeguard its trade, while the canal was building. They constructed a new cut and lock at Barnton (1771), and another at
Acton Bridge in 1778, appointed more lock-keepers and drastically
reduced tolls on paving stones, road materials and limestone. In
1775 those on salt and merchants' goods also came down to 1s (5p)
under the Act of 1760. By 1765 the trustees, whose trade and
revenues were steadily rising, seriously began to repay the debt,
which then stood at £25,470. By 1770 it was down to £21,000,
and in July 1775 it was liquidated, which meant that future profits
went to the county. These payments began in 1771, but future
capital expenditure was to mean that for many years thereafter
surplus revenue was ploughed back, or further sums borrowed
which had to be repaid.

In May 1777 the Trent & Mersey Canal was finished. Luckily
for the Weaver, the last section to be built had been that between
Middlewich and Acton. Combined with the effect of the 1775 toll
reductions, the revenue of the river fell from £7,079 in 1774 to

D

£4,525 in 1779, and the tonnage from 122,069 to 90,851. The Winsford trade was especially affected, which included that by land with the Potteries and with Middlewich. For the five years to 5 April 1778 this trade had averaged 11,510 tons; for the next five it averaged 5,297, clay and flintstones upwards, and cratesware downwards, being especially concerned.

From 1780, however, trade recovered very quickly, thanks to the rapid development of the salt trade, and by 1783 had passed any earlier level. Notably, the Winsford trade, which up to 1785 had never exceeded 15,000 tons, had climbed to 31,434 by 1790, and was to go steadily ahead, not only in absolute figures, but in relation to that from Northwich. The trustees helped this development by the work they did on the upper river. In 1778 they began to replace the timber locks with new ones of brick and stone, first at Vale Royal, and then, in the years to 1805, at Newbridge, Hartford and Hunts. In 1789, also, they built quays at the upper end of Witton Brook, just below Witton bridge.

Lower down, the salt proprietors wanted a cut and lock made below Frodsham bridge, so that flats could wait there for the tide, and not five miles higher up at Pickerings, so saving time. The trustees decided that their powers did not extend below Frodsham bridge, but built a cut and lock above it, at Sutton Marsh, by 1781, though they could only take tolls when the river would not otherwise have been navigable up to Pickerings. It was not until the nineties that a horse towing-path was made alongside the navigation down to Frodsham bridge, and even then men probably continued to tow below that point when sailing was not practical.

The trustees also encouraged means of transhipment between canal and river. In 1780 they improved the road between the river at Northwich and the canal at Broken Cross, building a warehouse there and appointing a wharfinger, and another at Northwich, appointing an agent at Longport to collect cratesware for transhipment, and using some boats of their own. But this trade lost money, though considerable tonnages of clay and merchants' goods were carried, and in 1784 the trustees gave up carrying, and sold the Broken Cross warehouse. In 1783, also, they paid for the repair of the Middlewich–Winsford road, in the hope of retaining some Middlewich traffic, but it is difficult to say whether they did so.

Here are averaged revenue and tonnage figures for the Weaver from 1759 to 1791:

Years from 6 April	Toll revenue £	Salt tons	Coal tons	Total tonnage tons
1759–61*	4,143	42,113	13,533	61,820
1762–64	4,289	48,709	15,521	72,927
1765–67	4,662	51,526	17,111	79,467
1768–70	5,902	64,872	23,841	101,453
1771–73	7,396	79,750	32,630	127,982
1774–76	6,194	74,181	26,853	114,140
1777–79	4,858	70,716	20,333	97,532
1780–82	5,310	75,021	25,441	106,319
1783–85	6,958	99,232	32,721	139,346
1786–88	7,634	106,245	41,140	153,286
1789–91	8,546	119,500	44,304	171,719

* 3½ years from 30 September 1758.

The river was prosperous, but the coming of the canal did mean that its dependence upon salt and coal was even more emphasized.* For in 1762–4 it had carried 8,697 tons of other goods; in 1777–9, on a greater total, only 6,483, and in 1789–91, on a total over twice as large, only 7,915.

From its opening the Sankey Brook Navigation had been successful. As early as 1772 an opponent described the shareholders as 'revelling in near twenty per cent for their capital annually'.[29] But soon after its opening the demand from the Weaver, from Ashton's refinery at Dungeon and Blackburne's at Liverpool, and from the coastal and Irish trades, was such that not enough was left for the Liverpool domestic consumer, and what did find its way to him was more expensive than it had been at first. A writer said in 1762 that coal which had been 7s† (35p) a ton when the canal opened had become 8s 6d (42½p).[30] He accused the 'engrossers of the Navigation coal', presumably the coalowners, and probably Sarah Clayton and her nephew Jonathan Case, the biggest producers, for the owners were in most cases also the freighters. Other irritations were added to the Liverpool sale: shortage of the better grades, complaints of short measure, which the navigation company tried to counter by advertizing the penalties laid down in their Act,[31] and failure to sell small quanti-

* The links are exemplified in an advertisement of 1801 for the sale of a third share in the Warburton salt works at Winnington, third and quarter shares in the Gerard's bridge colliery on the Sankey Brook Navigation, and a third share in four Weaver flats.[28]

† In fact, the price advertized in April 1758 had been 7s (35p) alongside a ship, 7s 4d (36½p) or 7s 6d (37½p) delivered.

COALS

To be SOLD by

WEIGHT,

Twenty Hundred to the Ton, and 120lb to the Hundred,

At the Proprietors Coal-Office, Opposite the *New Machine* on *Nova Scotia*, at the following Prices, *for Ready Money only*:

	Delivered to Fire-keepers, *per Ton.*			Delivered to Shiping *per Ton.*		
	£.	*s.*	*d.*	*£.*	*s.*	*d.*
Peter Leigh, Esq'rs Coal -	0	7	2	0	6	6
John Mackay, Esq'rs. do. -	0	7	0	0	6	4
Thomas Case, Esq'rs. do. -	0	6	10	0	6	2
Sir Thomas Gerrard's do. -	0	6	6	0	5	10

Any person taking a FLAT LOAD, may have any of the above said Coal, paying the Cost at the Pits, River Dues, Freight and Cartage. And to accomodate Poor Housekeepers, or such as cannot purchase a Ton at one Time, smaller Quantities will be delivered at the Yard, at four pence half-penny per Hundred, of 120lb.

Sworn Agents will attend constantly at the said Coal-Office, to whom the Public may apply.

By Order of the Proprietors.

3. A Sankey Brook broadsheet of 1770 advertizing coal for sale

ties, as did the Duke of Bridgewater at Manchester. There were also complaints of flats being delayed in the Mersey, perhaps without reflecting that they were paying no toll. The result was much correspondence in Liverpool newspapers, and interest in connecting the coalfields round Wigan, which were not served by the Sankey or the Bridgewater Canal, to Liverpool by a canal.[32]

The first scheme for a canal to Liverpool had been put forward in 1765, when the Duke, negotiating with the promoters of the Trent & Mersey,[33] suggested that the Bridgewater Canal might be continued by an aqueduct over the Mersey at Runcorn and on to Liverpool, which would have enabled Worsley coals to reach the port. There had been opposition from Liverpool and Warrington men who feared that an aqueduct would obstruct flats and barges moving on the river tide, and it had not been included in the Bill. However, a Liverpool group had been interested in the idea, which was revived at the end of 1768 as a combined road bridge and aqueduct carrying a narrow canal. At that time there were no locks on the Bridgewater Canal, and among the craft using it were the small narrow boats from the Worsley mines. Therefore, a narrow boat waterway to Liverpool was practicable. At this time, however, the idea of making both it and the lower section of the Trent & Mersey upwards from Preston Brook a barge canal was being considered. Brindley seems to have considered that a broad canal across the aqueduct would be impracticable, and that the Liverpool supporters would have to press for their aqueduct against those who wanted a barge waterway. Liverpool Corporation did indeed threaten to take legal action to prevent the widening of the Trent & Mersey, but the aqueduct idea was dropped, and a decision taken to build Runcorn locks, connecting Runcorn with the tideway, of barge size.

Meanwhile, what was to become the Leeds & Liverpool Canal (see Chapter III) had been considered since 1764, and actively promoted from 1766. By 1768 a route had been surveyed for it that by-passed the Wigan coalfield, and brought it into Liverpool in a great half-circle by way of Burscough. Although there were vague proposals for a branch to Wigan, the absence of anything in the Act left the pits still reliant upon the winding Douglas, on which improvement work was so slow that it was unlikely to provide a plentiful supply of coal to supplement the Sankey. The Act was passed in 1770, and work began in November between Liverpool and Newburgh. In September, however, the Liverpool Canal was proposed, the promoters having in mind to build the Mersey aqueduct from the Bridgewater Canal, by which it would connect with the Trent & Mersey, and then take the canal by way of Appleton, Cronton, Halewood and Toxteth, eventually to join the Leeds & Liverpool at North Lady's Walk. A branch could then be built into the coal area of Whiston and Prescot, and if necessary extended towards Ashton-in-Makerfield and Bolton, Bury, Rochdale and Halifax. The scheme offered a footbridge over the Mersey on the aqueduct, the junction of the Bridgewater, Trent & Mersey and Leeds & Liverpool, an opportunity for industrial development along the banks in Liverpool, and an addition to the town's water supply. But it was the possible

branch to the coalfields that attracted attention. A meeting in
October seems to have brought Wigan into the list of possible
places to be linked; surveys were ordered, and a deputation sent
to see the Duke.

For ten months nothing seems to have happened. Then a meeting was held in August 1771, and soon afterwards a proposed
route was published: from a separate terminus on the south side
of Liverpool it would run via Walton, Huyton and Cronton to
Appleton, where a flight of locks would lead to the Mersey
aqueduct. The canal would continue above the locks, over the
Sankey Canal near Newton and by Bamfurlong to Wigan to join
the Lancaster Canal, whence a branch could join the Douglas
Navigation and the Leeds & Liverpool. The scheme was later
extended upwards towards Chorley and a junction with the Leeds
& Liverpool near Cuerden.

Such a canal, running right through the Prescot and Whiston
coalfield, crossing the Sankey's line, and direct to the Wigan area,
was an obvious threat to the Sankey company. So efforts were
made to conciliate them by offering a junction. Instead, the Sankey
proprietors put forward their own alternative, a branch from
Winwick on their canal to Ashton-in-Makerfield, with branches
to Ince and Pemberton, which would enable them to tap the
Wigan coalfield; they seem also to have planned the enlargement
of their extended canal to take 80–100-ton barges. They sought,
and said they had obtained in a quarter of an hour, the £24,000
they needed for the extension. The Liverpool promoters in turn
sought £160,000 for their own scheme, which was now modified
to begin in the Leeds & Liverpool Canal near Liverpool and end
in the Lancaster Canal extension near Wigan. In this year of 1771,
89,720 tons were carried on the Sankey, 45,568 for Liverpool,
44,152 for Warrington, the Weaver, and elsewhere. In approxi-
mately the same period 30,525 tons of coal in all was carried on
the Weaver.

The Leeds & Liverpool now moved, to buy control of the
Douglas Navigation and so to get access to the collieries on its
banks, and to ally themselves with the Sankey. The two companies
now acted together, to discredit the Liverpool scheme outside
Parliament, and defeat it within. A Bill for it was introduced in
January 1772, with support from Liverpool and Wigan corpora-
tions, which dropped the Mersey aqueduct and a possible extension beyond Wigan to Chorley, but the opposition was too strong,
now that access to the Wigan coalfield would soon be obtained

via the Leeds & Liverpool, and it was withdrawn in committee. The Liverpool Canal idea was briefly revived in 1792 as a threat against the Leeds & Liverpool by Liverpool Corporation if they did not lower tolls, and, in the form of a junction of the Bridge- water, Sankey and Mersey & Irwell by a Mersey aqueduct, in 1825 by Francis Giles the engineer who was to build the Sankey extension to Widnes in 1830. Having allied themselves with the Leeds & Liverpool, the Sankey were of course unable to do any- thing about their own projected extension towards Wigan.

But though the project failed, its object was attained. Wigan coal was brought in by the Leeds & Liverpool Canal once it was opened, via the Douglas Navigation, in October 1774, while in January 1774 the Duke, though his canal was not yet finished, was also selling coal, and earning credit by doing so, in small quantities down to 24 lb for a penny, the same rate as for a cart- load.

> 'For this humane act, the blessings of those who have few friends shall be upon him, and the prayers of the poor shall proclaim him their benefactor.'[34]

The Sankey now faced serious competition from two directions. In October an advertisement announced that it was appointing its own coal agents in Liverpool, to prevent short measure and cheating, and that prices would be reduced

> 'by a saving on the first cost, by paying ready money to the Coal Owners, by reducing the freight and cutting off the unfair profits and advantage hitherto taken by the Dealers or Re- tailers',[35]

to 6s 6d (32½p) to 7s 2d (36p) a ton to householders, or 5s 10d (29p) to 6s 6d (32½p) delivered to shipping, according to the coal's origin. Quantities, down to one hundredweight of 120 lb would be sold at 4½d, which was a little cheaper than the Duke's 5d. The proprietors seem now to have entered the carrying business themselves in order to reduce charges to the public.

In April 1779 the canal line of the Leeds & Liverpool was open through to Wigan without using the Douglas, and imports of Wigan coal to Liverpool by it increased rapidly, from 31,401 tons in 1781 to 137,790 tons ten years later. The Sankey was also to some extent affected by coal from the Bridgewater Canal carried past Preston Brook and up the Trent & Mersey to Anderton and other landing places, from 1777 onwards.

Until the middle of the eighteenth century St Helens had been a village, and we can perhaps date its growth from the opening of

the canal, and more precisely from 1773, the date of an Act
enabling the British Cast Plate Glass Manufacturers to establish
there the first plate glass works in the country. By 1780 not only
these, but the Ravenhead copper smelting works also, were open,
and new collieries were being sunk. As industry developed, the
canal also began to carry coal and other raw materials to works
within the St Helens area, and take away their finished goods.

No. *1316*

A JUST, true, and perfect REPORT or ACCOUNT given to *James*
Crabing the Collector of the Rates and Duties for
SANKEY BROOK Navigation, by *John Maddock*
of *Dungeon*, having the Command of the Flat or Vessel
called the *Witton* of *Dungeon* Number *413*
navigating *Sankey* the said Navigation, of the QUANTITY, QUALITY,
and WEIGHT of all the Goods, Wares and Merchandizes, and other
Commodities and Things, which are in, and belong to, or have been dif-
charged from, or taken out of the said Flat or Vessel, since this present
Time of the said Flat's Entrance into the Limits of the said Navigation, and
for which the said Duties have been paid. Dated at SANKEY this
Day of *June* 178*9*

Golborne

For Duties as under,   To the Proprietors of Sankey Brook Navigation   Dr.

To 40 tons Cinders   £ 0 " 13 " 4

Draught of Water.   RECEIVED the   Day of
F.   A.   from   Pounds
Feet. Inch. Feet. Inch.   Shillings and   Pence in full
                         for Duties of the above-mentioned Goods, for the Use
of the Proprietors of Sankey Brook Navigation, by

You are to send the tonnage of the above   Collector
by the Bearer of this

4. A Sankey Brook permit of 1789 for 40 tons of cinders carried in the *Witton* of
Dungeon

The company had paid its first dividend in April 1761,[36] and by 1785 its £155 shares were considered to be worth £300, which suggests it was paying about 10 per cent, or £15 a share.[37]

In 1788 the Mersey & Irwell, anxious to extend their navigation downwards while yet avoiding the difficulties of the Mersey, had the idea that they might link their own line near Woolston with the Sankey's near Winwick, and 'extend it from the end of that Canal at ffidler's fferry to Runcorn in conjunction with the proprietors of such canal',[38] and decided to discuss the idea with the Sankey committee. In January 1789 plans of a Woolston–Bewsey cut and a Fiddler's Ferry–Runcorn Gap extension were before a special meeting of the Mersey & Irwell's shareholders, and approved subject to estimate. Their idea was now to build both lines themselves, and so a sub-committee was appointed to negotiate with the Sankey for the passage of Mersey & Irwell craft. They seem to have been confident that the Sankey would co-operate, but after a long time of discussion, the shareholders were told the following year that it had been impossible to agree on terms. (*To continue the history of the Weaver and Sankey Brook Navigations, turn to Chapter VI.*)

CHAPTER III

The Douglas and the
Leeds & Liverpool

++++++++++++++++++++++++++++++++ ◆ ++++++++++++++++++++++++++++++++ ++++

IN 1712, Thomas Steers surveyed the River Douglas from the
Ribble estuary to Bridge mill above Henhurst bridge, Wigan.[1] The
principal object was to substitute water for land carriage of Wigan
coal and cannel to and across the Ribble, and so to widen its
markets up and down the Lancashire coast, particularly northward; also to provide a better outlet for the inland manufacturing
towns. The carriage 'is very chargeable, and, to many, very
dangerous: their Road being cross Rible sands. Two miles over,
covered each Tide with Water; and in the Passage whereof, yearly,
several Persons, and Goods, are lost'.[2] A Bill was promoted in 1713
to make the river navigable to Wild Mill, backed by George
Kenyon of Peel Kenyon Hall, M.P. for Wigan, a Mersey & Irwell
supporter, Peter Shakerley, M.P. for Chester,[3] inhabitants of
Wigan, Liverpool, Rochdale, Bolton, Manchester and Lancashire
north of the Ribble, and 'several Thousands of Persons' from the
Fylde.[4] George Kenyon observed that Steers' estimate of return
on capital was modest, and wrote: 'I am satisfied ye profitt will
be double to what he mentions and ye charge not near so great.'[5]
But the landed interests of the riparian owners prevailed and the
Bill was rejected by the House of Lords.[6]

After a brisk interchange of pamphlets in 1719, support from
Wigan Corporation, 'and many Thousands of others, Owners of
Land, and Inhabitants' and considerable parliamentary opposition
from some local landowners and farmers, and from established
merchants of Wigan and Ormskirk, which nearly defeated the
Bill,[7] William Squire and Thomas Steers were authorized by an
Act[8] of 7 April 1720 to make the River Douglas (alias Asland)
navigable from the Ribble estuary to Miry Lane End, Wigan,

which would be 'beneficial to Trade, advantageous to the Poor, and convenient for the Carriage of Coals, Cannel, Stone, Slate, and other Goods and Merchandizes . . . and be a Means to preserve the Highways'. Eleven years were allowed to complete the navigation works, after which the commissioners appointed by the Act were empowered to appoint new undertakers. A single maximum toll of 2s 6d (12½p) a ton was authorized for all traffic except manure, which had to be carried free for landowners within 5 miles of the river.

Thomas Steers we know. William Squire was a Liverpool alderman concerned in the salt trade and in promoting the Weaver Navigation. Behind the Bill, but unnamed, was Squire's brother-in-law, Richard Norris, a merchant of the town and a former member of Parliament, entitled, it was later alleged, by a secret bargain, to one-third of the undertaking and its profits, partly for his help in getting the Act. He was the man to whom Thomas Patten wrote in 1698 about his ideas for making the Mersey and Irwell rivers navigable. Steers was supported before the parliamentary committee by William Marsh, who was soon afterwards to support the Weaver Bill, and John Sumner. The promoters had argued that coal and stone prices would be less because 20 miles of land carriage would be saved; that goods for Manchester, Bolton, Bury and Rochdale could be brought more cheaply by the Douglas, along with lime for burning near the coal pits; and that less goods would need to be transported over the treacherous Ribble sands.[9]

In June, during the South Sea Bubble stock exchange boom, the undertakers issued 1,200 £5 shares against a quarter of the profits, and soon these were selling at £70 each. This quarter was vested in trustees for the benefit of the shareholders, the rest in Squire, to be disposed of in shares for the benefit of himself, Norris and Steers. It is not known whether they were issued. The estimate had been £10,000, with a revenue of £1,000 p.a., of which £6,000 had now been raised. But in August the bubble burst, and soon Douglas shares were selling at £3 3s. Some years later, some shareholders put the promoters into court, alleging that the scheme was impractical, that they intended to 'make a Bubble thereof and to raise Money from all such Unwary Persons as they could draw in'. They said that Steers had only pretended to start work, by paving the river banks for a little way, building part of a lock and a boat too big to pass it.

Norris said he had nothing to do with the matter; Squire denied any deceit; Steers described the work he had done—buying land, stone and timber, building a lock, and carrying goods along 5 miles of the river. He said that whereas he had spent £900 on getting the Act and on his work, he had only received £800 from Squire, and would need £7,000 more to finish. If he were telling the truth, and if all the £6,000 had been called in the first place, the rest of the subscription had vanished.[10]

Local landowners took up the scheme again in 1733,[11] but action does not seem to have followed until 1738, when the commissioners met for the first time, and an agreement was made with a colliery owner in Orrell to deliver 800,000 baskets of coal at 3s 2d a score* on the river banks near Gathurst bridge. The coal was sold in the Fylde and north Lancashire, although in 1743 the undertakers complained that the colliery owner was competing against them by land sale at Poulton. This agreement appears to suggest that the greater part of the river was already navigable to Gathurst bridge; alternatively it might have been conditional on the making of the navigation to that point. In March 1740 two new undertakers were appointed by the commissioners, Roger Holt of Wigan and Alexander Leigh of Hindley Hall,[12] who pushed forward the work with more vigour. Steers seems not to have been concerned with these developments: from 1736 onwards he was building the Newry Navigation in Ireland, and from 1738 carrying out new dock work for Liverpool corporation. Given that the half of a 36th share which changed hands in 1746 for £112 7s 7d (£112·38) represented somewhere near cost price of the work and also of the 'Boats, Barges and other Vessels now trading upon the said River which belong to the proprietors or undertakers',[13] then the work done subsequently to Steers' efforts probably cost about £7,000, and the carrying fleet some £1,000 more.

By 1740, coal and stone were regular cargoes,[14] and in 1742 the commissioners certified that the river was navigable in terms of the Act.[15] By 1754 Edward and Henry Holt had joined the undertakers, when they made an agreement to charge only 1s a ton for coal, cannel, limestone, slate, soap, ashes and stone in order to encourage a small partnership to build two barges for carrying on the river.[16] In 1761 the undertakers were Alexander Leigh, who seems to have provided most of the money, Lord Pollington, David Poole, Edward and Roger Holt and John Chadwick.[17] This strengthening of the controlling body was probably made in

* A basket was 72 lb, 20 to the score.

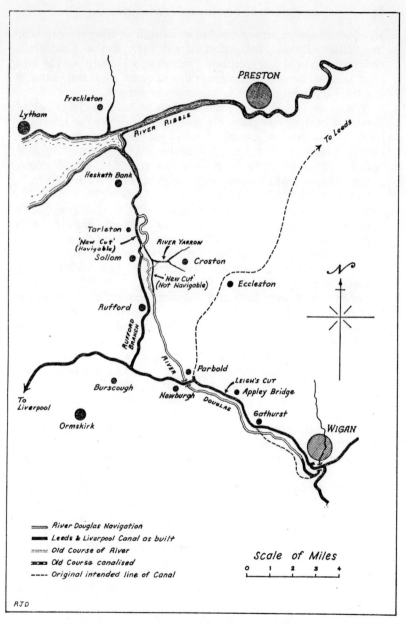

5. The Douglas Navigation, showing the changes at Sollom in 1805

an effort to secure improvements as a result of the promotion of
the Sankey Brook Navigation in the early 1750s. Trade had
developed in coal to Liverpool, Preston and Lytham, and to Ireland, whence there was a return traffic in grain, meal and butter,[18]
but the Liverpool coal trade was now threatened.

A start on 'Leigh's Cut', intended to by-pass the river below
Gathurst bridge, was probably made in 1753,[19] as the improvement works evidently were of sufficient magnitude to produce
strong criticism. That year 'A Disinterested Burgess of Wigan'
had this to say when Sir John Savile, as part of his election cam-
paign, sought credit for assisting Leigh to improve the river,

'As to Mr Leigh's Navigation, I would never contribute towards it, because I always thought it a wild impracticable
scheme, of certain Injury to many Thro' whose Lands it was to
pass, and likely to end in nothing but the Ruin of the Projector.
The Success has answer'd my Expectation; and I am sorry to see
the Misfortunes in which it has involved one whom I long
loved and respected'.[20]

If Leigh indeed were in financial straits, he weathered the storm
well enough to live another nineteen years, and by 1767 Sir John
had joined the undertakers, and Josia Poole had replaced David.[21]
In 1759 Miry Lane, which led to the head of the Navigation from
the Warrington turnpike at Pool bridge, was re-made at the
undertakers' expense, but Leigh's Cut was still incomplete when
the Leeds & Liverpool took a hand in 1771.[22]

In its final form as a purely river navigation there seem to have
been eight locks, two between Wigan and Crooke, one above and
one (on a lock-cut)† below Gathurst bridge, one above and one
below the present Appley Bridge, and two between that point and
Newburgh, the upper again on a lock-cut. There was a short
side-cut from the river to a basin at Miry Lane End.[23]

Trade northwards up the coast prospered: 'all the sea-coast
parts northwards* are supplied by means of the River Douglas,
which carries the coals from the neighbourhood of Wigan to the
mouth of the Ribble'.[24] Limestone from north Lancashire and
slate from Westmorland were brought back as back-carriage.[25]
This was written soon after the Douglas had been replaced by the
Leeds & Liverpool Canal's artificial cut, but undoubtedly the old
navigation had provided a well-established foundation for the
trade.

Alexander Leigh sold his majority holding of shares to the

* Of the Ribble.   † The remains can still (1970) be seen.

canal company on 26 November 1771. Leigh's son, Holt Leigh, bought a navigation share after his father had sold his to the canal company. He was a Wigan solicitor, and did various pieces of legal business for the canal company.[26] Alexander Leigh died on 24 November 1772, but by then the fortunes of the Douglas were bound up with the Leeds & Liverpool Canal.

Manchester men had failed in 1753–4 to get an Act for a canal to Wigan. The town had supported the Bridgewater Canal plan of 1759, but the local collieries were dependent on road transport and the Douglas for their coal exports. But a change was coming.

The success of the Sankey Brook, the opening of the Duke's canal to Manchester and the 1762 Act for its extension to Runcorn, the completion in 1763 of the first part of Britain's longest canal, the 25-mile Lagan Navigation,[27] and John Smeaton's report in the same year on a possible Forth & Clyde Canal, convinced men that canals were practical and necessary modern improvements. More, they now seemed the obvious answer to the age-old problem of exchanging goods between the principal ports. The result was a flurry of canal-building in the air between 1764 and 1766, followed by a rapid getting down to earth: schemes for canals to link not only Forth to Clyde, but Mersey to Trent, Trent to Severn, Irwell to Calder, and Mersey to Aire. The first, as the Forth & Clyde Canal[28] was authorized in 1768; the second and third, the Trent & Mersey and the Staffordshire & Worcestershire,[29] in 1766; the fourth, after a false start in 1766, not until 1794 as the Rochdale (see Chapter X). The last became the Leeds & Liverpool.

Joseph Priestley, who worked for the company later and ought to have known, gave the credit for its beginnings to an engineer, John Longbotham:

'The Duke's success drew forth the attention of Mr. Longbotham, a native of Halifax, who, after inspecting and examining the works on the Duke's Canal, projected the scheme of making a similar canal from Leeds to Liverpool, and for this purpose took an actual survey of the country between those two places, laid down a plan and prepared an estimate of the expense, which he produced at sundry meetings of gentlemen and land-owners interested in promoting the scheme.'[30]

Longbotham found a ready listener in John Hustler, a Quaker wool merchant of Bradford.[31] The result was a public meeting at the Sun Inn, Bradford, on 2 July 1766 'to consider . . . a navigation that will connect . . . Hull, Leeds, Wakefield, Bradford,

Keighley, Skipton, Coln, Burnley, Clithero, Blackburn, Wigan, Liverpool, Preston and Lancaster'.[32] The advantages were thought to be the cheap and easy distribution of goods imported at Hull and Liverpool; the carriage of limestone from Craven, coal from Lancashire and Yorkshire to the Pennine areas for lime-burning and domestic use, and stone, slates and flagstones to the ports for transhipment. Land carriage was then quoted as costing 1s (5p) per ton per mile, against which it was estimated that coal could be transported for 1½d, limestone for 1d, and merchandise for 2d a mile, at a total saving of some £200,000 p.a.[33] Longbotham was asked to do a preliminary survey while the promoters sought wider support by setting up a Lancashire committee based on Liverpool and one in Yorkshire on Bradford.

By the beginning of 1768 Longbotham had submitted a route from the end of the Aire & Calder Navigation at Leeds up Airedale to Gargrave, thence over the watershed to Colne, down the valleys of the Lancashire Calder and the Ribble to near Preston, and thence across the west Lancashire plain by way of Ormskirk in a great circle to Liverpool. This line was approved. Later, however, Brindley was asked to report on Longbotham's survey at the request of Liverpool Corporation, who had contributed £200 to preliminary expenses and now offered to pay £50 more towards Brindley's fee.

Some dissension now showed itself between the two committees, the Yorkshiremen (who controlled the finances) ordering no more money to be paid out or subscriptions accepted until the Lancashire committee had raised a sum equal to Yorkshire's. On 9 January 1769, however, simultaneous public meetings were held in Bradford and Liverpool to open the subscription lists to the general public. Brindley had by now largely approved Longbotham's plan (his assistant, Robert Whitworth, had done most of the field work). He stated the length of the proposed line as 108¾ miles, 42 ft wide at surface to take Aire & Calder wide boats, and 5 ft deep. He estimated the cost at £259,777, and future income from tolls at £20,000, leaving a balance of £3,000 after paying some £4,000 p.a. in working expenses and 5 per cent interets on capital.[34] Lord Thanet of Skipton castle headed the subscription list with £1,000, followed by John Stanhope of Horsforth with £4,000. By mid-February it was reported that £40,000 had already been subscribed in Liverpool.[35]

A Bill was prepared, with a supporting petition from Liverpool Corporation, but too late for the 1769 session. An argument now

Page 67 Weaver Navigation: (*above*) the Anderton lift before its reconstruction in 1908, showing also the salt chutes; (*below*) the old basin of Weston Point docks on 29 April 1924. Five steamers are discharging raw materials for the Potteries

Page 68 Sankey Brook Navigation: (*above*) Robert Daglish's works, by the Ravenhead branch, in 1845; (*below*) barges at the Sankey Sugar Company's wharf at Earlestown

began about the proposed line in Lancashire. Liverpool wanted one that ran less directly across the county, and which served towns that the Yorkshire committee felt could be adequately served with branches. They there⌐   ⌐mp'oyed two Lancashire surveyors, John Eyes and Richard Melling, to plan a line more to their liking. On 14 June 1769 Longbotham was instructed by the Yorkshire committee to take the following letter to Brindley in Lancashire:

'Sir, Some of the Lancashire Gentlemen being very warm for almost an Entire alteration of the Line of the proposed Canal through that County (the Circumstances of which the Bearer Mr John Longbotham will explain) we earnestly desire you will as Expeditiously as possible settle with him the proper means of satisfying them how far it is Eligible by a view of it or otherwise as you think necessary.'[36]

Brindley deputed Whitworth to check Eyes's and Melling's line for the Yorkshire committee, who evidently anticipated a certain lack of co-operation from their Lancashire partners when they instructed Whitworth:

'If the Liverpool Agents do not Employ a proper person to attend you and point out the said New Line you are to take such a Survey of the County as will qualify you to Judge of its propriety only.'[37]

Whitworth reported that Eyes and Melling had taken inaccurate levels at Rishton resulting in an error of 35 ft in the embankment required at Burnley. Having found this, and being pressed for time, he had gone no further. It was sufficient for the Yorkshire committee, who promptly rejected the Liverpool scheme on the grounds that it would increase the length of the canal by at least 20 miles, would cost twice as much as Longbotham's Lancashire line, and that the present association and subscription were based on the plan originally produced at Bradford the previous year. Further, to settle the matter it was resolved that no one in future but Brindley, Longbotham or Whitworth should be employed on surveys at the expense of the General Subscription. But they were too late; on the same day a meeting in Liverpool instructed P. P. Burdett of Liverpool, assisted by Richard Beck, to do another survey.

The Liverpool anxiety to alter the line arose from the lack of important coalfields upon it, the failure of the collieries on the Sankey Brook to produce the quantities of coal for which a sale was waiting, and therefore the urgent need for an alternative

E

source of supply. This obviously lay in the Wigan coalfield, which could not, however, compete with the St Helens collieries while its only means of water transport was by the roundabout and hazardous Douglas and coastal route. They therefore wished to re-plan the Lancashire portion of the Leeds & Liverpool to leave Longbotham's line near Colne and run by Burnley, Blackburn, Chorley, Wigan, Ormskirk and Bootle to Liverpool. The committee were taking no chances this time, and appointed Henry Berry and Melling to check Burdett's line. They also agreed to levy 10s (50p) per £100 subscription on the Lancashire subscribers to pay the costs.

In September Hustler and Abraham Balme hurried over to Liverpool in an attempt to carry Longbotham's line, and agreed that Brindley should be asked to arbitrate on the two routes, after which a General Assembly of the subscribers should be held finally to decide the matter. Brindley duly reported to the Yorkshire committee that the deviation between Leyland and Liverpool, to serve Ormskirk, would be both shorter and easier to construct, but for the remainder advocated Longbotham's line, with branches. Having got wind of this, the Liverpool committee (for the second time) resolved to withdraw their subscriptions and form an entirely independent committee only a week before the general meeting to be held at the Black Bull, Burnley, on 11 December,[38] at which Brindley's estimates of £174,324 for Longbotham's line of 66 miles in Lancashire and £240,881 for Burdett's of 83 miles were presented to the subscribers. It was resolved that Longbotham's line should be adopted, and a Parliamentary committee was appointed to promote a Bill, whereupon three Liverpool committeemen, attended by Burdett, presented a resolution from several of their subscribers withdrawing their subscriptions, which was accepted. What happened in the subsequent four weeks is not clear, but on 10 January 1770, at a further meeting at Leeds, the objecting Liverpool subscribers offered to reinstate their subscriptions if the Liverpool end of the canal could be built simultaneously with the Leeds end, to which the Yorkshire committee readily agreed.[39] Thus the controversy ended, but whether the large majority behind the more powerful Yorkshire committee deterred the Liverpool men from carrying on alone, or whether they were simply bluffing, is not clear. Wind of the Liverpool Canal schemes to link Wigan and south Lancashire pits both with Liverpool and with the Trent & Mersey Canal (see p. 55), with possible extensions into Yorkshire, which emerged the following September, may have influenced the decision.[40] Alternatively, and likelier, the decision to connect the canal to the Douglas may have been made at this time; if so, it would have been the deciding factor.[41]

There was a little opposition to the Bill, but with the powerful support of Liverpool Corporation, on 19 May 1770 the company received its Act[42] authorizing a canal from the River Aire at Leeds bridge to the North Lady's Walk, Liverpool, '. . . and from thence to communicate with the River Mersey'. The main opposition had been from the Douglas proprietors over the proposed aqueduct near Newburgh. It would be too low to pass masted vessels, so provisions were made for the Douglas proprietors to build connecting cuts to the canal on each side, with locks as necessary. Conditions were incorporated safeguarding both parties' water supplies, and the canal company was to pay £500 compensation to the Douglas proprietors within 3 months of completion. Thus river craft unable to pass beneath the aqueduct would be enabled to lock into and out of the canal on either side of it, a somewhat clumsy arrangement but one which seemed to satisfy both sides for the moment. More important, Wigan coal would thereby secure its inland route to Liverpool and the Act specifically referred to the mutually beneficial effect of communication. The authorized capital was £200,000 in £100 shares, work to be deferred until the entire amount was raised, with additional capital of £60,000 if found necessary. Interest at 5 per cent was to be paid on calls until completion.

The full capital was raised inside two months and a single committee of both Lancashire and Yorkshire proprietors was elected, meeting alternately in Yorkshire and Liverpool until 1775 when the separate Liverpool committee was re-formed to conduct affairs between Liverpool and Wigan in a subsidiary capacity, an arrangement which lasted until 1850. Brindley was appointed chief engineer at £400 p.a., and Longbotham clerk of works at £160 p.a. Subsequently Brindley asked to be released from his appointment and Longbotham agreed to act in both capacities. Work was authorized from the Douglas crossing to Liverpool, between Skipton and Bingley, and from Shipley to Leeds. Two treasurers were appointed, James Hollingshead in Liverpool and Hustler in Bradford, with respective office clerks, the boundary between their jurisdictions to be Padiham. Both offices were to exchange books every fourteen days and keep each other informed. But Bradford kept the ultimate control, where John

Eagle was appointed law clerk and Joseph Priestley book-keeper to the clerk of works and accountant, at £100 p.a. This was reinforced in 1771 when Hustler was appointed sole treasurer. The next year Priestley was instructed to take all the affairs of the company under his care, was provided with an office in Bradford and had his salary increased to £170 p.a.

Contracts were quickly let and work proceeded on both sides of the Pennines. The easier cutting in Lancashire led to the first boats being launched on a small section between Newburgh and Liverpool, probably for contractors' use, on 25 July 1771, occasioning a small celebration among the workmen.[43] This raised the problem of water supplies, as the company was forbidden under its Act to take water from the Douglas. It will be remembered that Alexander Leigh was making a lengthy cut to by-pass the Douglas from below Gathurst. For years work had been going on desultorily, doubtless for lack of funds. In November 1771 an offer to sell his majority shareholding (29 out of 36) was recorded by the committee, but more likely he had been approached first, for the need was great and, Leigh's cut by now having reached close to their line, the time was ripe. The company agreed a figure of £14,500, and the purchase was confirmed by an Act of 24 June 1783.[44]

But there was more to it than this. The scheme to cross the Mersey with a canal to join the Duke's and Trent & Mersey Canals, with branches on the Lancashire side to Liverpool (connecting with the Leeds & Liverpool Canal) and north-eastwards towards Ashton-in-Makerfield, tapping many pits, was gathering momentum. The Wigan coalfield was added following a meeting of the promoters in October 1770, and after an inactive period of ten months the scheme appeared again as a canal from Park Mills, on the south side of Liverpool, through Everton, Kirkdale, Derby and Huyton to Appleton, where it would lock down to the Mersey crossing. Branches would connect with the Leeds & Liverpool at North Lady's Walk, with further locks or a tramroad down to the Mersey, and with collieries in the Prescot area. Inland, the level at Appleton would be continued across the Sankey Brook Navigation by an aqueduct north of Newton, and so to the Wigan coalfield, joining the projected Lancaster Canal extension to the Bridgewater. A further branch to Wigan itself and the Douglas would provide another junction with the Leeds & Liverpool.[45]

Realization that the Leeds & Liverpool from Newburgh would

not compete effectively with the Sankey increased support in Liverpool, accompanied by accusations in the Leeds & Liverpool committee that Longbotham was in error over the levels between Shaw Green and Liverpool, to disprove which Jessop had to be called in. The Liverpool Canal scheme was now a serious rival and had to be fought; attacks therefore were made on several fronts. The first move was to purchase Leigh's shares in the Douglas; it was followed by suggestions that Liverpool could be supplied with water from the canal. At Wigan, the Corporation was promised a maximum toll of 1s per ton for merchandise shipped from the town, in return for their support in opposing the Liverpool Canal. Lastly, forces were joined with the Sankey proprietors and landowners on the projected route, each party agreeing to bear one-third of the cost of opposition. Aided by some of the more dissident Leeds & Liverpool subscribers, the Liverpool Canal reached its target of £160,000 and in January 1772 the promoters petitioned Parliament for leave to bring in a Bill for a straightforward Liverpool–Wigan canal, omitting the Runcorn aqueduct and the branches. But they were outnumbered by the opposition and their petition was rejected.[46] It cost the Leeds & Liverpool £244 in expenses and the price of the Douglas purchase at a time when they could ill afford it. By April, 20 miles of canal had been finished in Lancashire and 14 miles in Yorkshire at a cost of £48,888.[47]

As soon as they had secured control of the Douglas, the Leeds & Liverpool set about completing Leigh's cut and making a junction; work was in progress by August 1772. In October Longbotham's contract was renewed at £500 p.a. in return for his entire services, although in 1773 he was permitted to attend the Parliamentary committee on the projected Leeds & Selby Canal, which he had surveyed, and in which a number of Leeds & Liverpool proprietors were interested. The 8 April 1773 saw the opening of the first section of the canal to navigation, from Bingley to Skipton. Two boat loads of coal were sold in Skipton at half the normal price, 'The Bells were set ringing at Skipton; there were also bonfires, illuminations and other demonstrations of joy',[48] and the committee turned its attention to the matter of drawing up bye-laws. In Lancashire, by February 1774, the canal was navigable from Liverpool to Newburgh and thence up Leigh's cut to join the Douglas at Dean lock, Gathurst, some 3 miles below Wigan, a total mileage of 31½. A short stub was made at Newburgh ready for the main line. With 23 miles almost completed in Yorkshire, the works had cost £219,517, or £4,000 per mile.[49] The next month, on 21 March, traffic from Skipton was extended to below the newly-opened junction with the Bradford Canal (see p. 80) at Shipley, several thousand spectators witnessing the descent of the five-rise locks at Bingley by five laden boats (the first taking 29 minutes), in 'amazement and delight.'[50] By June the canal was open to Gargrave,[51] and there were moves afoot to promote a Bill for a branch canal from Settle to Barnoldswick which, however, failed to materialize.[52] Forty lime-kilns had been erected or were in course of completion between Skipton and Bradford. In October a ceremonial opening took place between Liverpool and Wigan, for which some hasty repairs to the River Douglas had been authorized above Gathurst, and a number of the proprietors sailed up the canal to the accompaniment of music, flags, two 21-gun salutes, and bell-ringing.[53]

Money was now extremely short. The original capital and eighteen months' income had been spent, to the tune of £227,363,[54] in constructing 55 miles of canal, and in September 1775 Hustler reported that he had insufficient funds in hand for the next pay day. The committee ordered him to borrow up to £2,000. Next month there was insufficient cash to pay the interest due to the proprietors, who had to accept stock placed to their credit in lieu. Meanwhile Longbotham had resigned in June. He had of late been constantly harried by the committee, who, justifiably perhaps, felt that he was not devoting all his energies to the canal's business. He had recently purchased coal mines at Upholland from William Berry, to which he was authorized to construct a side cut, and had formed a packet-boat concern on the opening of the canal to Liverpool. Differences arose over his accounts, which were referred to arbitrators, and even then the company had to threaten legal action to recover their award. Hustler carried on the superintendence of the canal works until Richard Owen was appointed engineer in July 1777.

Construction continued spasmodically towards Leeds despite arguments over the line to be taken below Armley which Jessop had to be called in to sort out, and finally sufficient funds were mustered by additional subscriptions to complete the junction with the Aire about ¼ mile above Leeds bridge, leaving that length of river under the company's control as far as the commencement of the Aire & Calder Navigation at the bridge. The grand opening ceremony was held on 4 June 1777, watched by 20–30,000 people. On arrival of the procession of boats from

Apperley Bridge, which they had left at 8 a.m., the proprietors were met by a party from the Aire & Calder Navigation who accompanied them to the New White Cloth Hall for the usual junketings.[55] In all, 58 miles of canal were now open, from Gargrave to Leeds with 29 locks falling 267½ ft, and an 8-arched aqueduct over the Aire at Dowley Gap near Bingley; and from Wigan down the Douglas to Gathurst, and thence by canal to Liverpool, with two locks falling 17½ ft and single-arched aqueducts over the Douglas and the Alt.

During this period, important decisions had been taken regarding the Lancashire section of canal. Several proposals were considered for a connection to the Mersey at Liverpool, either by locks or by a tramroad, but inability to reach agreement with the Corporation led to the scheme being dropped.[56] In 1775 an agreement was made with the administrators of Leigh's estate to rent the remaining shares in the Douglas, with an option to purchase at the end of 21 years. Early next year there was agitation among the Liverpool proprietors for extension of the canal from Gathurst to Wigan, in order to cut out the old river entirely, and a new cut from Newburgh to Sollom on the tidal Douglas above its confluence with the Ribble estuary to by-pass the lower half of the river. The committee suggested that the Lancashire men should raise additional capital among themselves for these purposes and authorized work on the Wigan section as soon as they had contributed £5,000. The sum of £3,000 was raised in additional shares in two months, upon which the committee agreed to let work commence as soon as £10 calls were paid, but progress was slow and the canal does not appear to have been completed to Wigan until 1780, with two locks.* It was constructed on the north side of the river, not the south as originally envisaged, in order to avoid a crossing on the level at Gathurst.[58] Henceforth the canal from Wigan to Newburgh was known as the Upper Douglas Navigation. In 1777 contracts were let for the Lower Douglas, or Rufford branch, and Owen reported that it was completed by October 1781, falling by 7 locks to a tide lock into the river at Sollom. To complete this work, and also to purchase six remaining shares in the Douglas Navigation from Holt Leigh (Alexander's son) by instalments, more money had to be found.

---

* An example of its attractiveness is an advertisement of May 1781: a colliery for sale at Orrell near Wigan is described as 'with a good and commodious Rail'd or Plank Road that Coals may be got down at an easy Expence to the Leeds Canal',[57] whence there was a good sale at Liverpool, Preston or Lancaster.

Interest due in 1778 was again paid in the form of additional stock; the Liverpool party advanced £1,700, and again £5,000, on security of future tolls, and the possibility of a 5 per cent loan was investigated. A credit balance of £3,808 in April 1779 prompted the General Assembly somewhat rashly to declare that a £2 10s (£2·50) dividend would be paid in 1780, which in the event had to be rescinded, and a resolution passed that no more improvements were to be made after the Lower Douglas works had been completed.

However, trade was growing and money was coming in. Coal traffic increased with the opening of the Upper Douglas, albeit slowly at first as coalowners were not anxious to build new wharves and staithes, with the result that transfer from the old river to the new cut was a gradual process. Passenger boats commenced to ply between Gathurst and Liverpool, tolls being levied at first at ½d per 2 miles per passenger, later consolidated into an annual sum. In 1775 Longbotham & Co. and the Union Company were each charged £90 p.a. for packet boats on this run. Tonnages on coal, slack, culm, and potter's clay were reduced in order to encourage the traffic, but once the Upper Douglas had been finished coal dues were advanced by 6d (2½p) a ton on the old river to force traffic on to the new canal. The build-up of traffic on both sides of the Pennines is shown as follows in the toll account:[59]

	Yorkshire £	Lancashire £	Douglas Navigation £	Total £
1772	—	—	162	162
1773	121	—	365	486
1774	1,146	365	514	2,025
1775	1,528	1,489	843	3,860
1776	2,438	1,714	1,160	5,312
1777	2,492	1,994	1,509	5,945
1778	3,017	2,545	1,790	7,352

Simultaneously, despite the shortage of ready money, the value of one £100 share had risen to £139 in 1778.[60]

In March 1781 a credit balance of £2,766 was reported to the General Assembly and in the following October, Owen announced that the Lower Douglas was now open and, without amendment of the order, would qualify for the additional 6d (2½p) per ton coal dues, as it superseded the lower reaches of the old river entirely. This would tend to restrict the recovery of coal carrying rather than the reverse, so the order was postponed for six months. Meanwhile, trial tolls of 1s (5p) for coal and limestone shipped to and from the Ribble and 3s (15p) for merchandise from Liverpool to the Ribble were authorized. Owing to the high cost of the Douglas improvements, and Sir Robert Holt Leigh's[61] demands for the first instalment on his shares, no dividend was declared yet. As some £13,000 had been borrowed on the surety of a few individual committee members it was decided to include borrowing powers in the Bill for retrospective authorization of the Douglas purchase, although in the event only powers to lease the tolls for up to 21 years were granted (except those on the Douglas to which the remaining shareholder's consent had to be obtained). Powers to borrow up to £20,000 specifically to purchase those remaining shares were, however, incorporated, and in the same Act of 1783 coal tolls on the Bradford Canal were protected from under-cutting within 6 miles of the junction at Shipley, and the position regarding General Assemblies was regulated. The previous frequent meetings were reduced to twice a year, alternately in Lancashire and Yorkshire.[62]

In the summer of 1782 Owen was discharged and John Harrison appointed superintendent, in charge of maintenance and day-to-day operations. The importance to the canal of the road network in the Leeds–Bradford–Halifax area is illustrated by the company's opposition to moves by the turnpike trusts to increase their charges. They felt the canal would 'be much prejudiced if any Additional Tolls should be laid upon coals passing upon the said Roads'.[63] A first, and solitary, distribution of profits 'divided according to stock held' was made in 1783, perhaps injudiciously, as by next January more money had to be borrowed on credit of the tolls in order to pay Leigh's next instalment, and in July 1784 debts amounted to between £17,000 and £18,000. It was firmly decided to declare no more dividends until the debts had been discharged, and by October there was enough in hand to pay off the balance due to Leigh and make a start on them. A suggestion to encourage traffic to and from Leeds and the Bradford Canal by reducing tolls, at the expense of increasing them between Newburgh and Liverpool, was rejected at the next Assembly, although the opportunity was taken to help Bradford pits compete against coal coming off the Aire & Calder by reducing tolls on downward coal traffic at Shipley and increasing them on upwards traffic from Leeds.

By the beginning of 1785 the net profit had risen to £8,013 and more debts were paid off. Somewhat ominously, water shortages

in Yorkshire were reported. At the beginning of 1786 the Leeds
& Liverpool entered the quarry business by leasing the Earl of
Thanet's limestone quarries at Skipton (see Springs Branch Canal),
which they continued to do until the present day, and in the
second half of the year a £2 dividend was paid. The Wigan coal
trade was by now very profitable and the Liverpool proprietors
sought enlargement of the basin at Liverpool to accommodate the
increasing traffic and expedite the development of yet more pits.
To this end an attempt was made to stabilize prices for 10 years
provided the pit-head prices remained similarly constant, but the
enlargement of Liverpool basin was frustrated by the dominant
Yorkshire proprietors who in their turn, because of the interests
some of them held in the Bradford Canal, were anxious further to
reduce the Bradford dues to increase traffic on that side.

In 1789, Robert Whitworth was asked to report on the cost of
completing the canal, which he estimated at £169,818, including
a summit level tunnel at Foulridge. Whitworth optimistically
stated

> '. . . I will find it necessary to lay the head level 53 ft below the
> summit at Foulridge-lane, and to carry the canal, for about
> 1,500 yards, in a tunnel, underground. This tunnel, compared
> with what has been done in other canals, will be a small affair;
> and there is good reason to suppose from the nature of the
> ground and the materials which are at hand, it will be easier to
> make than most that have been executed'.[64]

Another application to Parliament for borrowing powers was
authorized. There was opposition from millowners on the River
Aire to Whitworth's proposal that water should be taken from it
to feed the summit level, and from landowners on the deviation
between Colne and Whalley, where Whitworth proposed to keep
to the south side of Pendle Water and the River Calder instead of
the north bank as originally authorized, to avoid a large aqueduct
at Whalley. Lord Sefton opposed the overflow weirs proposed in
the Alt valley near Aintree, and the owner of Broughton mill
near Skipton feared for his water rights. They were all pacified by
various means, the latter by taking the tenancy of his mill, and an
Act was obtained on 9 June 1790. It authorized a deviation from
Lomeshaye, near Colne, through Marsden (now Nelson), Ighten-
hill Park, Padiham, Altham, Clayton, and Great Harwood to
Whalley, with provision for a section 120 yd wide at Dean Clough,
doubtless to form a reservoir. Restrictions on water supplies were
onerous: water was not to be taken from the Aire or its tributaries

above Gargrave, from the rivers Ribble and Hyndburn, nor from streams supplying Martholme mill, Great Harwood. After completion of the summit level, Howden Beck was to be diverted back into the Aire. The provisions under the 1783 Act for borrowing £20,000 were repealed and the company authorized to borrow up to £200,000 to complete its line. Bradford coal owners gained parity in tonnage rates with coal coming into Yorkshire from Lancashire, but not the long-sought advantage over coal coming up the canal from the Aire & Calder.[65] Whitworth was approached to act as engineer, which he agreed to do for 600 guineas (£630) p.a., the same salary he was receiving as engineer to the Forth & Clyde Canal, now nearing completion. He left his elder son to finish the Forth & Clyde and took up his appointment on the Leeds & Liverpool, assisted by his younger son William. No time was lost in borrowing £6,000 and ordering a start on the works, followed by another £20,000 and preliminary borings for Foulridge tunnel in September. From the first modest 2 per cent dividend, in 1786, a return of 6 per cent was now being paid.

In November 1790 the company suffered a blow in the death of John Hustler, who had done so much to promote and establish the canal. Now that Whitworth was engineer, Harrison was made responsible under him for maintaining the Lancashire side and James Fletcher of Bradford, the Yorkshire side. The Leeds & Liverpool up to this time had been more closely identified with Hustler than with any other man. It was he who had ceaselessly campaigned for a waterway to 'unite the seas', once Longbotham had found the way; he who had canvassed for subscriptions; he who, largely by his own efforts, had smoothed down the Liverpudlians who had threatened to wreck the project before it started, and, once work did begin, had constantly travelled back and forth between Bradford and Liverpool for meetings, inspections, surveys and all the numberless tasks involved in co-ordinating works being carried out 50 miles and more apart. Financial control had been in his hands from the beginning and, despite the heavy debts incurred, he saw the value of a £100 share increase to £207 two years before his death, a toll income of over £17,500 the following year,[66] and a dividend of 6 per cent. For a canal little over half completed it was fair progress. (*To continue the history of the Leeds & Liverpool Canal, turn to Chapter VII.*)

The Bradford Canal

In 1744, a group of 'Gentlemen, Farmers and other Inhabitants of the Towns and Parishes of Bingley, Kighley, (sic) Kildwick, Skipton, and Carleton, and other Parts adjacent to the River Aire, in the West Riding of the County of York' petitioned for leave to bring in a Bill to make 18 miles of the river navigable from Inghay bridge, near Skipton, to Cottingley bridge, east of Bingley.[67] Although the course of the proposed navigation was followed by the Leeds & Liverpool 30 years later, it was really a forerunner of the Bradford Canal, for its object was to improve communications between the Craven district and Bradford. Cottingley was the nearest practicable point on the river from which goods could be unloaded. There the road from Keighley left the valley and ran over Heaton Moor to Bradford, the present road through Shipley not being constructed until about 1820.[68] The petitioners maintained that the navigation would make

'the more easy Conveyance, and cheaper Sale, of Coal, Lime, Wood, and several other Sorts of Goods, Merchandizes, and Commodities; the Prices whereof, by the heavy Charges of Land Carriage, occasioned by the Badness and Uneveness of the Roads, are very much enhanced, to the great Discouragement of Husbandry, and other Employments.'

The Commons referred the petition to a committee of the House, but thereafter it was dropped.[69]

Promotion of the Leeds & Liverpool revived interest in giving Bradford water transport, and in 1770 a group of fourteen merchants and others interested was formed to promote a Bill, including six who were members of the Leeds & Liverpool committee, John Hustler and Abraham Balme among them. An Act was obtained quite quickly, on 29 April 1771, empowering twenty-eight proprietors to raise a capital of £6,000 in £100 shares to construct a canal, of similar dimensions to the Leeds & Liverpool, from the latter at Shipley to Hoppy bridge, Bradford (the present Forster Square covers the site). An additional £3,000 could be raised if needed, 5 per cent was to be paid during construction, and the company was empowered to make reservoirs and take water from 'such watercourses running into a Brook called Bowlingmill Beck as shall be found within the distance of Two thousand yards of Hoppy Bridge aforesaid'.[70]

Balme appears to have supervised construction of the canal and been responsible for its finances, while John Longbotham was consulted on the engineering side, but by 1776 Priestley was evidently attending to the administrative and legal matters.[71] The precise opening date was not recorded in the minutes, but on 12 March 1774 Balme paid 16s (80p) to 'the Ringers at the arrival of Mr Balme and Mr Leaches Boats'.[72] By this time the Leeds & Liverpool was open from Skipton to Bingley and there was water in it at Shipley; indeed it had been declared 'navigable' for 13 miles upwards from a point 2 miles below Shipley in late 1773;[73] the official opening from Bingley to Thackley (on the Leeds side of Shipley) did not, however, take place until 21 March, nine days later. The Bradford Canal was $3\frac{3}{8}$ miles long and fell 86 ft from Bradford by ten locks. (*To continue the history of the Bradford Canal, turn to p. 181.*)

The Springs Branch or Lord Thanet's Canal

Lord Thanet, of Skipton Castle, owned a large acreage of limestone rock which was let for quarrying purposes, and in 1772 the Leeds & Liverpool committee were asked to consider varying their line at Skipton to give better access to the quarries at the back of the castle, at a cost of £300–£400. They declined, and in the following year of 1773 his Lordship's agents (he was a minor at the time) obtained an Act on 10 May to make a canal from The Springs near Skipton Castle to the Leeds & Liverpool at Hebble End Close, Skipton.[74] The Earl's quarries were 530 yd from the Leeds & Liverpool,[75] and in 1785 that company leased from the Earl the 'Canal, Waggon Road, Lime Rocks &c . . . at or near Skipton for . . . eleven years' at £134 per year. The quarry was at that time being worked by Mercer Flatts Lime Company, whose rights were taken over together with 'Utensils, Waggon Way, Staith and Dock'. When the lease was completed, Hustler was instructed to 'prepare proper wood for Sleepers for making the necessary Waggon Road up to Haw Bank',[76] although no further action seems to have been taken. Evidently a rapidly growing demand for limestone made it worth while to open up the deposits in a big way, as Haw Bank was some $\frac{3}{4}$ mile beyond the existing quarry and about 200 ft higher. So began quarrying operations which are still carried on today, and which have been executed under the control of the canal concern, directly or indirectly, until the present time.

In 1786 negotiations were opened to extend the Springs Branch

Canal a further 240 yd in order to give better access to the Haw Bank works, the company offering to pay Lord Thanet 1s 6d (7½p) for each £1 per annum expended, which his agent declined with the suggestion that the company should make it at their own expense and lease the necessary land at £20 a year. The Yorkshire committee of the Leeds & Liverpool decided to defer the work until his Lordship should come of age, perhaps hoping for better terms, but meanwhile purchased another acre of limestone land. (*To continue the history of the Springs Branch, turn to p. 180.*)

PART TWO—1790–1845

CHAPTER IV

The Mersey & Irwell and the Bridgewater, 1790-1824

++++++++++++++++++++++++++++++++ ◆ ++++++++++++++++++++++++++++++++

WHEN our period begins, the Bridgewater Canal had for thirteen years been connected with the Potteries, the Trent, Birmingham and the Severn by means of the Trent & Mersey Canal at Preston Brook. An indirect link with London by way of the Thames at Oxford was opened that year, and a much better one through the Warwick lines of canal and the Grand Junction in 1800.[1] The Mersey & Irwell, however, had local connections only, with the Weaver, the Sankey Brook and later the Ellesmere Canal to Chester.* With the Bridgewater Canal there was no link. Both waterways also received and despatched goods by road transport between their own lines and places as far distant as, for instance, Sheffield.

In 1790, however, the Old Quay† company heard that a canal from Manchester to Bolton and Bury was being discussed, and at once made it known that they would welcome a junction 'upon fair terms';[3] these were agreed, and in the next year the Manchester, Bolton & Bury Canal was authorized to join the Irwell near their quay. Though the final connection was not made until December 1808, the canal had been completed to its basins at Oldfield Road some twelve years before (see Chapter IX), whence traffic could be exchanged with the river.

The Manchester, Bolton & Bury's promotion was soon followed by a revival of the 1766 scheme for a Rochdale canal from Manchester to join the Calder & Hebble at Sowerby Bridge. Its pro-

---

* The Wirral line of the Ellesmere Canal from Ellesmere Port to Chester was opened for commercial traffic in February 1796. Early in 1797 the Mersey & Irwell sent two flats to start carrying on it, and seem to have continued the trade.[2]

† Mersey & Irwell.

moters soon chose a junction with the Bridgewater Canal at Castlefield, and got their Act at the third attempt, in 1794. The Manchester, Bolton & Bury, backed by the Mersey & Irwell, tried both to defeat the Rochdale project, and also themselves to get a connection with Yorkshire and Hull, either by a canal from Bury to Sowerby Bridge, or from Bolton to join the unfinished Leeds & Liverpool at Red Moss above Wigan. Both failed. The Mersey & Irwell therefore put all its efforts into building up the Liverpool–Manchester trade, and gained a larger share than the Bridgewater. That canal's managers depended more on their coal sales, the considerable local trade down the Runcorn line, and their growing interchange trade, first with the Trent & Mersey, then with the Rochdale and the canals that were built from it, the Ashton-under-Lyne, Peak Forest and Huddersfield, and finally with the Leeds & Liverpool after the two were linked via Leigh in 1821.

By 1793 the Mersey & Irwell, their 'Navigation having become very considerable' had accumulated a balance of £5,000. They decided to pay some of it out as a 30 per cent dividend. In the same year the veteran Hugh Henshall and Charles McNiven, then beginning his career as a local waterway engineer, surveyed the navigation and reported that if the locks and cuts were kept in good order, and millers prevented from lowering the water level, 'this Navigation would be capable of doing much more business than it ever has done and with greater dispatch and certainty to the Merchants as well as to the Navigation';[4] also the, annual repair bill would be less. The company, with money in hand, then did what was immediately needed, obtained an incorporation Act[5] to modernize their company structure, and turned their minds to further improvements, for trade was pressing hard upon the means of transport.

By now several cuts had been made by the former and present Old Quay companies to shorten the river line: at Mode Wheel, Stickings below Barton, Calamanco (Sandywarps), Butchersfield (with an additional lock) below Hollins Ferry, the old Woolston cut, and Howley.[6] But their heart was more in improvement below Warrington, and in 1796 they started to investigate a possible canal to by-pass the river section between Warrington and Runcorn Gap where craft were delayed during neap tides, in the hope of being able to improve on their current Liverpool to Manchester freight rate of 7s 2d (36p) a ton by operating at all times. Once again they talked with the Sankey Brook committee,

but once again the latter would not agree. So they employed
Thomas Morris of Liverpool, son of Brindley's assistant on the
Bridgewater, to seek an alternative. He reverted to the 1783
suggestion of a canal from above Warrington to the Hempstones
just above Runcorn. His broad estimate was approved in June
1797, and cutting from Latchford below Woolston to Runcorn
started in 1799, finance being provided by calls on the shareholders, who were meanwhile limited to 5 per cent dividends and
5 per cent interest. Only two shareholders dissented: the Duke of
Bridgewater with five shares and his representative at shareholders'
meetings, John Marsden, with ten.

Having delivered this blow to the Bridgewater Canal with one
hand, the company moved smartly with the other to stop the
Manchester, Bolton & Bury's proposed Bill to cross the Irwell
and join it. They minuted that 'every possible exertion should be
made to prevent such Act being obtained'.[7] It was, and they
succeeded, though their own chairman, Matthew Fletcher, who
was also a committeeman of the Manchester, Bolton & Bury and
a principal supplier of its coal, must have had some difficult
moments. However, his help in getting the Runcorn cut started
against obstructions from Sir Richard Brooke's trustees, whose
land was affected (Brooke when alive had opposed the Duke, we
may remember), and in defeating the threat of a Mersey bridge in
1801, earned him the company's thanks and an inscribed silver
cup worth £100. In that year the Old Quay seems first to have
started to carry coal and limestone, the coal probably first shipped
at Bank Quay, Warrington, for carriage to Manchester and intermediate wharves, for they quoted a toll of 1s 8d (8½p) for coal
over the whole length, wharfage included, and 1s 6d (7½p) for
limestone. The old figure of 3s 4d (16½p) was maintained for
other goods.

The cut was finished late in 1803, but the company then decided to extend it beyond the Hempstones to a point just short of
Runcorn Gap, and about a mile above the Runcorn locks of the
Bridgewater Canal, the last mile and a half or so being along the
river's edge. It was opened in July 1804.[8] To build it, £75 seems
to have been called on each share, yielding £37,500, to which
must be added sums ploughed back from profits. These calls were
repaid to the shareholders between 1810 and 1816 to restore the
shares to their original value and the paid-up capital to £10,000.*

* The minute books do not make the number of calls clear, but we have assumed
that the sums repaid were those that had been called.

The cost was later given as £48,000.[9] Their opening announcement told the public that their flats were now locked and sealed, to prevent pilferage and damage, and to keep cotton and other goods dry and clean, and that they had much increased their warehouse accommodation where craft could be loaded or unloaded under cover.

The 7¾-mile cut started with a rising lock* off the navigation at Latchford, and ran level on the Cheshire side of the river to the entrance lock into the Mersey at Runcorn, a saving of over 3 miles in distance in comparison with the old river course, and much more in time and trouble. The engineer was probably Charles McNiven. At Runcorn the canal entered a small basin, whence a lock admitted craft to the river. Water was supplied to the new canal by a long and winding feeder from the old Woolston cut. It crossed the river above Woolston lock, and entered the canal just above Latchford lock.† Directories now noted that 'in consequence of the late improvements . . . the delays formerly occasioned by the neap tides are now wholly done away, and vessels sail daily'.[10] The old channel to Warrington remained navigable, and was used when the new canal was being repaired, and for local traffic, especially coal from the Sankey. Even after the cut had been built, the Mersey & Irwell still hankered after a connection with the Sankey, though the motive was probably now to get better access to their coal. Discussions again took place in 1813, but were dropped, there being 'little prospect of the Scheme being accomplished'.[11] Soon afterwards a reduced toll of 1s (5p) a ton for Sankey coal was decided upon, and coal supplies for carriage upstream on the navigation seem then to have improved.

By this time, the company had extended their Old Quay accommodation, and were operating a considerable number of craft. In 1796, after a strike for more money, they had sent their superintendent Peter Wright with John Wright their clerk to deal with the men. The two came back with an interesting agreement that seems to have lasted. Its main provisions were:
(a) increased wages of 16s (80p) p.w. for a captain, 13s (65p) for the first hand, and 6s (30p) to 9s (45p) for the second hand or boy;
(b) bonuses to the crew for doing two trips on one spring tide,

* Protected by reverse gates against Mersey floods.
† When the Woolston new cut (see p. 98) was made later, this was replaced by a feeder from the new cut which again crossed the river by a trunk, this time just above Paddington lock.

and for delivering cargo at Liverpool on the second day after loading at Manchester;

(*c*) yearly bounties to all hands for good behaviour, five guineas to the captain, two to the first hand, one to the second;

(*d*) cost of living allowances for the wives and children of captains whose homes were in Liverpool or Manchester;

(*e*) the captain to choose his crew, subject to the superintendent's approval;

(*f*) a week's notice on either side, and no flat to be left during a voyage.

Later, eight annual bounties were added, for those captains who had done the most trips in a year with the least complaints, after allowance had been made for repair time, and all boys on the flats were made 7-year apprentices, with 10 as the lower age limit. These bonus arrangements lasted until 1831, when revised rates were substituted.

In January 1811 the company agreed with the Manchester, Bolton & Bury to operate carrying services from Bolton and Bury over their joint lines to Liverpool, seemingly to replace the retiring firm of Rothwell & Addison, whose craft and stock they bought for £730. Carrying began soon afterwards.

Until the Runcorn cut was made, the company does not seem to have employed lock-keepers. Presumably flat crews or horse towing men did the job. But in 1806 lockhouses were ordered to be built, as 'many Accidents and Inconveniences which happen from time to time at the Locks and Weirs would be thereby prevented'.[12] In 1804 the Mersey & Irwell got a lease of their existing wharf at Liverpool, some more accommodation there, especially for their important timber trade, and preferential berthing in Manchester dock, which was becoming overcrowded by everyone's vessels using it. About 1807 they took the whole dock on long lease, with permission to turn it into a wet dock. This was done by 1813. They now made it known that 'Sloops or vessels having cargoes to forward by this navigation are admitted free of dockage into the canal at Runcorn, to discharge their cargoes into the company's vessels plying on their navigation, as also into their newly erected Wet Dock . . . (at) Liverpool'.[13] From 1802 onwards the Bridgewater concern was also extending its dock and accommodation at Liverpool.

In 1805 the Mersey & Irwell company considered a possible canal link with the Rochdale Canal* which would also provide

* See the account of the Manchester & Salford Junction Canal in Chapter V.

them with additional wharfage within their own land round Atherton Street, and got John Nightingale, the Manchester, Bolton & Bury's engineer, to estimate it. The cost came out at £20,131, and nothing was done, but it led to the company employing Nightingale as their first full manager-engineer at the then high salary of £500 p.a., a house, horse-keep and expenses when away from home. When Nightingale died in 1814, they split the job, Thomas Lingard being made manager and Arthur Gilbody* engineer.

Meanwhile, changes had been taking place on the Duke's canal. The passing of Acts for the Ashton-under-Lyne Canal in 1792, and for the Rochdale, Huddersfield and Peak Forest in 1794, offered the Duke the future prospect of trade with Yorkshire through two Pennine waterways, as well as a promising local trade in coal, cotton and merchandise up to Rochdale, and in limestone with the Peak District. The Ashton and its link to Castlefield through the short Piccadilly–Castlefield section of the Rochdale Canal was opened in 1800, as was its extension the Peak Forest. The Pennine connection by way of the broad Rochdale Canal opened at the end of 1804, the narrow and less important secondary route by the Huddersfield Canal not until 1811. Finally, the Duke obtained an Act[14] in 1795 to extend the Worsley line of his own canal onwards to Pennington near Leigh. Incorporating a small part of the cut made for the Hollins Ferry branch after the 1759 Act, it was opened about the end of 1799. The authorized toll was still the old 2s 6d (12½p) for any distance on the Duke's canals, but, as Joseph Priestley of the Leeds & Liverpool wrote in 1802 in connection with that company's proposed branch to Leigh, 'The Duke possesses all the Lands adjoining the Termination of his Canal at Manchester, so that no other Staiths can there be procured than his, but his Staiths & warehouses are open to the public, paying him 1s 2d per Ton'.[15]

Until the Trent & Mersey was completed in 1777, the Duke was the only carrier at Castlefield. Then Hugh Henshall & Co., the Trent & Mersey company's own carrying department, arrived, and carried to and from the Trent & Mersey and Birmingham. Not until about 1790 did Worthington & Gilbert, themselves linked to the Duke's affairs, start in business. Pickfords came to Castlefield in 1794; by 1804 twelve firms of carriers worked there, and by 1813 there were three fly-boat services to London. By 1821 there were twenty-two firms, mainly operating to the connecting

* In 1818 Gilbody resigned, and was succeeded by Richard Phillips.

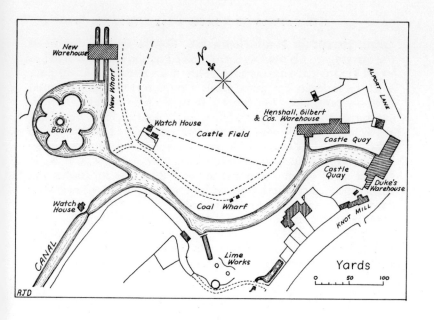

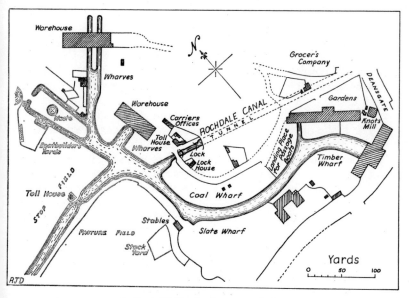

6. Castlefield basins in 1790 and 1825

canals. Except for Hugh Henshall & Co, the Duke did most of the carrying on his own waterway, aided by the authorized toll of 2s 6d (12½p) for any distance. This discouraged short-distance work by independent firms, while a trade to Liverpool required not only canal craft, but those able to use the tideway as well as accommodation at the port. Some of the Duke's craft were built at Worsley; others were bought, or constructed to his order. When he died in 1803, he seems to have owned 60 flats and 46 lighters. Probably later, fly-boats were worked between Manchester and Leigh, Warrington and Runcorn for light and perishable traffic. These were wider than narrow boats, narrower than barges, and were sometimes called bastard boats.

It seems that in the 1790s, relying upon rising prices and costs to justify him, the Duke began to disregard the 6s (30p) freight and toll limitation of his Acts. In 1794 and again in 1797 he advertized[16] his freight rates as follows:

	Cotton		Goods	
	s	d	s	d
Manchester and Liverpool	10	6 (52½p)	7	2 (36p)
Runcorn			6	2 (31p)
Preston Brook	8	10 (44p)	6	2 (31p)
Acton (T & M)			7	2 (36p)
Stockton	6	8 (33½p)	4	2 (21p)
Burford Lane			4	2 (21p)
Broadheath			3	6 (17½p)

Between Liverpool and Manchester he was not restricted, but the cotton rate from Preston Brook to Manchester seems to be illegal, even if one puts the odd 8d of the Stockton rate and the 2d on goods to Preston Brook, to wharfage and similar charges.

The Duke died on 8 March 1803. The title became extinct, but a life interest in his canal property went to the Marquess of Stafford, and was then entailed upon his second son, Francis, who was later to take the name of Egerton and be created Earl of Ellesmere, and his heirs. Under the Duke's will, trustees were established—at first, Sir Archibald MacDonald, Chief Baron of the Exchequer, the Bishop of Carlisle, and the manager of the canal at the time, that remarkable character Robert Haldane Bradshaw. In the will Bradshaw was given the management of the canal, collieries and local estates for life or until resignation, was to have Worsley New Hall and Runcorn House free of rent, rates and taxes, and was empowered to appoint his successor.

Both concerns had taken an early interest in steam traction. In

June 1793 trials of John Smith's steamboat were made on the Sankey Brook Navigation.[17] Early in 1794 the Mersey & Irwell minuted:

> 'A person in Liverpool having produced to the Committee the Model of a Boat navigated by Machinery & having a paper signed by the Mayor and several other respectable Gentlemen of Liverpool who had subscrib'd different Sums of Money for encouraging the Scheme, Mr. Wright was directed to pay him five Guineas'.[18]

One guesses that this was Smith. Tomlinson tells us that in 1797 Smith's steamboat travelled along the Bridgewater Canal from Runcorn to Castlefield. William Sherratt of the Salford firm of Bateman & Sherratt watched the trial and, when two years later the Duke tried a steam craft at Worsley, it was fitted with a Sherratt engine.[19] A little later the *Charlotte Dundas*, successfully tested on the Forth & Clyde Canal in 1802, was brought to the Duke's notice. He ordered similar craft to be built for his own canal, but after his death in 1803, the trustees cancelled the order.[20]

In August 1806 the Mersey & Irwell decided to enter the passenger-carrying business between Manchester and Runcorn, and to organize river connections to and from Liverpool. They ordered Nightingale to get boats built. He moved quickly, for on 18 February 1807 a party of shareholders were given a trip to Runcorn in one of the new boats before the public service started on 1 May. The down boats left Manchester at 08.00 and arrived at Runcorn at 16.00, having done the journey an hour faster than those on the Bridgewater canal. Up boats took the same time as the trustees', leaving Runcorn at 10.00 in summer and 08.00 in winter to arrive at Manchester eight hours later. Fares were the same, but 'private rooms, for the accommodation of parties, may be engaged for the day'.[21] The navigation's packet wharf at Manchester was on the Salford side of the Irwell near New Bailey bridge, where waiting rooms were built beneath the roadway. The Warrington stop was originally at the Black Bear bridge, but later the boats were taken to the more convenient Warrington bridge, where passengers who wished could transfer to the Liverpool coach. In two respects the Mersey & Irwell boats had the advantage. At Runcorn their passengers, when changing from the Liverpool river boat to the navigation packet, only had to cross a wharf, while those by the Bridgewater had to walk up the flight of locks, and have their luggage carried, to the packet waiting at the top. And 'within a dozen miles of Manchester, the water of the canal is black as the Styx, and absolutely pestiferous, from the gas and refuse of the manufactories'.[22] That of the river was some-what cleaner. This competition caused a serious fall in the trustees' packet-boat takings:

Years	Average takings £	Years	Average takings £
1791–93	3,864	1803–05	5,422
1794–96	3,673	1806–08	4,814
1797–99	4,168	1809–10 (2 yrs)	4,221
1800–02	5,181		

It also caused the trustees to make immediate arrangements for boat connections at Runcorn to and from Liverpool instead of coach interchanges at Stockton. These Mersey packets were sail-ing ships, but a steamer, the *Elizabeth*, was launched in 1812. She was not a success, being sold in 1816 and then converted to a horse-drawn packet. But early in 1816 it was reported that 'two new and elegant Steam Packets to sail betwixt Runcorn and Liverpool, are now building, and will be ready to sail early in the spring; the one to meet the late Duke of Bridgewater's Boat, the other to meet the River Mersey and Irwell Navigation Company's Boat for Manchester.'[23] These came into service in 1817, taking two to three hours for the run. Thereafter steamers normally worked between Liverpool and Runcorn.

The Duke's packet boats, carrying parcels, bundles of cloth and groceries for country stores as well as passengers on business or pleasure, were popular. In 1794 fares from Manchester were:

To	Front Room s d		Back Room s d	
Altrincham	1	0 (5p)		9 (4p)
Lymm	2	0 (10p)	1	3 (6p)
Preston Brook	3	0 (15p)	2	0 (10p)
Runcorn	3	6 (17½p)	2	3 (11p)
Worsley	1	0* (5p)		6* (2½p)

* Front room, 1s 6d (7½p) return; back room, 9d (4p).

An 1802 directory said:

'The sail from Manchester to Runcorn, in the Packet Boats, is very amusing . . . at Lymm the boat stops a quarter of an hour, and passengers have the opportunity of getting refresh-ments at a neat and clean public house . . . Runcorn is become an astonishing place of business . . . it is a place of summer

resort for sea bathing, being very much recommended by physicians for its saline as well as salubrious properties.'[24]
The Worsley service was extended to Leigh in 1800.

In 1824 the services on the Runcorn line were a boat from Manchester at 08.00, connecting at Warrington with coaches for Liverpool and at Preston Brook for Chester, and arriving at 17.00. In the other direction the boat left Runcorn at 10.00, and arrived at Manchester at 18.00. There was also a Saturday market boat from London bridge (Warrington) at 05.00, arriving at 10.00 and returning at 16.00. From Runcorn, the *Duke of Bridgewater* and *Eclipse* steam packets sailed about high water for Liverpool, calling at Weston Point, where in the summer they connected with the *Lady Stanley* packet from Northwich. Between May and September extra canal packets were run to connect with the tide steamers. On the other line were twice-daily boats between Manchester and Worsley, with a once-weekly extension to Leigh. In addition, there was a daily service at 06.00 (summer) and 07.00 (winter) from Manchester to Wigan, Scarisbrick (where conveyances met the boats to take passengers to Southport), and Liverpool.[25]

By 1815 the Mersey & Irwell were taking steam seriously, and asking for experiments with steam-packet boats, and a packet hauling a flat. They considered that if they did not themselves take the initiative, 'certain Adventurers will be attempting to put Steam Packets on the old River to the prejudice of this Company'.[26] So they sent their engineer Arthur Gilbody and a sub-committee to Scotland to find out what they could at Glasgow and Greenock. These came back discouraged, reporting that 'as Steam Boats and Engines are now constructed and navigated, it is not . . . practicable' to haul loaded flats by steam, for a 24 h.p. engine would be needed to tow three loaded flats from Warrington to Manchester. The weight of the engine and coal would be 22–4 tons, and the draught more than the 4 ft available. In addition, they saw navigational difficulties, for 'the River Mersey is greatly circuitous in its Course, the Water is shallow, the Cuts are narrow, the Locks are numerous, and difficult to approach and quit'.[27] Therefore they did not think steam haulage practicable yet on their own navigation.

Competition from the Mersey & Irwell seems to have held the Bridgewater Canal's takings and profits steady in the decade following 1790. Then in 1800 the Duke and the river company decided to offer identical freight rates (including tolls) between

Liverpool and Manchester. These were advertised in the *Manchester Mercury* for 15 July 1800. They showed heavy increases, part presumably due to the last few years' price rises, but part the consequence of ending competition. The rate for timber, iron, bricks, etc. was now 10s (50p), for corn 11s 8d (58½p), most groceries 13s 4d (66½p), tea, sugar and tobacco 15s (75p), and both cotton and Manchester manufactured goods 16s 8d (83½p).

The effect of this rates agreement, added to that of the additional trade brought by connecting canals—this itself increasing with the rapid growth of the national waterway network, as well as from the Leigh branch—was to cause a sharp rise in profits, even though waterborne supplies from collieries on the Ashton Canal were now able to compete with those from Worsley. A profit fall after the Mersey & Irwell opened their Runcorn & Latchford canal did not greatly alter the position. Here are averaged figures:

Years	Receipts £	Profit £	Trade to and from Manchester & Liverpool tons	Total trade tons
1791–93	64,772	18,774	117,010	283,195
1794–96	61,738	23,409	108,126	271,417
1797–99	66,628	24,441	105,326	287,467
1800–02	98,641	43,587	107,820	326,628
1803–05	117,349	50,736	126,583	345,190
1806–08	116,925	44,466	121,490	346,005

For the years from 1806 to 1824, the average profit remained at about £44,500, though for the prosperous year 1824 it reached £80,697.[28]

In November 1808 the Mersey & Irwell found it necessary to watch a Bill for a branch canal from the Leeds & Liverpool at Wigan to meet the Duke's at Leigh, 'which space, it is said, is almost a continuous bed of excellent pit and cannel coal'.[29] This would also 'open a new line of Water Carriage between the Towns of Liverpool and Manchester'[30] that would be all canal, though roundabout. The Manchester, Bolton & Bury were strongly opposed, because they had themselves hoped to join the Leeds & Liverpool (see Chapter IX). It seems likely, however, that when the Old Quay's superintendent called on his Bridgewater opposite number, an understanding was reached, for the Mersey & Irwell seem not to have formally opposed the Bill. It was lost, but the understanding remained, its object being to continue cooperation between the two concerns on the Liverpool–Manchester route,

A rates agreement was again reached, and in September 1810 the
trustees and the Mersey & Irwell once more published identical
notices of higher rates for carrying in their own craft side by side
in the columns of the *Manchester Mercury*:[31]

	Manchester– Liverpool per ton		
	s	d	
Timber, iron, lead, clay, bricks, etc.	13	4	(66½p)
Grain, tallow, soap, etc.	15	0	(75p)
Provisions, hides, ropes, flour, sacks of meal, etc.	16	8	(83⅓p)
Clog soles, coffee, tobacco, loose horns, bark, etc.	18	4	(91⅔p)
Cotton, wool, bale goods, linen, tea, hops, glass, oil, spirits, etc.	20	0	(£1)

This was a mistake. There was an outcry from the merchants,
and early in 1811 Benjamin Sothern of the Bridgewater saw
Nightingale of the Mersey & Irwell about an application from
some of them either for a reduction in freight rates, or for warehouse accommodation should they become carriers themselves.
The latter company agreed to lower any freights that the two
officials thought too high, but meantime the independent Grocers'
company had been formed to carry on the Duke's canal, and
started operations in March 1811. By 1825 they had 15 flats.

In 1812 the Mersey & Irwell proposed considerable freight
reductions, up rates to vary from 12s 6d (62½p) and 13s 4d (66½p)
on most goods to 18s 4d (91½p) on wines and spirits, cotton and
linen, the down from 10s (50p) to 12s 6d (62½p), these being a
good deal lower than those of 1810 and by no means high for the
times. They asked Bradshaw to make similar reductions, and the
absence of further minuting perhaps suggests that he did. In
August 1813, finding other carriers offering a still lower rate for
upstream timber, they cut their own, and decided that 'it is the
Interest of this Company to carry upon the same Terms as any
other regular Carriers'.[32] This policy of meeting any other outside
price, including the Bridgewater's, then became their practice.

Identical rates were thus quickly dropped in favour of a loose
understanding between the two waterway concerns that if one
made a change, the other should follow. For instance, in 1816 the
Mersey & Irwell learned that back carriage on the Duke's canal
cost only 13s 4d (66½p) irrespective of cargo, whereas their own

figure was 16s 8d (83½p); they promptly reduced. Again, in 1821 they found that Bradshaw had cut the cotton figure to 15s (75p), and followed him.

The Mersey & Irwell now entered a prosperous period that lasted almost to the end of its independent life. The dividend, which had fluctuated between 3 and 5 per cent while the Runcorn & Latchford Canal was being made, and until 1813, then rose at the same time that capital repayments were being made, until it stood at 20 per cent in 1816. In 1817 it rose to 30 per cent, in 1823 to 35, and in 1829 to 40 per cent. We must of course remember that even a 40 per cent dividend needed only £4,000 p.a., and that the assets actually employed were far larger than the nominal capital of £10,000. By 1825, for instance, the company had spent £100,000 on warehouse accommodation alone.

In 1819 the river company started on a major improvement, when they decided to replace the existing short Woolston cut by a longer one, starting just above the upstream point of the old cut, but running for 1¾ miles to rejoin the river further down, so by-passing an additional curve. This was opened on 14 February 1821 at a cost of £20,000. A new lock, Paddington (Dobson's), at its lower end, replaced Woolston lock at the foot of the old cut. The Mersey & Irwell, 28¾ miles long, was now only a few hundred yards longer than the Bridgewater Canal. It was another 16 or 17 miles to Liverpool. In 1822 they passed to another improvement. Unable to pass more than about 20 craft each way on an average tide through their tide-lock at Runcorn into their small basin above it and so to the Latchford cut, they decided to provide a second parallel and larger lock that would open into a much larger new basin. Craft could be locked in and out of this by a second lock to the river, but the basin would also have a separate pair of tide-gates to be used when the tide-level equalized, so increasing capacity to 140 craft a tide, more than all those, company and independent, then using the navigation. Thus they would avoid 'all those inconveniences and delays which are so seriously felt and daily experienced at the entrance into the River from the Duke of Bridgewater's Canal'.[33]

The Corporation of Liverpool, under powers claimed as conservators of the river, but with no wish to see a coastal and foreign shipping port grow up at Runcorn, promptly told the Mersey & Irwell that their works would affect navigation and must be removed, and applied to the Lord Chancellor for an injunction. The company kept their nerve, got counsel's opinion that they

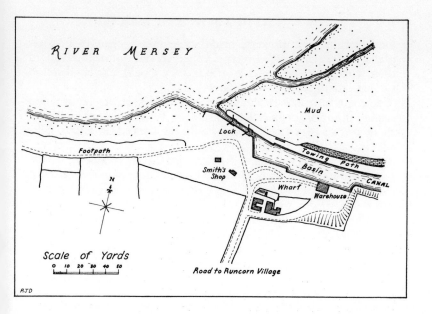

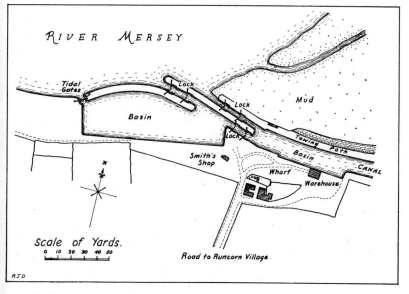

7. The Runcorn terminus of the Mersey & Irwell Navigation before and after the building of the new lock and basin in the 1820s

were within their powers, made some minor changes in their plans, and went ahead. Liverpool then served notice that should their works later be found injurious, they would take legal action to abate them, and the controversy died.

In their turn, the Bridgewater trustees decided to lay down a second flight of locks at Runcorn, even though the management there said in 1825 that 60 craft could be worked on a tide. This left the existing flight below the top staircase pair, and ran diagonally across the ends of the existing basins to a point on the river below the old exit. The new flight ended in an extension of the tidal dock, when access to the river was through a last pair of gates when tides were suitable. The work was started in 1825, and the locks were probably in use by 1827, an extra toll of 8d being charged, though this was never confirmed by Act.[34] Later the top pair of locks were themselves doubled.

A branch from the Leeds & Liverpool Canal at Wigan to the Bridgewater at Leigh was at last authorized in 1819 and opened at the end of 1821. The many towns served by the Leeds & Liverpool were now linked to Manchester, as was Manchester by a third waterway to Liverpool. This new alignment of routes may have been one cause of revival of the Duke's old idea for a canal from his line at Sale Moor to Stockport, for this would have given the Leeds & Liverpool and the Bridgewater access to Stockport and the useful new coal-producing area beyond it, without using the roundabout line by the narrow-boat Ashton. Plans were drawn in September 1822[35] by James Gilbert, engineer, and notices appeared in early 1823 for a $13\frac{7}{8}$ mile long canal from the Bridgewater at either Sale Moor or Stretford to Stockport and on to Hope Green near Poynton, with a $4\frac{1}{8}$ mile railroad extension to Kerridge near Bollington. The project was naturally opposed by the Ashton and Peak Forest companies, but it may have helped to revive the Macclesfield Canal scheme to connect the Peak Forest at Marple with the Trent & Mersey by way of Macclesfield and Bollington that was taken up again in 1824 and carried through.[36]

Though the tendency of rates from 1810 onwards was always downwards, bye-trading grew on the Bridgewater's Manchester and Liverpool run: in addition to the Grocers' company, David Bellhouse & Co started in January 1823, mainly in timber, the Manchester & Liverpool Union company in November 1823, mainly in corn, and the Rochdale & Halifax company, working through from and to the Rochdale Canal, in January 1824. On the

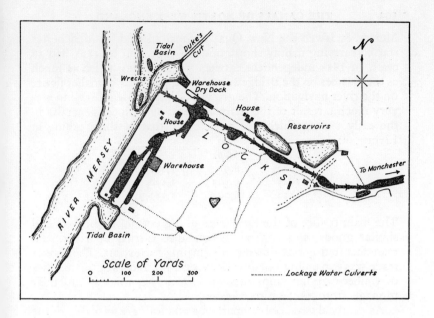

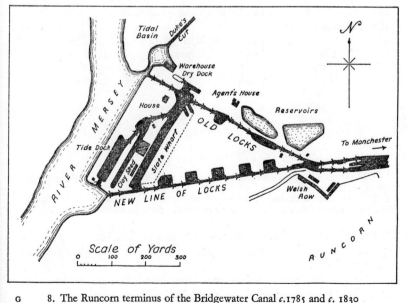

G   8. The Runcorn terminus of the Bridgewater Canal *c.*1785 and *c.* 1830

Mersey & Irwell the New Quay company based on Manchester started carrying mainly shop goods in 1823, and by 1825 had 18 craft. In 1825 independent carriers were moving twice as much as the trustees on the Bridgewater Canal, probably a smaller figure on the river navigation. The growth of independent carrying was very much a result of the sharp increase of business generally in the early 1820s, which was reflected in that of ships calling at Liverpool:

Year	Ships	Tons
1822	8,910	1,010,819
1823	9,507	1,120,114
1824	10,001	1,180,914

The main traffics of the time were grain, cotton, timber, oil and similar goods, and general merchandise carried up river, and manufactured goods downwards, mainly for export. The timber trade was expanding notably: between 1822 and 1824 the number of timber-carrying ships increased from 384 to 609, and their tonnage from 100,000 to 160,000.

As nearly always, only imperfect statistics[37] are available of the volume of Liverpool–Manchester trade on the three waterways. For the Mersey & Irwell we have figures of company flats loaded at Liverpool and know roughly the proportion of upwards to downwards trade:

Year	Flats loaded	Approximate tonnage*	Approximate total tonnage†
1816	2,483	80,697	93,112
1817	2,689	87,392	100,837
1818	3,071	99,807	115,162
1819	2,903	94,347	108,912
1820	3,282	106,665	123,075
1821	3,234	105,105	121,275
1822	3,337	108,452	125,137
1823	3,550	115,375	133,125

* The average cargo of a loaded flat was 30–35 tons. We have taken 32½ tons for the purpose of this table.
† This column estimates total tonnage on the route by adding two-thirteenths, the proportion of down to up trade, to the totals of the previous column.

These figures are for the company's own craft. One may perhaps guess that not more than 10 per cent should be added for the independents.

For the Bridgewater line, we have the following figures for carryings by the trustees' craft and by independents:

Year	Liverpool–Manchester			Manchester–Liverpool			Grand total
	Trustees	Bye-traders	Total	Trustees	Bye-traders	Total	
	tons	tons	tons	tons	tons	tons	tons
1815	23,633	35,195	58,828	4,407	12,828	17,235	76,063
1816	24,785	30,930	55,715	3,326	8,543	11,869	67,584
1817	24,764	32,552	57,316	2,190	11,037	13,227	70,543
1818	30,755	38,132	68,887	2,939	11,192	14,131	83,018
1819	22,737	41,932	64,669	2,357	8,705	11,062	75,731
1820	25,817	44,887	70,704	2,202	8,438	10,640	81,344
1821	27,470	49,122	76,592	2,545	11,037	13,582	90,174
1822	33,515	44,982	78,497	2,828	11,609	14,437	92,934
1823	30,279	59,975	90,254	2,790	10,418	13,208	103,462
1824	31,836	69,625	101,461	3,453	12,768	16,221	117,682

To these should be added those for the traffic coming on from Leigh and the Leeds & Liverpool by Kenworthy's and Pickford's boats:

	Liverpool–Manchester			Manchester–Liverpool			Grand total
	Kenworthy*	Pickford*	Total	Kenworthy	Pickford	Total	
	tons	tons	tons	tons	tons	tons	tons
1821	3,203	1,096	4,299	1,380	451	1,831	6,130
1822	3,335	3,780	7,115	1,513	2,164	3,677	10,792
1823	3,611	2,567	6,178	1,530	1,269	2,799	8,977
1824	4,653	2,277	6,930	2,408	1,632	4,040	10,970

* Kenworthy's began carrying in January, Pickford's in October, 1821. Pickford's gave up the route in December 1824, leaving only Kenworthy.

The Leeds & Liverpool Canal trade, we may note, was better balanced, and this route must have had some effect on both the Bridgewater and Mersey & Irwell routes in creaming off the scarce Manchester to Liverpool traffic.

CHAPTER V

The Impact of the L.M.R.

ON 2 October 1822 a newspaper notice appeared for 'a rail or Tram Road from Manchester to Liverpool'. The Mersey & Irwell got a copy of the plan and supporting documents and, having studied them, minuted that the line would 'materially affect the interests of the Company, if the Act should be obtained',[1] and decided both to oppose it and to alert other canal concerns. In February 1823 they were glad to hear that Bradshaw of the Bridgewater had 'expressed himself decidedly hostile to the projected Rail Road and would oppose it'. So had the Leeds & Liverpool and the Aire & Calder.

In August 1824 a sub-committee was despatched to see Bradshaw 'to ascertain what his views and intentions are about it'. Bradshaw told them that he 'should give the Scheme the most decided Opposition', and would help the Mersey & Irwell in theirs.[2] This should dispose of ideas that the two concerns worked closely together. Far from it. Thomas Lingard the Mersey & Irwell's superintendent spoke truly in 1825: 'there has been nothing like a combination existing between the two establishments; since I knew them, there has been a more than necessary jealousy between the two concerns'.[3]

The railway was, however, not the only potential competitor to the navigation companies. The Mersey & Irwell had to give a thought to Giles's not very serious plan to extend the Bridgewater Canal by a Mersey aqueduct to Liverpool, and both concerns to the proposed Manchester, or Manchester & Dee, ship canal.

Earlier proposals for a canal from the Dee to the Mersey[4] had been intended to support Chester's position as a port against that of Liverpool, but the Dee estuary was now seen as a more accessible starting point than the Mersey for a seagoing ship canal to Manchester. Such a line was surveyed in 1823 and 1824 by the Scottish engineer Robert Stevenson,[5] to take 400-ton craft and

run from Dawpool (between West Kirby and Heswall) by Frodsham, Lymm and Didsbury to Manchester. He was working for a
group not backward in appreciation of their own city:

'Manchester—itself the metropolis of the north of England,
and the central point to and from which manufactured goods
of every description are brought and forwarded, it has become
at once the great depot for the commerce of the world. Instead
of relying, as hitherto, on her inland communication with the
Mersey, she will extend her powerful arm to the ocean, and
draw to her own bosom the beneficial results of her enterprise
and industry',

as the prospectus[6] put it when seeking a million pounds to build
the 45-mile canal. A Bill was introduced, opposed, and thrown
out on standing orders early in 1825.[7]

The promoters then got William Chapman to study the scheme
again, and in 1825 he reported in favour of a smaller canal 51 miles
long to take 250-ton vessels. This, he thought, would be big
enough, for out of 3,240 craft entering Liverpool in a year, 2,118
were under 100 tons. Larger craft could tranship to lighters at
Dawpool docks. His estimate, however, was £1,569,000. He
quoted[8] interesting figures upon the main motive for the promotion of such a canal, the effect of the Liverpool dock and town
dues, some of them payable whether goods transhipped there or
not.

Charges on 500 bags of imported cotton	£	s	d	
Liverpool dock and town dues	19	15	10	(£19·79)
Carterage and porterage	15	12	6	(£15·62½)
Brokerage @ ½ per cent	31	5	0	(£31·25)

	£	s	d	
Liverpool charges	66	13	4	(£66·66½)
Freight to Manchester	41	15	0	(£41·75)
	£108	8	4	(£108·41½)

Charges on 20 cases of exported manufactured goods	£	s	d	
Liverpool dock and town dues		11	8	(58½p)
Carterage and porterage		18	4	(91½p)
Brokerage @ 2s 6d per package	2	10	0	(£2·50)

	£	s	d	
Liverpool charges		4	0	0	(£4·00)
Freight from Manchester		1	0	7	(£1·03)
	£5	0	7	(£5·03)

In 1826 Mr Dumbell of Mersey mills, Warrington, wrote a pamphlet[9] which, while not opposing Chapman's scheme as regards Manchester, suggested that the Mersey also needed improvement to Warrington by the building of a barrage and locks at Runcorn Gap. Finally, in 1828 Telford, Stevenson and Nimmo reported upon a 7-mile ship canal from Hilbre islands off West Kirby parallel to the north coast of the Wirral to Wallasey, to avoid the difficult Mersey entrance channels.[10] Dumbell's proposals was developed further in 1837, when local businessmen financed a survey.[11] This was carried out by Sir John Rennie, who proposed a ship canal 16 ft deep between Liverpool and Warrington, that could without difficulty be carried on to Manchester.[12] After which such schemes merged into those of the early 1840s (see p. 120) for the enlargement of the Mersey & Irwell.

We have gone far beyond the ship canal threat of 1825, which ended with the Bill's failure in the same session as that for the railway. Let us now look at the two navigations, the Mersey & Irwell and the Bridgewater, as they were during the railway controversy of 1825.

The Mersey & Irwell were still charging independent carriers the 3s 4d (16½p) toll authorized in 1721, though this now applied to a navigation starting at Runcorn and not at Bank Quay. It worked out at 1½d a ton/mile, a cheaper merchandise rate than most canals. Coal and road materials were cheaper, manure free. The Bridgewater's toll was 2s 6d (12½p) for any distance. This was theoretically cheaper, but as the trustees could charge what they liked for wharfage, 'the public pay as much by one conveyance as the other', as Mr Dumbell said in 1826.[13] In the Old Quay company's vessels the inclusive freight and toll charge from Liverpool (not Runcorn) was 15s (75p) for cotton, 12s (60p) for grain and 8s 4d (41½p) for timber, in the Bridgewater's 15s (75p), 10s (50p) and 8s 4d (41½p). Upwards traffic in timber was stored free at Liverpool until it could be shipped, and goods arriving at Manchester could be warehoused free for three weeks. Downwards traffic was collected free by the company's carts in Manchester:

'The Old Quay Company's servants usually call at the warehouse to know whether we have any goods, and what time they will be ready, and their carts call for them at the time we request them to call, and they take them down to ship them on board their vessels. There is no charge made for the use of the Company's carts, nor for collecting the goods'.[14]

These were finished textiles, the downwards rate on which was 10s (50p) a ton. The Mersey & Irwell's witnesses before the parliamentary committee pointed out that the cheaper rate offered by the railway promoters must be considered not only against the navigations' rates, but against the free services they also provided.

Quantities carried were considerable. The railway's counsel in 1825 said that in 1810, 110m. lb of cotton had passed upwards to Manchester, and in 1824 over 160m. lb. At this time the Mersey & Irwell's inwards trade was one-half timber, one-quarter cotton, one-eighth grain, and one-eighth sundries. The total trade between the two cities was some 250,000 tons a year, but it was unbalanced, only some one-sixth or one-seventh of the craft getting a downwards loading of bale or other goods, and this must also be borne in mind when charges are assessed.

Trade being good, the Mersey & Irwell were led to rationalize their fleet, deciding to build new and larger flats instead of repairing older and smaller ones. Thereby fewer craft would carry more goods at less cost. In 1825 they had 64 vessels of their own, with a carrying capacity of over 2,000 tons, and were building 6 more; the Bridgewater trustees had 75 with others building. The two navigations therefore owned 139 out of some 250–260 vessels in the Liverpool–Manchester trade, a total which compares with about 200 in 1811.

In 1824 and early 1825, boom times, trade was very good, and delays occurred, both by congestion in Liverpool docks, waiting for empty craft, and pressure on warehouse space. A reasonable time for the Liverpool–Manchester run by the Mersey & Irwell was 12 to 15 hours, flats loading overnight for delivery the next day but one. Transit times on the Bridgewater were much the same, with a little more delay on upwards than on downwards traffic. If someone wanted faster delivery, they would probably use John Kenworthy's fly-boats on the Leeds & Liverpool.

Pilferage, the curse of canal carrying, had, Lingard claimed, been ended on the Mersey & Irwell, who had not had to prosecute for ten years. Loaded vessels:

'are covered and chained up, and sealed, the counterpart of which is sent to Liverpool, and when the vessel is sent there it is matched with the part left on, so that they could not open it without its being detected'.[55]

And here let us say that a myth must be gently put aside—the myth that the Liverpool & Manchester Railway[16] was a response

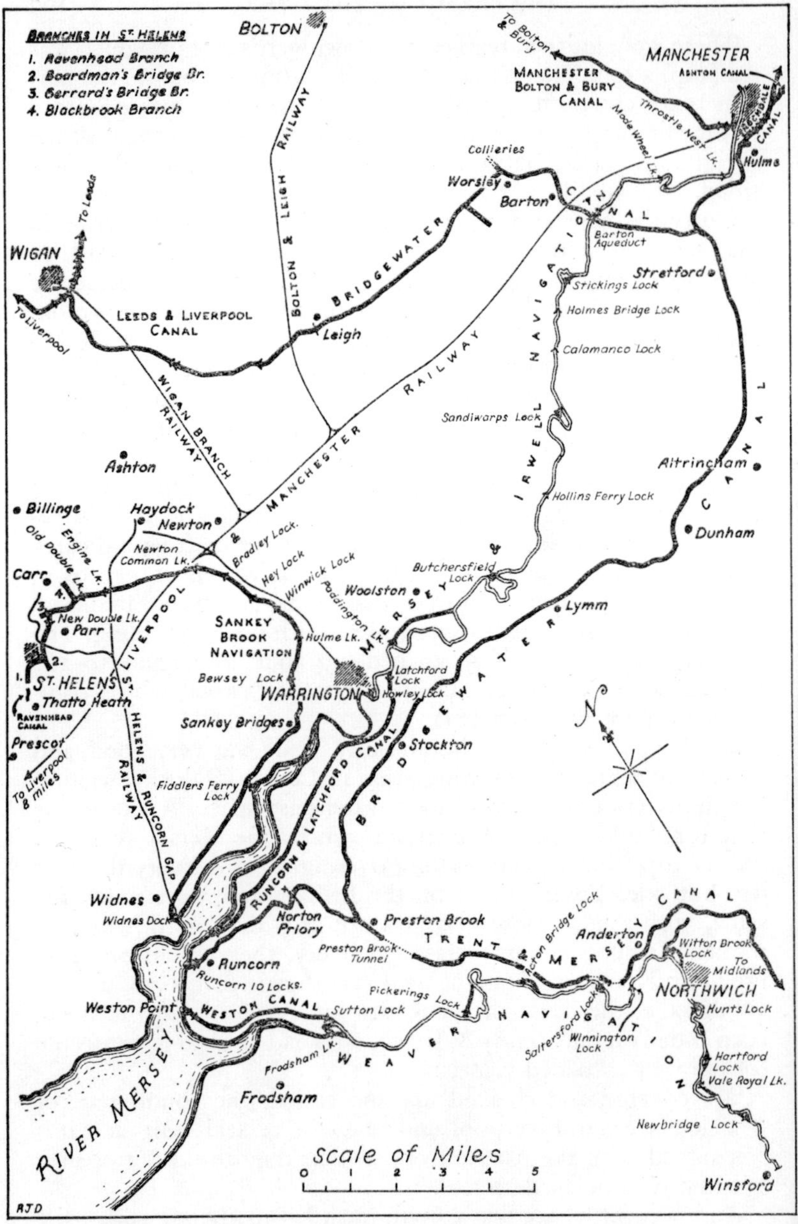
BRANCHES IN ST. HELENS
1. Ravenhead Branch
2. Boardman's Bridge Br.
3. Gerrard's Bridge Br.
4. Blackbrook Branch
BOLTON
To Bolton & Bury
MANCHESTER
ASHTON CANAL
MANCHESTER BOLTON & BURY CANAL
ROCHDALE CANAL
Throstle Nest Lk.
Mode Wheel Lk.
Hulme
BOLTON & LEIGH RAILWAY
Collieries
Worsley
Barton
Barton Aqueduct
To Leeds
WIGAN
To Liverpool
BRIDGEWATER CANAL
Stretford
Stickings Lock
Holmes Bridge Lock
LEEDS & LIVERPOOL CANAL
Leigh
Calamanco Lock
MANCHESTER & RAILWAY
WIGAN BRANCH RAILWAY
Sandiwarps Lock
MERSEY & IRWELL NAVIGATION
Ashton
Altrincham
Hollins Ferry Lock
Billinge
Haydock
Newton
Engine Lk.
Old Double Lk.
Newton Common Lk.
Bradley Lock
Dunham
Carr
Hey Lock
Winwick Lock
Butchersfield Lock
Woolston
Paddington Lk.
Lymm
New Double Lk.
Parr
SANKEY BROOK NAVIGATION
Hulme Lk.
ST. HELENS
ST. HELENS & RUNCORN GAP RAILWAY
LIVERPOOL
Bewsey Lock
Latchford Lock
WARRINGTON
Howley Lock
Thatto Heath
RAVENHEAD CANAL
Sankey Bridges
Stockton
N
Prescot
To Liverpool 8 miles
RUNCORN & LATCHFORD CANAL
Fiddlers Ferry Lock
Widnes
Widnes Dock
Norton Priory
Preston Brook
Acton Bridge Lock
Anderton
Witton Brook Lock
To Midlands
Preston Brook Tunnel
TRENT & MERSEY CANAL
Runcorn
NORTHWICH
Runcorn 10 Locks.
Pickerings Lock
Hunts Lock
Weston Point
WESTON CANAL
Sutton Lock
Saltersford Lock
WEAVER NAVIGATION
Winnington Lock
Hartford Lock
Frodsham Lk.
Vale Royal Lk.
Frodsham
RIVER MERSEY
Newbridge Lock
Scale of Miles
0 1 2 3 4 5
Winsford
RJD

9. Waterway lines based on the Mersey in 1833

to inefficiency and monopoly charges by the waterways. Apart from pro-railway sources, such as Joseph Sandars' pamphlet[17] and the weak evidence in the Bill of 1825, there is little independent evidence of strong feelings or complaints against the navigations. Both had steadily improved their lines,* provided more efficient craft and better warehousing and service; both had frequently reduced their freight charges, and neither was a monopoly carrier on its own line.[19] More, the Mersey & Irwell, having a very small nominal capital, could operate on low profits and yet plough considerable sums back, while the Bridgewater had no shareholders to satisfy, though against this it seems likely that necessary capital expenditure had been held back by the terms of the Duke's will.[20] As we shall see, the river company took the building of the Liverpool & Manchester very calmly. Once opened, the railway never succeeded, in its first dozen years, in carrying more than one-third of the total traffic between the two towns, and remained more frightened of price cutting by the waterways than the other way round. The motive for its building surely lay much more in hope of a profitable share in Manchester's prosperity, which itself was partially a product of the benefits of well-conducted water transport throughout the cotton area.

The Mersey & Irwell did some lobbying. There had been rumours that Lord Derby favoured the railway; however, he told them that he would not agree to it passing through his land, and Lord Stanley that he would oppose it. At the end of 1824 they again considered extending their navigation to Hunt's Bank, gave more thought to steam haulage, ordered steam cranes for Manchester, Howley and Liverpool, and built half a dozen new flats to cope with the 'increased Business of the Concern'.[21] With the railway threat hanging over them, however, they postponed action to build new warehouses. They already had extensive accommodation at Manchester: seven warehouses, and five timber wharves with 13 cranes, where up to 75 craft could be worked.

Both the Bridgewater trustees and the Mersey & Irwell successfully opposed the Liverpool & Manchester Railway Bill of 1825. The railway case was poorly made, and against the carefully presented position of the water companies, the rather foolish misstatements of the leading counsel for the Bill stand out: 'The

* Imports of raw cotton, much of it carried on the navigations for use in Lancashire mills, were 5·2m. lb in 1781, 56m. lb in 1801 and 123m. lb in 1821[18]. Increases of this order are evidence of efficiency, relative, of course, to contemporary standards.

shortest line by the Canals includes a distance of fifty miles at
least' (both were about 45 miles); 'You can never send goods
upon these Canals where they have to pass through a vast number
of locks' (there were ten in this distance on the Bridgewater,
twelve on the Mersey & Irwell); 'There are bye-carriers on these
Canals, but the tolls which are exacted, and the impediments that
are thrown in the way by the owners of the Canals, who are
carriers as well as owners, and who own the warehouses, are such
that those bye-carriers can get no profit' (this must have surprised
the carriers in question, whose business was growing as fast as
they could build craft to carry it); and finally, 'the present monopoly', a curious remark, picked up by endless historians, to apply
to a route with three competing waterways, on which two companies and at least seven major carriers were working, and upon
which the toll, taken on the full 45 miles to Liverpool, was about
⅔d per ton/mile on the Bridgewater, and just under 1d on the
Mersey & Irwell, in those cases where it was fully charged.

The Mersey & Irwell did not rest in their victory, but in May
1825 asked Telford to survey their navigation and suggest possible
improvements, and in June minuted that it was 'very important
to proceed with all possible dispatch in the various Works which
are calculated to improve the Navigation and to facilitate the
conveyance of Vessels',[22] the cost to be borrowed and then repaid
from a sinking fund. By early August they had the recommendations, and moved to carry them out.

But now occurred a change of heart by the Marquess of Stafford.
Whereas R. H. Bradshaw remained only a little less adamant
against the railway, Lord Stafford saw that the pressure of potential traffic on the Liverpool–Manchester route would be too much
for the existing waterways. He realized, too, that beyond the
economic reason lay a surge of interest in railways, a merchants',
manufacturers' and financiers' movement based upon great
engineering inventions, which was at any rate partly directed
against the Bridgewater Canal because of his own position as a
great property-owner, as well as against waterways as techno-
logically obsolete. Therefore a ship canal, or an enlargement of
the Mersey & Irwell, would not be a full answer to the new mood.

Lord Stafford took time to think. He consulted Telford, and as
a result invested in the Birmingham & Liverpool Junction
Canal,[23] meant to answer the demand for a railway from Birmingham to Liverpool. He also got James Loch to consult Josias
Jessop, engineer of the Cromford & High Peak Railway, and

made enquiries in the north about locomotive capabilities. And then, on what he felt was the balance of public advantage, with an understanding also of a difficult public relations situation, he allowed William Huskisson finally to persuade him to support the railway. Attacks on the canals came out of their revised prospectus; in exchange he subscribed £100,000, one-fifth of the capital they raised, with the right to nominate three directors to the board: these were Captain James Bradshaw, son of his superintendent, James Sothern, later to be the latter's successor, and Loch his principal agent. To placate the elder Bradshaw, he also allocated £40,000 to canal improvements.[24] This paid for the new Runcorn locks and warehouses at Liverpool and Manchester.[25]

Meanwhile the Mersey & Irwell had been preparing for further opposition to 'a Scheme so pregnant with injury to the interest of this Concern'[26] by having the railway's levels checked, when they were horrified to read in a newspaper that the Marquess of Stafford had subscribed for 1,000 shares and that he and his family had withdrawn their opposition. An official rushed to Captain Bradshaw, 'who expressed his astonishment at the arrangement the Marquess of Stafford had made with the Railway Committee. That he* was satisfied it had been entered into contrary to Mr Bradshaw's advice and opinion and in direct opposition to his ffeelings & that it would have the effect of making him a more strenuous Opponent to the Measure'.[27] But there was nothing to be done, and in May 1826 the railway got their Act.

Two months later Liverpool Corporation sought an injunction to prevent the company continuing their Runcorn improvements, now nearly finished, on the grounds that these and other works in the tideway were causing an increase in silting. Thereupon the company, fortified by legal advice that Liverpool's claim to be conservators beyond the limits of the town 'appears to be a usurpation',[28] decided to continue. They emerged victorious from a battle of injunctions, and finished their work in peace. There does seem to have been shallowing of the tidal river at this time, but Thomas Jevons, writing in 1828,[29] thought the new jetties and pier heads at Liverpool docks were responsible.

Between the passing of the railway's Act and its opening, the Mersey & Irwell made some freight reductions, but without panic, and usually following others. At end-1827 the Warrington–Manchester rate for flour came down from 8s 4d (41½p) to

---

* It is not clear whether this 'he' refers to Captain Bradshaw or to Mr Eccles, the Mersey & Irwell's representative—probably the latter.

6s 8d (33½p) to conform to the Bridgewater and other carriers, the Liverpool–Manchester rate having earlier been reduced from 12s 6d (62½p) to 10s (50p). In early 1829, following the Grocers' Company, some other long-distance freights came down to 10s (50p). On the other hand, the company were not unfriendly to the Liverpool & Manchester now they had become a fact of life. In July 1828, for instance, they sold them land so they could change the prospective position of their Manchester station.

From 1828 the Mersey & Irwell were concerned with several problems: further improvements to their navigation and craft, pressure for a Mersey conservancy, renewed arguments over alterations in the tideway and opposition to various Mersey bridge proposals, and of course, relations with the railway, the Bridgewater, and the other water carriers. These had best be taken separately, but the reader must remember that many coincided in time, and each influenced the others.

They did not carry out their most ambitious project, a cut from near Barton for some five miles to Butchersfield, though it was often discussed, but they did build a new cut near Stickings lock, nearly a mile long, to replace 2,112 yd of river, and a short new one at Butchersfield, where they constructed two additional parallel locks. They also appointed a travelling inspector to see that vessels were not held up, settle local business on the spot, and watch for ill-treatment of horses.

In 1835 the Mersey & Irwell company started a long effort to get access to the cut through 'No Man's Land' just above the entrance to old Runcorn locks and below their own entrance, and to remove certain projections into the river there. In early 1839 the trustees agreed to round off the rocks at the entrance and to allow free navigation through the cut, on condition that they could widen its entrance and improve the entry to the old locks. The Mersey & Irwell had doubts about this concession, but the two sides reached agreement in February 1842.

By early 1830 steam towage was being used between Liverpool and Runcorn by the St George's Steam Packet Company at Liverpool and probably others, but not yet by the Mersey & Irwell or the Bridgewater. The company then ordered a tug, to be engined by Bateman & Sherratt of Salford and to cost not more than £1,300, in April 1831 started to convert an old flat to another, and later built a third. They reckoned that three would be enough, two for regular work and one in reserve and for jobbing in the docks. These tugs were to help the sailing flats, not to replace them.

They minuted that tugs were only to tow flats with sails in cases of actual necessity, and that the practice must stop of 'Flats with sails, which could safely proceed to their destination, coming to an anchor in various parts of the River and waiting the Steamer to tow them, whereby Time is lost, the Engines unnecessarily used and strain'd, and a greater quantity of Fuel required'.[30] By mid-1832, however, some flats had been dismasted, being towed to and from Runcorn by tugs and above it by horses,* the boats being given a square sail to be used to help the horses when possible. These tugs were at first only used to tow the Mersey & Irwell's own craft, but after refusing the New Quay company towing services below Runcorn in 1832 on the grounds of not enough steam power, they agreed in 1834 to provide them. The Bridgewater began to use steam tugs in 1833[31] on the tideway, but not the canal.

By 1833 the company had settled upon a new design of flat, recommended by their engineer Samuel Wylde, but still of the same general type, with nearly vertical stern, boom that did not project beyond the rudder, and mast that could be struck. This had one-third more capacity, and one in wood and one in iron were ordered as experiments. These were in use by early 1834, and were so successful that four more were immediately ordered. Lingard also designed a decked iron flat specially for timber carrying. Steam tugs and bigger capacity flats between them increased average cargoes to 39 tons.

The tidal Mersey presented a real problem. The Mersey & Irwell, Bridgewater trustees, Sankey, Weaver and Ellesmere & Chester all went their own way, and there was no central authority concerned with maintaining a navigable channel and the avoidance of silting between Ellesmere Port and Warrington. Liverpool, as we have seen, considered itself to have a traditional claim to the conservancy; the Crown and the Duchy of Lancaster, who had foreshore and land rights, were also concerned. From 1829 meetings of all these bodies were held, but no one wanted Liverpool to be in charge, no one really wanted to pay for a conservancy, and everyone wanted to limit its powers were it to be set up. In early 1837 Liverpool decided to prepare a Bill giving itself control. The Mersey & Irwell and the Bridgewater trustees protected themselves, but the Bill failed, as did another in 1842. The problem was not solved until later.

* At this time the company were themselves providing the towing service, using their own horses and drivers in regular stages.

Concern lest a bridge over the tideway of the Mersey might obstruct navigation by sailing flats, or alter the set of the tides, went back to November 1800, when Ralph Dodd put in a parliamentary notice for a bridge near Runcorn, though he went no further. In 1813 there was serious talk of one, which the Mersey & Irwell thought would be 'a very serious Obstruction and Injury to the Navigation'.[32] They had engaged Mylne to advise them, and canvassed support from the Sankey, before learning that the scheme had been postponed. It came up again in 1815 and 1816, the company again mobilizing opposition, and in 1819 as part of a proposed new road from Liverpool to Northwich that got as far as a Bill. These were all road bridge schemes, but from 1830 onwards they became projects for carrying rails across the river. In 1831 the company were negotiating with the committee of the railway that became the Grand Junction from the Liverpool & Manchester to Birmingham, and agreed to one across the river and canal below Warrington that cleared the river adequately, but the canal at a level that would compel flats to lower their masts, on payment of £1,000 compensation. The line was opened in 1837. We must remember that not only the Runcorn & Latchford cut, but the river to Warrington, was well-used, the latter by some 7,000 flats a year, though 'the trips are at present made with difficulty owing to the shallow water and narrow channels combined with the number of Vessels grounded each Tide betwixt Runcorn and Fiddler's Ferry'.[33] Because of neap tides, craft could only pass on some two-thirds of the possible days.

The opening of the Liverpool & Manchester Railway on 15 September 1830 passed unminuted by the Mersey & Irwell, and produced no immediate reaction except that in January 1831 they followed a Bridgewater cut in cotton freights to 10s. But the railway was carrying more cheaply on many commodities, and the Liverpool committee reported that there were numerous requests for freight reductions. They talked to Bradshaw of the Bridgewater, but he 'declined to give any pledge thinking it better that each party should be left at liberty to exercise his own discretion altho he admitted that the matter was well worthy of consideration'.[34] However, John Moss of the Liverpool & Manchester, who had attended some of the talks between the Bridgewater and the Mersey & Irwell, 'pledged himself that the Railway company would not charge less in any case than the full rates they were authorized to receive under the powers of their Act unless they should be oblig'd to do so, by any other Carrier charging a lower rate',[35] and asked for a Mersey & Irwell rates list. A request from the New Quay Company to cut tolls to 1s 6d (7½p) was refused, whereupon they threatened to go out of business, a threat which they continued to make, but not to carry out. The Mersey & Irwell were hampered in answering by not being able to learn what Bradshaw was doing about tolls and freights. Eventually they did find out that he had agreed to allow the Grocers' Company 1s a ton off tolls, and followed him.

Whereas in these first difficult years of adjusting to the railway, the Mersey & Irwell's superintendent supported, and was supported by, his committee, things were different with the Bridgewater.[36] From the time that the Marquess of Stafford had subscribed for railway shares, his views were expressed on the Liverpool & Manchester's board by James Loch. He foresaw railway extension, realized it could not sensibly be resisted, and envisaged the value of his employer's holding growing as that line linked with others. But R. H. Bradshaw thought more narrowly of the canal's interest. On broader lines of policy, such as the attitude to be taken to the building of the Grand Junction Railway to Birmingham, Loch's general views prevailed, even if somewhat modified. But in matters of canal rates, Bradshaw took his own line. Convinced that the railway's high running costs were its weakness, he determined to cut rates, to show where the strength of canal transport lay, and to revenge himself on Lord Stafford for his desertion.[37]

In December 1831, hearing that Bradshaw and the railway were allowing 1s 8d (8½p) a ton off tolls, the Mersey & Irwell again followed. Some further price cutting ensued, though the Mersey & Irwell held up against the panic cuts of the New Quay company, but still Bradshaw would not come into a rates agreement, even when the railway company suggested it: 'Mr Bradshaw declines having anything to do with any Meeting of Carriers . . . intending to pursue such courses as Circumstances may render necessary and advisable'.[38] The company was now feeling the need for economies and made some staff redundant.

Lord Stafford died in 1833, soon after he had been created Duke of Sutherland. His railway shares went to his eldest son and successor, his life interest in the Bridgewater trust, with its canal and colliery property, to his second son Lord Francis, who took the name of Egerton, under the terms of the Duke's will. Nevertheless, Loch served both as agent. In October 1833 the difficult Bradshaw was persuaded to resign. His son, Captain Bradshaw, intended for the succession but over-strained by conflicting loyalties, had, however, committed suicide a month earlier. As he had power to do, he therefore nominated James Sothern, son of Benjamin and long a member of Bradshaw's staff, as his successor at Loch's suggestion. Sothern was elderly and as awkward as Bradshaw himself. However, in April 1834 a meeting was arranged between Lord Francis Egerton, Loch, the Mersey & Irwell and the Liverpool & Manchester. After it the railway produced a list of proposed freight increases, to which Sothern agreed if the Mersey & Irwell would. In fact, freight rates were not increased, but continued at current rates, all three bodies agreeing in February 1835 that these and similar arrangements for warehouse rents 'be faithfully adhered to and that no deviation be made by any of the three Parties without notice being given in writing to the others'.[39]

The Bridgewater, its trade only partially, of course, competitive with the railway, had stood up fairly well to the shock of its new competitor. Receipts fell from £175,997 in 1830 to £142,251 in 1833 though, oddly, passenger takings increased from £4,340 to £5,292; profits from £47,650 to £17,473. Tonnage had increased from 716,568 to 764,860, but the direct Liverpool–Manchester trade had only risen from 91,793 in 1831 to 105,572 in 1833, whereas the railway's figures for those years were 77,271 and 113,248.[40]

In mid-1835 the Mersey & Irwell seem to have decided that co-operation with the Bridgewater and the railway was a losing policy. In June they seriously took up the idea of building a canal, the Manchester & Salford Junction (see p. 126) to give them-selves a link to the Rochdale Canal and its connections (it was authorized in 1836), and in July Lingard reported to his committee that the railway was steadily increasing its carrying business, though he doubted whether it yielded them a profit. He pointed out that the Mersey & Irwell could not keep business by carrying at the same rates as the railway—the basis of the current agree-ment—because that concern could offer facilities which could not be matched. Therefore he recommended cuts, cotton for instance from 10s (50p) to 9s 2d (46p). These were agreed. Within a few days Henry Booth of the Liverpool & Manchester was round asking the company to rescind their reduction, but met with a refusal. He tried again in November, asking for freight revisions and an interview, and again was told that it was 'not expedient to make any alterations'.[41]

In July 1836 Thomas Lingard of the Mersey & Irwell died, after 'long, zealous and faithful services'. In 1835 the company had had to drop their dividend from 40 per cent to 25, at which level they maintained it (except for 12½ per cent in 1840) until 1841, but they were still powerful and competitive. In Manchester their wharves and warehouses extended most of the way between the river and Water Street from the Liverpool & Manchester's bridge to Liverpool Road station and Bridge Street. Beyond Water Street they owned a big block of land from Charles Street to Quay Street and back to Atherton Street, into which, in 1832, they had laid rails across Water Street to carry timber. The New Quay company's wharves were a little lower down the river, between the railway bridge and the turnpike road.

Thomas's successor, T. O. Lingard, favoured an aggressive improvement and charging policy. As soon as he had been appointed, he set off to visit canal and dock works at Leeds, Goole and Hull. Meanwhile, in April, the Bridgewater had cut its tolls below those of the Mersey & Irwell, who followed. T. O. Lingard now tried to agree with the Bridgewater, but reported in September that 'owing to the present state of the Disputes between Lord Francis Egerton and Mr Sothern it appeared impossible to effect any such alteration'.[42] Nevertheless, the existing Mersey & Irwell rate cuts were beginning to show results: for the eleven months ending June 1836 their tonnage was 147,520, against 119,359 for the same period the previous year, and for the nine months to the end of March the takings had been £44,399 against £39,173 for the comparable period. Traffic was some 100,000 tons a year from Liverpool in the company's own craft, and 20,000 tons of down goods from Manchester. To these figures had to be added 20,000 tons of goods carried by the New Quay company on the Mersey & Irwell, 30,000 of traffic to and from coasters and Irish trade vessels putting in at Runcorn, and averaging 46 tons a vessel, plus some 60,000 tons of toll-free traffic to Warrington by the river. Some 40 tons was the navigation limit, but vessels of 150–200 tons drawing 10 to 12 ft could reach Runcorn, and 100–120 tons, drawing 7 to 8½ ft, Warrington on spring tides.

Successful packet-boat services were still being run. Here is the Bridgewater's 1841 timetable on the Runcorn line.[43]

H

Manchester–Runcorn

	A	F	B	E	C	D	Front Room s	Front Room d	Back Room s	Back Room d
Manchester	08.00	08.00	10.00	13.00	16.00	17.00				
Stretford								6		4
Altrincham	10.00	10.00	12.00	15.00	18.00	19.00		9		6
Dunham							1	0		8
Lymm					19.30	20.30	1	6	1	0
London Bridge (Warrington)	13.00		15.00				2	0	1	3
Preston Brook	14.00		16.00				2	6	1	6
Runcorn	15.00		17.00				3	0	2	0

	A	B	C	D
Runcorn		09.00	11.00		
Preston Brook		10.00	12.00		
London Bridge		12.00	14.00		
Lymm	06.00				
Dunham					
Altrincham	07.30	14.30	16.30	16.00	18.00
Stretford					
Manchester	09.30	16.30	18.30	18.00	20.00

A Except Saturdays   C Winter   E Except Sundays
B Saturdays only   D Summer   F Sundays only

N.B.—In Summer extra packets were run through between Manchester and Liverpool in 7 hours.

On the Worsley–Wigan–Scarisbrick line, boats left Manchester for Worsley at 10.00 daily, and at 17.00 (winter) and 18.00 (summer), taking two hours. They seem then to have gone on to Astley Green to terminate. They were two-class, charging to Barton 6d first class, 4d second, Worsley 9d (6d), and Astley Green 1s 2d (9d). In addition, a boat left Manchester every weekday at 08.00 for Scarisbrick, on which higher fares were charged, as follows: Barton 10d (6d), Worsley 1s 4d (8d), Astley Green 1s 8d (1s), Leigh 1s 10d (1s 3d), Wigan 2s 6d (1s 9d), Scarisbrick 4s (2s 6d). Children over two and under seven paid half-fare. At Scarisbrick a coach met passengers for Southport, charging 1s, and also private carriages.

At the end of 1843 swift packet boats of the new light kind were attaining 12 m.p.h. on the daily journey from Manchester* to Runcorn. These were built very lightly of iron and drawn by two horses at a gallop, the horses being changed several times on the run. By 1845[44] the fast packets, *Water Witch*, *Swallow*, *Eagle* and *Dolphin* were providing two daily services to Runcorn in 3½

* An omnibus on hire to the trustees carried passengers between the basin and the town.

hours, leaving Manchester at 09.30 and 15.00 (Sundays exc.), the former having a coach connection to Chester. From Runcorn the trustees' steamer *Blanche* (it had been the *Duke of Bridgewater* in 1835) and others chartered by them, worked to Liverpool. There was also a boat to Altrincham at 08.30, and to Lymm at 15.55 (Sundays exc.) and 17.30 (Sundays exc.). On the canal's other line, a boat now ran to Worsley only at 11.00, through to Leigh at 17.45,* and to Scarisbrick at 08.30. Fares were unchanged, except that the through fare to Liverpool was quoted at 3s 6d (2s 6d), only 6d more than that to Runcorn.

In addition to regular packets at fixed times, the Mersey & Irwell also put on swift boats during the 1830s. These, horse-drawn though sometimes sail-assisted, were timed to catch the best tides at Runcorn, and so to enable passengers to make the fastest voyage between Liverpool and Manchester. In 1835 the steam boat *Eclipse* was working to and from Liverpool in connection with the packets. On 4 July 1838, however, the company put the stern-wheeled *Jack Sharp*, carrying 150 passengers, on the river, and in the same year the iron screw steamer *Countess of Ellesmere* started to work a pleasure service on the Irwell down to Pomona Gardens, on the site of the present Ship Canal docks, followed later by the *President*.[45] They also instituted through summer services between Liverpool and Manchester in seven hours, and these may have been worked by *Jack Sharp*. In 1843 through fares, Liverpool to Manchester, were 3s best cabin or 2s cabin, or 1s 6d and 1s, Liverpool to Runcorn.[46]

In March 1837 Lingard drew up a paper on rates and management policy suitable for the Mersey & Irwell and the Bridgewater, and sent it to the latter. In the same month Lord Francis Egerton, tired of being defied by Sothern, bought him out for £45,000, and appointed James Loch as superintendent. He in turn appointed George Fereday Smith manager of the Bridgewater trust. Smith, then only 25, with an engineering background, became active in canal business, and was to remain so until the trustees sold their canals in 1872.[47] At last Egerton and Loch could follow a coherent policy. For the next eight years Loch as Bridgewater superintendent tried to agree rates with the other carriers, and as railway director to encourage such pooling agreements. It was a sensible policy, based on the genuine competitive power of the navigations and the water carriers. After some months of discussion, agreement was reached between Lingard, Loch and the carriers

* This was returning to Leigh, having left there at 07.30.

with railway consent on an upward adjustment of rates that brought them almost back to 1832 levels. Peace descended temporarily, except for the building of the Hulme locks by the trustees in 1838 to link their canal to the Mersey & Irwell near Castlefield, the opening of the Manchester & Salford Junction a year later, and its purchase by the Mersey & Irwell in 1842. All the Manchester waterways were at last linked, but the effects were masked.

The rates agreement also greatly benefited the Liverpool & Manchester Railway's merchandise receipts:

	Passengers £	Merchandise £	Coal £	Total £
1836	133,901	93,184	7,550	234,635
1837	133,855	86,106	6,069	226,029
1838	141,054	112,337	6,912	260,303

One great advantage the waterways had to set against the railway's speed, the ability to deliver goods direct to ship's side in their own craft, whereas what went by rail had to be moved by cart to the ship under the management of a forwarding agent. B. W. Clapp, for instance, writing of the Manchester merchant John Owens, says of the railway 'he travelled on it himself, sent letters by it, and goods too if they were in danger of being shut out of a vessel. In the ordinary course of business, however, the carriers on the Bridgewater canal and on the Mersey and Irwell Navigation provided a better service'.[48]

Lingard's study of recent waterway enlargements in Yorkshire combined with previous studies made for a possible ship canal and steadily increasing Manchester disgruntlement with Liverpool's town and dock dues to produce a strong feeling about 1840 in favour of a waterway that would enable seagoing ships to reach Manchester. 'Every morsel of bread put into the mouth of the working man in Manchester has, before he saw it, been subject to the tax of Liverpool town and dock dues',[49] as a propaganda sheet of 1841 put it. These dues had risen from £2,781 in 1756 to £12,377 in 1796, £92,546 in 1816 and £221,000 in 1836, and in that year it was alleged that Liverpool got half its dues from merchandise brought to Manchester.[50] The Mersey & Irwell company commissioned their own enlargement study from H. R. Palmer. His *Report on the Improvement of the Rivers Mersey and Irwell . . . for the Navigation of Sea-Going Vessels*, dated 29 June 1840, proposed an enlarged line to end at Regent Bridge, Manchester, with extensive new cuts, and below Woolston lock a new canal to Bank Quay and on past Fiddler's Ferry and parallel to, but nearer the river than, the St Helens Canal extension (see Chapter VI) across Cuerdley Marsh to join the river above Runcorn. He recommended six large locks over the whole route, to take a 400-ton steamer or four flats, to supplement the existing small locks. There was to be a railway drawbridge at the Grand Junction Railway crossing. He gave no estimate of cost. The Mersey & Irwell's committee thought a new company might be formed to carry out improvements along the lines of Palmer's report, present shareholders having an option to transfer their holdings, and the 1841 annual general meeting agreed in principle to the need for reconstruction. But too much else was happening for action to be taken.

In September 1838 a proposal was put forward, with the encouragement of the Ellesmere & Chester company and for a time of the Bridgewater trustees, for a canal* 16 miles long from the Bridgewater at Altrincham to the Ellesmere & Chester at Middlewich, the company to have a capital of £500,000. It would have improved the canal route from Manchester to the Potteries and Birmingham at the expense of the Trent & Mersey, Peak Forest, Ashton and Macclesfield companies, all of whom opposed it. The project came to nothing.[51] By this time the Bridgewater, as part of the canal line to Birmingham, was beginning to feel the competition of the Grand Junction Railway, opened thence from the Liverpool & Manchester in 1837; heavy price cutting followed in 1840 and 1841. With pressure added on the Macclesfield Canal and by the Anderton company on the Weaver, in 1841 the trustees started carrying with their own boats on the canal lines to the Potteries by the Trent & Mersey and on the Macclesfield route.[52] This was a temporary move, the trade being soon handed back to independent carriers. But it was to be made again later.

In October 1838 the Manchester & Leeds Railway from their Oldham Road terminus in Manchester were considering a connection either with the Bridgewater Canal or the Mersey & Irwell, and preferred the latter in default of rail connections to the Liverpool & Manchester and Manchester, Bolton & Bury Railways. The Liverpool & Manchester made difficulties, and in January 1840 representatives of the Manchester & Leeds talked to Lingard. In February the railway formally enquired whether the Irwell could be made navigable right up to the railway's property

* The Manchester & Birmingham Junction Canal.

on the banks of the Irk, beyond the statutory end of the navigation. The Mersey & Irwell suggested that they should extend their waterway to Hunt's Bank, and the railway their tracks to the Irwell, as they had power to do, 'which would enable the Railway Company to load and unload their carriages out of and into the Company's flats'.[53] A few days later Lingard gave the railway his personal pledge that the extension to Hunt's Bank would be made in 1840; tenders were then sought, and in July work started by direct labour. At the end of October it was reported to the railway's board that 'the *Mary* had succeeded in making a voyage to Manchester direct from Dublin and was now unloading her Cargo of Potatoes near the Victoria Bridge and that it was intended to freight with a load of Meal the next Voyage'.[54]

It may have been the combined prospects of a highly profitable link with the Manchester & Leeds Railway, exhilaration at the idea of rebuilding their waterway as a ship canal and the amount of support for it, and realization of their good competitive base in any event, that caused the Mersey & Irwell's shareholders' meeting of June 1840 to tell Lingard 'to take such steps as he may find desirable to withdraw from the carriers' agreement',[55] though advice to do so had probably come from him in the first place. Notice was given in July.

This annoyed everyone, and both the railway and the Bridgewater, who with the independent carriers had stuck to the agreement, retaliated to a point where the river company had to protest, and join a new rates agreement made in April 1841. The Mersey & Irwell may by now have been rather less ebullient, for the Manchester & Salford Junction had been an immediate failure, and the snags in too wholehearted a co-operation with the Manchester & Leeds Railway were becoming obvious. When that company in early 1841 invited the Mersey & Irwell to become through carriers on their railway and their own navigation between Liverpool and Leeds, they cautiously refused, though re-offering 'every facility for transferring goods carried along their Navigation to and from the Railway'.[56] However, this caused the Manchester & Leeds to put on the screw by starting carrying talks with the New Quay company, and reducing its freight charges through to Liverpool.

In December 1841 the L.M.R., anxious at its small share of cotton carrying and falling part in the transport of manufactured goods to Liverpool,[57] cut out of the rates agreement by reducing cotton freights. As usual, the Mersey & Irwell met the cuts. This time the Bridgewater and the Mersey & Irwell found themselves on the same side; James Loch on the railway board tried hard for peace, even threatening to remove the Duke of Sutherland's money from the company. The Mersey & Irwell made matters worse by agreeing in February 1842 with the Manchester & Leeds Railway for the two companies to start carrying immediately between Hull and Liverpool, the arrangement to extend also 'to all Goods heretofore using the Leeds & Liverpool Canal',[58] The railway company seem to have turned to the Mersey & Irwell not only because of the services they could provide, but as a means of attacking the Bridgewater, because they blamed Loch and his canal interests for their failure to get a rail link with the Liverpool & Manchester. Then the Mersey & Irwell backpedalled, explaining to the Bridgewater that they had not intended their agreement with the Manchester & Leeds to be exclusive to them, whereupon that company deserted the Mersey & Irwell and in June 1842 combined with the Liverpool & Manchester (who had now agreed to make the rail link between the two lines) to offer through carriers from Liverpool to the Manchester & Leeds better rates than those of the waterways.

Meanwhile total traffic on the Mersey & Irwell was increasing. It had been 183,924 tons in 1839, 212,663 in 1840, and 219,794 in 1841, though an increasingly large proportion was carried by outside carriers, partly as business grew generally, partly because Lingard reckoned that the company made more profit that way.*

Another rates agreement of May 1843 favoured the water carriers. Under it the Liverpool & Manchester undertook not to carry a greater share of the total trade than the average proportion of the last five years, and to pay the waterways 3s 6d (17½p) a ton on any excess. But the railway interpreted the agreement differently from the river company, and soon there was trouble. James Loch, anxious to keep the agreement, was told by the Mersey & Irwell that they would continue to keep their freedom unless the railway would maintain the agreed rates. An acute bout of price-cutting broke out between all three concerns, the Mersey & Irwell reducing freights from Manchester to Liverpool to 5s (25p), and both they and the Bridgewater remitting all through tolls for goods between Liverpool and Manchester. This may have been brave, but it further damaged the Mersey & Irwell's already shaky financial position, and seriously frightened the shareholders,

---

* In these years the company carried 131,499, 127,975, and 117,080 tons respectively.

whose dividend had fallen to 20 per cent for 1842 and was to be 10 per cent for 1843.

Loch now realized that there was only one way to carry out his policy: the Bridgewater must control the Mersey & Irwell. Lord Francis Egerton offered £800 a share, or £400,000, and agreed to take over the company's mortgage debt of about £110,000 and certain other liabilities, transfer to be on 1 January 1844.* The money was temporarily raised in bonds, and later, in 1848, borrowed from the Law Life Assurance Company on mortgages of certain properties of the Bridgewater trustees and the Mersey & Irwell.

Rate cutting ended in December 1843, when it was agreed between the parties that 'measures would be at once adopted to put an end to the contest and to restore the rates of charge by the several lines of conveyance between Liverpool and Manchester. And it was at the same time agreed that in the negotiations required for that purpose, 'the Cmᵉᵉ of the Old Quay Co should bear a part as hitherto so that the proceeding shall not appear to arise out of the acquisition of their navigation by Lord Francis Egerton'.[59] A few days later James Loch was appointed principal agent of the Mersey & Irwell.

After an Act of 1845 had authorized them to do so, the Bridgewater trustees bought the navigation from Egerton, the shares being transferred on 17 January 1846. The purchase caused speculation in the press. The *Railway Times* of 13 April 1844 reported that Lord Francis had it in mind to convert the Bridgewater Canal to a railway that would then be continued to Ellesmere Port, while the Mersey & Irwell remained as a waterway. This report was probably inspired by the agreement of 1844 for the trustees to rent for £4,122 p.a. the craft and accommodation at Ellesmere Port that had been used by the Ellesmere & Chester Canal Company to operate a cross-river tug and barge service to Liverpool. This arrangement lasted until 1852, when the Shropshire Union, as it then was, terminated it and resumed its own services.

So ended the independent Mersey & Irwell, its shares having appreciated from £20 in 1779 to £800† in 1843, having at one time reached £1,350. Its life ended for the unusual reason that it

* Evidence by a Bridgewater representative upon the Ship Canal Bill of 1885 said that the total sum paid was £550,800.

† The price Lord Francis Egerton paid for them. This was, however, much higher than the market price in that year, which was about £380 in May and £370 in September.[60]

was too independent and self-confident: the Bridgewater a few years later[61] said that 'owing to the aggressive character of its management and the difficulty of binding it to the terms of any Agreement Lord Ellesmere* was induced . . . to purchase it', having been told by the Liverpool & Manchester Railway that if he did so, 'that Company would enter into a friendly agreement with respect to the Traffic'. The result of the purchase was to give the Bridgewater preponderance in the Liverpool trade. The average tonnages carried† by the three concerns in the six years 1839–44 had been:

	Tons	Tons
Bridgewater Canal	200,856 ⎫	
Mersey & Irwell	141,813 ⎭	water 342,669
Liverpool & Manchester Railway		rail 164,625

Policy was henceforward to be with the Bridgewater trustees. But the Mersey & Irwell company remained in shadowy existence, with an occasional meeting, until the early days of the Manchester Ship Canal. Until then, also, the Old Quay's carrying business was continued separately from that of the trustees, and later of the Bridgewater Navigation Company. For 1844, without the Mersey & Irwell's figures, the trustees' profit on waterway operations was £85,439. They had carried 350,529 tons of their own trade, including coal, while 936,011 tons had been conveyed by independents.

Meanwhile James Loch had been making changes in the general conduct of Bridgewater business. He tightened up the way it had been run under Sothern. Believing that small carrying concerns were likely to be more efficient than large ones, he also encouraged the former as much as possible at the expense of the trustees' own business. It was therefore ironical that, when independents gave up as rates were cut, the trustees had to step in to maintain trade, and so found themselves carrying further afield than they had been accustomed, on the Macclesfield Canal and beyond in the early 1840s, and to the Potteries via the Weaver and Anderton (see Chapter VI) when in 1848 they took over the Anderton company.

He and Fereday Smith had also been improving facilities, though the constitution of the Bridgewater Trust made money for

* Formerly Lord Francis Egerton.
† These figures only refer to through traffic between Liverpool, Manchester and beyond. Those quoted earlier also included intermediate traffic.

large capital expenditure difficult to find. A new dock, the Egerton, was built between 1837 and 1839 at the south end of Liverpool's line of docks for the timber trade, and in 1845 a half-tide basin was opened between the Duke's dock and the river to speed up flats' turnround time and enable coasters to discharge directly into them. At Runcorn the Francis dock was built in the early 1840s.[62]

On 8 August 1845, nineteen months after the Mersey & Irwell's purchase by Lord Francis, the Liverpool & Manchester Railway itself ended its independent life, when with the Bolton & Leigh it was absorbed by the Grand Junction, two directors of which the Duke of Sutherland could now nominate. In 1846 the Grand Junction in turn became part of the London & North Western Railway. In 1847 the Manchester & Leeds, absorbing two smaller companies, became the Lancashire & Yorkshire Railway. The great transport groupings were beginning.

Manchester & Salford Junction Canal

The Manchester & Salford Junction originated in a division of Manchester's waterways that lasted until 1838. On the one hand the Mersey & Irwell Navigation, prosperous and efficient, to which the Manchester, Bolton & Bury was connected at Salford. On the other hand the Bridgewater Canal, linked at Preston Brook with the Trent & Mersey, at Castlefield with the Rochdale, which in turn joined the Ashton that led to the Huddersfield, the Peak Forest and the Midland canals, and later at Leigh with the Leeds & Liverpool to those and many other towns.

It was the Bolton & Bury's interest, and less so that of the Mersey & Irwell, to obtain a junction between the two systems, so that additional trade and markets might be sought. Therefore most of the early initiatives came from the former. But it was not the Duke's interest to allow such a junction, for his canal was likely to lose more to the Mersey & Irwell than he could possibly gain from the Bolton & Bury. In 1790 the latter tried to encourage the Duke to join his canal to the Irwell—an unhopeful line to take. In 1799 they planned to cross over the Irwell to make a junction with the Rochdale, but their moves towards a Bill foundered on Mersey & Irwell opposition; and in 1801 thought of putting to the river company what, thirty-five years later, was to be the Manchester & Salford Junction Canal, 'a Navigable Tunnel from the Old River Navigation towards the Rochdale Canal'.[63]

In late 1805 the Mersey & Irwell themselves proposed a cut

from near Water Street that would provide more wharf space within their own land up to Atherton Street, and would then be extended to join the Rochdale Canal, presumably near Deansgate tunnel, at a total cost of £12,100. But that got no further. The next move was in 1824, when the Mersey & Irwell bought some land near Charles Street with the idea of making a road to connect their waterway to the Rochdale. In 1825, too, the Manchester, Bolton & Bury was talking of a possible link with the Bridge-water.[64] The idea was once more brought up at the June 1835 shareholders' meeting of the Mersey & Irwell, when a sub-committee was appointed to consider it. Within a fortnight this had decided that there was a good case, first, because the company was carting 30,000 tons a year between the two waterways, but charging only 6d (2½p) a ton for what in fact cost them 1s 8d (8½p) to do; therefore they would save £1,750 p.a. Second, in the previous 21 weeks, 438 craft had passed easterly and 4,233 westerly through the lock connecting the Rochdale Canal to the Bridgewater, carrying an average of 2,500 tons a week exclusive of coal. There was good hope that some of this business might be attracted to the Mersey & Irwell. Finally, the ground was suitable for making a canal, and the resultant relief of street congestion would gain local support.[65]

The idea seems to have originated in a group including Mersey & Irwell and Bolton & Bury committeemen and shareholders, as well as independents and carriers, though no one from the Roch-dale. By July the Old Quay company was willing to support a Bill and subscribe £10,000, whereupon a maximum toll of 6d (2½p) was agreed upon, to be reduced when dividends reached 7 per cent. The promoters also saw the Bridgewater's representa-tives, who proposed instead a link between the Mersey & Irwell and their canal at Hulme as a better way of achieving the same result. It was indeed a much cheaper one, but the Mersey & Irwell felt that it would leave them in the power of the trustees. By April the Bridgewater seem to have decided to make their Hulme junction. The Mersey & Irwell agreed that their craft would pay 2d to enter the Rochdale Canal, the Duke's to pay 2d to get to the Bolton & Bury. Estimates of traffic were made for the Junction Canal which envisaged an average of 5,704 tons a week (296,608 p.a.), of which 834 p.w. were seen as interchange traffic with the Rochdale, and the rest apparently as local, 2,200 tons of it coal, 620 tons Bolton stone and flagstones, and 600 tons merchandise off the Mersey & Irwell.[66]

In July 1836 the Act[67] was passed. It authorized a capital of £50,000 in £100 shares, which was subscribed as follows:

Shares		£	
100	=	10,000	Mersey & Irwell.
156	=	15,600	Mersey & Irwell shareholders as individuals.
235	=	23,500	Others.
491		49,100	

It enacted also that the new canal's water level should be 6 in above that of the Rochdale, from which no water should be taken. The first part of its course downwards used a private branch from the Rochdale 'to and under Lower Mosley Street', and users of this were given special access rights. Finally, both the Bridgewater trustees and the Liverpool & Manchester Railway were authorized to join it, the latter either by railway or canal.*

Construction began, with two Mersey & Irwell representatives on the managing committee and John Gilbert as engineer. Meanwhile the Bridgewater trustees, who had been empowered to make their own Hulme cut and three locks to the Irwell by the Salford Junction's Act, went ahead. These were opened on 20 September 1838, and provided an easy alternative to the new canal.

The canal, 5 furlongs long including the former branch, was opened to the public on Monday, 28 October 1839, with T. O. Lingard of the Mersey & Irwell as manager. It ran from the Irwell, passed under Water Street between Quay Street and Grape Street, and joined the Rochdale Canal near Great Bridgewater Street. There was a single entrance lock from the Irwell, and then three in duplicate, the upper two, under what was later Central Station, being staircase pairs, these having been built to handle the expected heavy traffic. A tunnel 499 yd long with a towing path was lit every 20 yd with gas. Because no water could be taken in at the summit from the Rochdale, it had to be pumped up from the Irwell. One steam engine stood above the Irwell lock to pump up from the river, and another above the upper pairs raised it again to the Rochdale level and stored it in a reservoir beside the flight.[68]

In March 1840 the Mersey & Irwell company began a branch canal near Quay Street to serve their land off the Old Quay, where

* In September 1838 the Liverpool & Manchester Railway indeed asked the Mersey & Irwell to sell them land to make such a canal, but were refused.

a potato market was to be established linked to the Irish craft now using the navigation. The market was open by August 1841, by which time the cut was probably completed. This was also joined to the Manchester & Salford Junction by an arm to above the Irwell lock.

The new canal started badly, with high running costs, work still to be done, and little traffic. In the first six months there had been trouble with the pumping engines, a lock wall had collapsed, and the Bridgewater trustees had insisted on the top lock being reconstructed on the grounds that it had not been built as the Act of 1836 had directed. A second Act[69] of April 1840 authorized the raising of another £25,000 by shares; when half this sum had been subscribed, the company might also borrow £10,000. It also gave the company powers to sell themselves to the Mersey & Irwell.

Two new shares, £100 nominal, were now offered at £25* each for every old share held, and were taken up as follows:

Shares		£	
200	=	5,000	Mersey & Irwell.
234	=	5,850	Mersey & Irwell shareholders as individuals.
312	=	7,800	Others.
746		18,650	

However, a revised estimate of traffic raised it slightly to 316,680 tons a year, with merchandise from the Mersey & Irwell now expected to reach 1,000 tons a week, and interchange traffic with the Rochdale 1,600 tons a week. This with other revenues would yield £8,807. Annual expenses were put, however, at the high figure of £4,169.[70]

This revenue sounded well, but did not materialize, and in April 1841 a deputation offered the canal to the Mersey & Irwell for £30,750 plus the debts, then estimated at £21,000.[71] As the river company had put up £13,000 already, this was hardly a bargain, and the offer was refused. In June the deputation was back, this time offering the Salford Junction for nothing if it were freed from all debts and liabilities at the date of transfer. The Mersey & Irwell committee, judging that the canal would probably be closed if they did not take it over, agreed in principle, and asked Lingard for a report.

As manager of both concerns, he was in a difficult position, saying that previous reports '(not only by myself but by everyone

* In fact, only £15 was called on these shares.

else) having caused so much disappointment, and hitherto apparently been so very erroneous'.[72] He referred to the 'present miserably defective traffic of the Canal', revealed that tolls for the previous half year had been only £531, whereas annual expenses including interest on loans and depreciation were £3,745 and that there was a deficiency of assets of £4,316, and a debt of £17,000. On the other hand, the Mersey & Irwell reckoned that the extra tolls they got for traffic passing on the Salford Junction plus rent of land, yielded them a small annual profit already, with the chance of increase.

In November the Mersey & Irwell encouraged traffic on the canal by remitting the river toll on limestone passing from it to the Bolton & Bury and by conveyance of 19 January 1842 they took it over. (*To continue the history of the Bridgewater undertaking, turn to Chapter XIV*.)

CHAPTER VI

Weaver Salt and Sankey Coal

++++++++++++++++++++++++++++++++ ✦ ++++++++++++++++++++++++++++++++

TRADE flourished. An advertisement of 1792 reads: 'Messrs Kent and Naylor are in want of Ten Flatmasters, capable of conducting the Salt Flats from and to Northwich, and up the Sankey Canal, whose emoluments will be, at least, Eighty Pounds per annum'.[1]

Weaver Navigation

Increasing business encouraged the Weaver trustees to all manner of improvements. In 1788 and the following years they widened Witton Brook, built a new quay, improved road access, and raised the lock. But these works suffered badly from salt subsidence. A new lock had to be built there in 1826; a year later the trustees decided to re-site Northwich lock and weir below the town, and when this was opened two years later, the new river level which it maintained enabled Witton Brook lock to be eliminated. Improvements were also made elsewhere on the river. In most cases new locks were constructed in new cuts designed also to cut off corners and so shorten the line: Vale Royal, Newbridge, Hartford and Hunts were rebuilt in the 1790s, and Butty Meadow eliminated.

In June 1792 salt proprietors at Liverpool, Northwich and Winsford petitioned the trustees to build a horse towing path so that bow-hauling by men could be done away with. They agreed, and in July ordered a path to be made from Frodsham to Acton bridge, and six months later that it should be extended to Anderton. The work seems to have been done by mid-1793. It was extended later through to Winsford. Horse towing on the Weaver was then done by independent men who hired themselves and their animals to flat captains needing them.

In 1788 a historic activity was conceived, when some Middlewich salt men suggested that

'if proper Quays and Engines with communications and other conveniences were erected and made at Anderton or Barnton for reshipping of Goods and Merchandize into the River Weaver from the Staffordshire Canal,* it would be an advantage to the River Weaver and accommodate the Trade thereon'.[2]
They were supported by a committee of manufacturers from the Potteries. Anderton was chosen, where the Trent & Mersey Canal at the top of a 50 ft high slanting bank came close to the river below. The trustees started to negotiate for land, and stubbornly continued with their plan in spite of opposition from the Trent & Mersey company. This last presumably reckoned that they would lose trade if salt on their canal were transhipped to the Weaver instead of continuing to Preston Brook, and also foresaw interference with towing, because their towpath was on the river side of the canal at Anderton, and transhipment would have to be done over it. However, after threatening action to eject the trustees from the land they had bought, they fell back on non-co-operation.

By 1793 a new cut had been made to a basin at Anderton, and sheds provided for the salt hand-carts which were the first means of transhipment, and which remained in regular use until 1940. These were loaded from the canal boats, and then moved to a stage above the basin, where their loads were tipped into Weaver flats. In 1794 the Weaver's engineer, John Johnson, was sent off to east Shropshire to study 'railed roads and other works there for shipping goods into vessels on the River Severn',[3] though it was not until about the end of 1799 that a tramway was provided for the carriage of rock-salt and merchandise, mainly for the use of J. Gilbert & Co., the carriers, who guaranteed to generate enough tolls to pay the costs. White salt continued to be transhipped by cart, but meanwhile a second wheeling stage had been built for it, and two cranes erected for general purposes. A second tramway, for 'goods, wares and merchandize', was provided in 1800, and then chutes for loading white salt. About this time also a traffic began in china clay upwards to the Potteries and crates for pottery downwards.

Meanwhile a more important development was taking place. In June 1796 the salt proprietors and flat owners suggested that the navigation should be extended from Frodsham to deep water in the Mersey at Weston Point, so avoiding delays by neap tides, and enabling flats to do a quarter more trade in the same time.

* The Trent & Mersey.

Page 133 Leeds & Liverpool Canal: (*above*) Bingley five-rise locks in 1955; (*below*) the entrance to the canal from the river Aire at River lock, Leeds, 1957

Page 134 (above) The original terminus and warehouse of the Leeds & Liverpool Canal at Wigan; (below) Stonebridge mill and bridge on the Bradford Canal c. 1900

After some token reluctance, the trustees in October set John Johnson to survey for a canal between these points. He did so, and a special meeting in December authorized a Bill.

Then came deadlock. The trustees proposed to pay for the extension by immediately raising tolls, for how else could they pay interest on the money they would have to borrow without burdening the current Weaver trade, or the county rates, with the costs of the extension? But the traders pleaded that they could not afford to pay higher tolls until they got better facilities. By 1799 the salt proprietors had agreed to subscribe £10,500 towards the new canal; it was not enough, and the trustees waited.

In 1803 they wondered whether to make a new basin and lock at Frodsham, then thought better of it, and gave parliamentary notice for a canal to Weston Point, in the hope that the salt proprietors would rise to the bait of 2d per ton on all goods. They did not, but in 1806 came the crunch. In January the trustees, conscious that during neaps, flats might wait several days at Frodsham lock, considered two plans: to make a basin and another lock at Frodsham for £16,000; or a canal to Weston Point, with a lock and basin there, usable at all times, for £40,000. Thereupon the salt and flat owners agreed to extra tolls until £20,000 had been paid, but the trustees asked for £24,000 (£40,000 less £16,000). The proprietors refused, and told the trustees to get on with Frodsham basin; then, fearful lest they should, they summoned the engineer Thomas Morris. He undertook to do the work for £38,000, towards which they agreed to contribute £21,000. Agreement was reached on £22,000 to be raised by extra tolls on the new canal and the Weaver, but the trustees, thinking Morris's proposals too vague and diffuse, insisted on the work being undertaken by their own John Johnson, accepting under penalty of £2,000 to do it in 27 months after the Act, and £1,000 a year after three years. A Bill was sought, and passed in 1807,[4] opposition from the Trent & Mersey being bought off by the trustees giving up their right to tranship 'pipe clay, flint stones and crates' of pottery at Anderton, and certain other goods if specified, though not salt, coal or limestone. A few days after the Act's passing it was 'ordered that Mr Johnson have leave to take down the Warehouse and Cranes and other Works now become useless at Anderton Basin and use the materials for other purposes on the River'.[5]

The trustees moved to buy land for the extension, borrow money, and start cutting with Johnson in charge. It sadly turned

I

out that their confidence had been misplaced; Johnson was not capable of a job as big as the Weston canal and basin. By November 1809, the 27 months having passed, they realized that they were well over estimate, with the canal almost finished, but not the basin and sea-lock. Telford was summoned from the neighbouring Ellesmere Canal, and reported in February that there 'had been great want of judgement and method in executing the work'. Poor John Johnson was dismissed after having worked for the Weaver since 1780, victim of his employers' over-confidence in his ability, and Telford himself was appointed consultant, with Samuel Fowls, who remained with the Weaver until his death in 1847, as resident engineer. To add to the trustees' troubles, their clerk, Thomas Chantler, was unable to repay considerable sums of the navigation's money, and had to be bankrupted.

Weston Basin was opened about the middle of 1810 without the intended piers. One of these was added at the south-western entrance about 1817, the other three years later. By 1819 the new canal and basin were busy enough to need a full-time harbour-master as well as a lock-keeper: they had been a success, and trade steadily increased.

Seemingly £32,900 was borrowed, and this had been repaid by the end of 1814. The rest of the cost, which totalled around £50,000, had been raised from the levy on tolls and from the navigation's considerable revenue, no transfers of surpluses to the county treasurer being made for some years. The new cut left the old navigation half a mile above Frodsham lock, and ran for 4 miles to the basin and tide-gates. On the new cut a lock was provided at the Frodsham end, at Sutton, another just short of the basin, and finally tide-gates. Toll-taking on the canal under the 1807 Act ceased in 1816; thereafter it was a free navigation until the Act of 1866.

In 1830, with the Middlewich branch of the Ellesmere & Chester Canal being built[6] not far from the Weaver's navigation head at Winsford, the trustees sounded that company on the possibility of a canal junction costing about £17,000, which would have given them access to Middlewich as well as to the Birmingham & Liverpool Junction and the Ellesmere lines. They also circularized traders and salt proprietors, asking their views. Opinion was that, Staffordshire coal being better than Lancashire for salt making, the salt works would take it through such a cut, which would also attract the upwards pottery clay, which could be shipped as back carriage in the coal boats, if the Weaver could offer transit times equal to the Trent & Mersey. On the other hand, it was likely that Bradshaw of the Bridgewater, who had already reduced tolls, would do so again rather than lose traffic. Water supply was a problem, for the Ellesmere & Chester could not afford to supply all that would be needed. Agreement on water sharing was reached, but then the trustees lost interest, because the Middlewich branch was unfinished;* probably because the Trent & Mersey's compensation tolls at Wardle lock at Middlewich where the branch joined their canal made the economics too chancy; and certainly because of railway projects which appeared to threaten competition, and made it less likely that such a through route would be profitable. Indeed a decision to oppose the Bill for the Grand Junction Railway from the Liverpool & Manchester line at Warrington to Birmingham because it would 'very materially impede and injure the Navigation both of the River Mersey and Weaver' was passed at the same trustees' meeting of 3 February 1831 that dropped the extension project.

The Bill failed, but obviously would be reintroduced. In September 1832 the trustees learned that the Bridgewater had made a 'great reduction' in merchandise tolls between Liverpool and Preston Brook, and a month later agreed to reduce their own charge for transhipment at Anderton from 1s (5p) to 8d a ton. In early 1833 the railway Bill was back in Parliament, and a deputation, including their engineer Joseph Locke, met the trustees to settle the railway crossing of the Weaver near Pickerings by the great 20-arched Dutton viaduct. It was agreed this should be 42 ft wide between piers, including two 6 ft towpaths. Necessary realignment of the waterway was to be at railway expense. The line opened in July 1837, and seems not to have affected the Weaver traffic.

Between 1832 and 1835 the important Barnton cut was built at a cost of £19,400 to shorten the bight of river from Saltersford towards Winnington. It was followed by two smaller cuts at Crowton and Aston Grange. At this time the locks on the navigation were: Weston basin (tide-gates into the Mersey), Weston Point, Sutton, Frodsham (side-lock into the Weaver estuary), Pickerings, Acton Bridge, Saltersford, Winnington, Hunts, Hartford, Vale Royal and Newbridge.

The trustees now had it in mind to double the locks starting

---

* It was opened on 1 September 1833.

with Winnington, but before doing so, called in William Cubitt to tell them whether the river could be made navigable for sea-going vessels. The engineer reported that this would indeed be possible, but inexpedient, for the cost would be greater than the advantages, and the result not so convenient for their staple traffics of salt and coal. Weston Point might, however, be used as a harbour for ships transhipping cargoes to and from the navigation. Gratifyingly, he told them that their river 'is on the whole the most perfect artificial Navigation I have yet seen',[7] and advised them to continue to straighten and deepen the channel, rebuild the older and repair the newer locks to produce one good stone-built set and then to duplicate them, and to improve their weirs to allow flood-water more easily to escape. They accepted his views, and started on Winnington, working to give the river a depth of 7 ft 6 in., with locks 88 ft by 18 ft, able to take craft carrying 100 tons or more. When Winnington was done, they moved in 1844 to Acton and in 1845 to Hunts.

Transhipment, mainly of salt, from the canal to the river at Anderton continued to increase. The white salt stages were enlarged in 1815, additional rock salt facilities were provided in 1822, and an Act of 1825[8] repealed the 1807 limitation of goods that could be transhipped. Some manoeuvring followed. In December Fowls was asked to estimate for continuing the Weaver navigation upwards to Middlewich either from Winsford or by way of the Dane, a move that threatened the Trent & Mersey's canal trade in salt, and in April 1826 that company were asked whether they in fact intended to use the Weaver for their Liverpool trade. No reply is recorded to this query, but probably the canal company followed their usual policy of keeping the matter open. Late in 1831, however, perturbed by Bridgewater policy, they were themselves surveying for possible locks to link their canal to the Weaver,[9] and indeed acquired the necessary land just upstream of Acton bridge. In 1832 another tramway was provided to transfer Staffordshire coal from canal to river, and a crane for timber and heavy goods going upwards. The coal trade did not flourish, so the tramway carried rock salt instead.

A firm of carriers, Alexander Reid & Co., in the spring of 1829 began a trade via Anderton to the Potteries in clay, flints and other raw materials for the Potteries, and crated goods back, and also in general merchandise and grain. Additional facilities and a quay were provided, in 1831 the approach to Anderton basin was widened and a second cut made to give two connections to the river,* and in 1832 the Weaver toll for Potteries goods was halved to 6d (2½p). Happily the trustees authorized the purchase of 10 dozen very best sherry and 10 dozen best madeira to encourage themselves. Though one or two other carriers participated, Reid's did most of the transhipment trade until in 1837 the Anderton Carrying Company was formed to take it over from them. The transfer business remained a steady one, averaging 31,087 tons of Potteries raw materials and crated goods, and 7,404 tons of grain and general merchandise, in its first fourteen years.

The Weaver trustees were good employers. In the bad times after the Napoleonic wars they tried to employ flatmen during the winters when trade was slack; they paid pensions to old employees, some of whom had been allowed to stay at work long after their best days, like the barrow-maker who was over 80 when he was pensioned in 1836; and they often employed widows of lock-keepers in the same jobs as their former husbands and at the same pay. And in 1837 they 'ordered that a Dinner be given to all the men in the Employ of the Navigation in honour of Her Majesty's Coronation, and that Mr Adams provide the same and be allowed Five shillings per head to include drink'.

A national wave of concern for the spiritual state of the working class, and for Sunday observance not only for religious reasons but to lessen the burden of work, affected the publicly-owned Weaver much more than it did most of the canal companies. It began in June 1839 by the trustees realizing that their own office was issuing craft passes on Sunday, and by receiving a petition from flat captains and hauliers asking for Sunday off. By August they had passed a bye-law prohibiting Sunday work, with a £5 penalty, and were thanked by over 400 watermen, though the rock salt proprietors disapproved.

But the trustees felt they should be more positive, and set up a sub-committee to consider providing church accommodation and religious instruction out of surplus revenue for those who worked on the river. An enabling Act[10] was passed in 1840. By the end of 1841 Christ Church, Weston Point, had been built with its parsonage house, and £150 p.a. salary for its minister charged against revenue. They even paid the choir and the man who lit the heating boiler, and provided books bought from the S.P.C.K. This was followed by Holy Trinity, Northwich, in 1842 and Christ Church, Winsford, in 1843. That done, they turned a former infant school held in a building near their office at Northwich into a school for

* See the plan on p. 37 of *The Canals of the West Midlands*.

the children of flatmen and hauliers, paying a schoolmaster £60 p.a. and collecting 1d a week from each child. These school pence were carefully brought to account. They amounted in 1854–5 to £5 17s 7d (£5·88), from which one deduces that many children were excused payment. It was so popular that the schoolroom had to be enlarged in 1844, while another was built at Winsford, and a third at Weston Point. It was a remarkable and efficient effort in care not only for their own employees, but for all who worked on the river, not unmixed with a real benevolence, as when in 1848 the trustees, discussing a falling off in school attendance at Winsford, asked the clergyman there to tell the schoolmaster 'that the exhibition of a little more kindness to the children might have a beneficial effect'.[11] The schools were transferred to the Church authorities from 1905, the three churches in 1929 also under an Act which empowered the trustees to contribute a substantial sum as endowment for the incumbents' stipends.

In 1833 the trustees decided to build a new west wall to the basin at Weston Point, thereby enlarging it on the south side to hold 20 more flats. Waiting for the tide was chronic: in the same year it was reported that out of 80 towing horses on the river, up to 30 would be waiting at the basin. A stable was built for them, with a room attached for their drivers. Enlargement was followed in 1837 by work starting on a second river entrance to enable the increasing numbers of craft to get in and out. This was finished about the end of 1839, and was followed by enlargement of the south side of the basin. By 1842 business was so brisk that two assistant harbourmasters were needed. A sea-wall was started about 1841, 300 ft long, outside the harbour against which flats could moor while waiting to get in, and in 1844 extended another 200 ft.

By 1836, Anderton had an 'immense increased trade', due partly to salt transhipment, but also to enlarging business in clay and merchandise, mainly in the hands of the Anderton Carrying Company. This company, in addition to shipping china clay upwards to the Potteries, and carrying merchandise, seems to have carried a range of goods in crates to take advantage of special tolls offered for crated goods, notably pottery. By 1843 the trustees came to the conclusion that the company was getting away with toll evasions, and raised the transhipment tolls at Anderton for goods with crates. The Anderton company, led by its chairman, Falkner, annoyed at the raising of rates they

had thought to be permanent, replied by giving notice of a Bill*
to amend the Weaver Acts to eliminate the payment of surpluses
to the county and to put control of the river into the hands of
those who paid the tolls. An exchange of press letters was
followed by the Bill itself, and a memorial to the Board of Trade
from the Liverpool earthenware merchants supporting it. The
trustees sent a counter-statement, but smartly agreed to a request
from the salt trade for the improvement of lock approaches on the
navigation. The Anderton company, having tried to get away
with not paying the additional toll, dropped their Bill. Once the
lesson had sunk in, the trustees relented in 1845, and restored
transhipment tolls roughly to where they were before. The
Anderton company in 1843 transhipped 33,345 tons at Anderton,
of which 12,835 tons was clay. If we add a large salt and small coal
transhipment, a considerable tonnage must have changed waterways each year.

In the years between 1792 and 1845, the trustees had seen an
enormous growth in their business, yet with little change in its
constituents. Total tonnage had increased from an average of
164,657 in 1792–4 to 778,715 in 1843–5. Salt traffic had quin-
tupled, coal increased about three and a half times. But within the
salt total, white salt had gone ahead of rock salt: in 1800–1 55,903
tons out of a total of 198,579 carried were rock salt; in 1845–6
112,731 tons out of 575,645. Toll revenue, averaging £8,172 in
1792–4, was £38,363 in 1843–5. Within the total tonnage, an increasing proportion was along the whole length of the navigation.
Here are the figures for the Northwich and Winsford trades in
1800–1 and 1845–6:

	Northwich		*Winsford*	
	1800–01	*1845–6*	*1800–01*	*1845–6*
Tolls (£)	10,814	24,103	4,594	14,562
Salt (tons)	145,698	346,034	52,881	229,611
Coal (tons)	60,534	83,995	37,746	59,014

The trustees had paid out of revenue for all the improvements
they had undertaken to ensure an efficient navigation for 90-ton
craft, and an adequate transit basin at Weston Point. Yet they had
also transferred about £500,000 of surplus funds in relief of the
county rates, not far short of £10,000 p.a.; since 1830, over
£16,000. Public administration could well stand comparison with
private. Here are the Weaver's averaged figures since 1791:

* There seems to have been an earlier Bill in 1838.

Years from April	Toll Revenue	Salt tons	Coal tons	Other tons	Total tons
1792–4	8,172	112,810	45,270	6,577	164,657
1795–7	10,762	144,746	54,046	8,160	206,952
1798–1800	12,920	164,559	85,397	10,875	260,851
1801–3	15,108	193,438	95,916	13,682	303,036
1804–6	16,621	219,981	104,845	9,854	334,680
1807–9	18,782	210,230	118,097	8,920	337,247
1810–12	20,273	217,897	123,341	9,551	350,789
1813–15	23,547	284,074	131,396	8,615	424,085
1816–18	17,082	238,314	94,873	11,199	344,386
1819–21	18,294	258,670	130,771	12,094	401,535
1822–4	20,071	289,568	97,836	15,757	403,161
1825–7	22,292	306,541	124,163	18,062	448,766
1828–30	28,287	402,849	134,642	31,841	569,332
1831–3	30,275	442,026	129,577	52,278	623,881
1834–6	27,857	403,305	121,912	71,403	596,620
1837–9	32,270	472,930	141,878	51,286	666,094
1840–2	32,513	483,944	135,128	51,595	670,667
1843–5	38,363	558,506	154,699	65,510	778,715

As the period ends, we get in 1844 and 1845 the first references to chemical works, upon which the navigation was one day to depend. (*To continue the history of the Weaver Navigation, turn to p. 376.*)

Sankey Brook Navigation

In the absence of the company's records, one can only glimpse the Sankey's development while the Weaver was so strongly going forward. We see, perhaps, a less progressive concern than the Weaver, isolationist, yet very prosperous in its own local business.

We use the word isolationist because the company so frequently rebuffed the Mersey & Irwell's suggestions for a junction. Before the latter had decided to build their Runcorn & Latchford cut to get a line free from the tidal troubles of the river between Runcorn and Warrington, they approached the Sankey in 1796 and 1797 to discover whether they would do better to join that canal and extend it themselves to near Widnes. But they got no encouragement. Even after the Runcorn & Latchford cut had been made, the Mersey & Irwell saw value in joining the Sankey, not now to extend it downwards, but to get access to coal that could be carried upwards, and in 1812 sounded the committee upon a

possible branch from their cut to the Mersey opposite Fiddler's
Ferry. But once more, in June of the following year, they had to
report failure. Yet the demand seems to have been there, for in
that same November colliery proprietors on the Sankey were
asking for rates on coal to Manchester. The Mersey & Irwell
fixed them low, at 1s a ton 'to encourage the Trade', but this
gesture had no effect in lessening the Sankey's aloofness.

On 26 June 1797 *Billing's Liverpool Advertiser* wrote:
   'An unusual occurrence took place at Newton Common, on
Friday the 16th . . . a vessel, heavily laden with copper slag,
passed along the Sankey Canal, without the aid of hawlers or
rowers, the oars performing 18 strokes a minute, by the
application of steam only . . . it appears, that the vessel after a
course of ten miles, returned the same evening to St. Helen's
whence it had set out'.

This was a boat fitted out by John Smith of St Helen's, with a
Newcomen engine working a paddle crankshaft through a beam
and connecting rod. According to Spratt[12] the first trials were
made in 1793.

Developments on the Weaver probably contributed to the
profitability of the company in the early years of the new century.
Dividends between 1805 and 1816 averaged as follows:

per £155 share

	£	s	d	
1805-7	44	15	4	(£44·76½)
1808-10	52	18	4	(£52·91½)
1811-13	54	18	8	(£54·93½)
1814-16	58	19	4	(£58·96½)

In 1815 the tonnage was 181,863,* and in 1816, 144,806½.* On a
5 per cent basis, the value of a Sankey share in 1814 was about
£1,200.[13]

Charges were low. Thomas Waring, engineer to collieries at
Blackbrook, said in 1825 that his pits were connected by railroad
to the canal, which carried all his coal at 1s (5p) a ton.[14] This was
the original toll of 10d from the 1755 Act, plus 2d for using the
extension to Fiddler's Ferry, levied on a ton that in fact meant
some 27 cwt. Yet the flourishing coal trade yielded high dividends
on the company's small capital: Thomas Case, a Sankey committeeman, giving evidence in 1829, said that an average dividend of

* We think these are nominal tons—at this time the canal company were carrying
27 cwt to the ton. Actual tonnages were probably 7/20ths greater.

33⅓ per cent had been paid since the canal opened. The dividend figures quoted earlier must therefore have risen still higher in the meantime. Most of this carrying was by colliery-owned craft. Toll-sheets for the period 9 to 21 January 1826 show cargoes from thirteen collieries, but only one flat with an owner-captain.

In their prospectus of 29 October 1824, the promoters of the Liverpool & Manchester Railway referred to

'coals from the rich mines in the vicinity of St Helens. . . . These coals at present pass along the Sankey Canal, and down the Mersey to Liverpool, a distance of about thirty miles. By the railway the distance will be shortened one-half'.

This line was to have run more to the north than the one built, within a mile of St Helens and past several of its canal-served collieries.

The colliery owners round St Helens, who were also much engaged in the salt trade, did not much need the Liverpool and Manchester Railway, but they did want a line to the Mersey which, they fondly hoped, would provide them with quicker and cheaper transport than the canal to Liverpool and the Weaver. In 1829 a group commissioned Charles Vignoles to make a survey, and a route was chosen from near St Helens to a proposed dock at Runcorn Gap (Widnes), which was to cross the Liverpool & Manchester Railway by a bridge with inclined planes on each side. It should perhaps be remembered that the present town of Widnes was built after the railway had been constructed and the canal extended. The promoters seem to have had little encouragement from the Weaver trustees. An authorizing Act was passed for the St Helens & Runcorn Gap Railway on 29 May 1830.[15] The lines were to cross the existing Sankey Canal twice, at Hardshaw Mill and Burtonwood, and twice more on the proposed canal extension, all on swing bridges. These were normally to be kept open, and engine drivers were to reopen them after their trains had passed.

In face of this threat, the Sankey proprietors decided to do what they had so long talked about—extend their line parallel with the Mersey for 3½ miles to Widnes also, with a dock and river entrance. There had been earlier proposals. The Sankey company had introduced a Bill in 1819 to extend to Runcorn Gap because 'by means of the shallowness of the . . . River, and of beds of sand in the same, the Navigation thereof, especially at neap tides, is greatly impeded', but they ran up against Sir Edward Brooke's opposition and had to drop it.[16] The need was still there: writing

in 1831, the Mersey & Irwell, referring to the river channel between Runcorn Gap and Warrington, minuted: 'The trips are at
present made with difficulty owing to the shallow water and
narrow channels combined with the number of Vessels grounded
each Tide betwixt Runcorn and Fiddler's Ferry'. When the
Sankey extension had been made, however, they expected it only
to be used at neaps: 'when their Canal is cut to Runcorn one half
of the flats will go up or down the River, and only just at Neap
Tides will all flats go up the Canal'.[17]

An additional demand was also showing. Up to about 1830,
most of the Sankey coal had gone to Cheshire; but thenceforward
a steadily increasing demand arose to load coasters and other
craft at Runcorn or Liverpool, many for Ireland. In addition,
coal was needed for the furnaces of a growing number of steam-
ships, naval, packet and commercial. In 1846 the St Helens company's secretary considered that of 693,000 tons of coal from the
St Helens field, 183,000 tons went to the salt works of Cheshire,
and 440,000 tons 'down the river', for steam vessels, export or the
coastwise trade.[18]

The authorizing Act[19] of 1830, passed on the same day as that
for the railway, also enabled the directors to form a new incorporated Company of Proprietors of the Sankey Brook Navigation, which would issue four new £200 shares for each of the 120
old £155 shares. The nominal capital therefore became £96,000.
Power was also given to borrow up to £30,000 to finance the
extension. Tolls, however, were still to be the 10d plus 2d of
former Acts, and the exemptions in that of 1755 were maintained.
A clause in the Act refused the new company

'Right of Property in the several Jetties or Stone Works which
may have been constructed from Time to Time by the Proprietors of the Sankey Brook Navigation in the Tideway . . .
or to sanction or authorize the Continuance or to prevent the
Removal of the same, on account of their being injurious to the
Navigation of the said River'.

This suggests that the old company had tried to improve part of
the Mersey's tidal channel by training works designed to deepen
it.

The canal extension was engineered by Francis Giles, and
opened in July 1833 to the Mersey at Widnes and to a new dock
there beside that built by the railway. Twin locks 79 ft × 20 ft,
rather larger than those existing on the canal, were built at the
Mersey entrance, whence the line was level to Fiddler's Ferry,

where the former entrance lock to the estuary was kept open for craft to or from Warrington. The railway was formally but ineffectively opened on 21 February 1833 and was working by the middle of the year, when coal began to be shipped from its dock. But it had cost some £200,000, much more than had been estimated, and for lack of money the company had been unable to build branches to all the collieries it had intended to serve. The hoped-for passenger traffic failed to appear, and its daily working was hampered by its two awkward inclined planes. Oppressed by its bond debt, unable to pay a dividend, finding it hard to maintain its track and work its trains for lack of money, it was the railway, not the canal, that struggled to survive. In July 1834 the railway's minute book noted sadly how difficult it was to get people to change their habits:

> 'the masters of Flats and others interested in them, accustomed to the navigation of the Sankey Canal, are in many instances still desirous of clinging to old usage and adopt the change reluctantly. By degrees these prejudices subside, and the manifest advantages of expedition and economy are gradually developing themselves and producing their proper influence'.[20]

In fact, after some mild rate cutting, both lines found themselves carrying more. But whereas in 1836 the canal carried 170,000 tons of coal against 130,000 by rail, in 1845 the figures were 440,784 against 252,877,* much of the canal's increase coming from new collieries in the Blackbrook district.

The Weaver trustees on 2 October 1834 noted that whereas by their Acts 63 cu. ft of coal, cannel or slack were declared to be a ton, this measurement caused uncertainty because of differing qualities. Their engineer had estimated that 63 cu. ft made about 27 cwt, but as the St Helens & Runcorn Gap Railway allowed 28 cwt, they would adopt the same measure.

After a confidential meeting between two committeemen of each party, a meeting of railway shareholders in February 1838 considered amalgamation with the Sankey. It was agreed in principle, and afterwards the two committees met and resolved that the union should take place.[21] But it did not, perhaps because of the railway's financial position. In 1842, however, the railway met the canal suddenly, when at 7 a.m. on 13 January a train of laden coal trucks near Pocket Nook found a swing bridge over

---

* Both railway and canal were charging 30 cwt as a ton in 1845. We do not know whether the above figures, quoted by Barker and Harris, are nominal or actual tonnages.

the canal open ready for a flat to pass, so that the engine, tender and two waggons fell in. The driver and stoker prudently jumped off in time. The canal had to be drained, but the *Railway Times* thought it would probably be necessary to dismantle the engine, as there was no tackle to lift it.[22]

It seems that in 1843 the canal company were considering another extension to their canal, this time upwards to the Mersey at Warrington, where it would have at last linked with the Mersey & Irwell.[23] This project may have stimulated renewed contact between the companies. Representatives of each met at the Sankey Navigation office early in January 1844,[24] with the result that the canal company agreed to sell to the railway for £300 per £200 share, equivalent to £1,200 on the original £155 shares, or £144,000 in all, and the transfer of their bond debt of £29,450. A new company, the St Helens Canal & Railway Company was to be formed, to which the canal shareholders were to subscribe one-third of 1,440 shares of £100 carrying a preferential dividend of 5 per cent, at the rate of one preference share for each share held, further profits to be divided rateably between these shares and the railway's older 1,200 £100 shares and 1,065 half shares of £50. The first authorizing Bill of 1844 failed on standing orders, but an Act[25] was subsequently passed on 21 July 1845.

The Act provided that the canal should be maintained, but that if later any part did not cover expenses, the company could after notice seek the Board of Trade's agreement to closure. This section was repealed in 1864 when the combined concern was transferred to the London & North Western Railway. The Act also gave the company power to buy Sankey Quays from Lord Lilford, and repealed the old provision that 63 cu. ft of coal equalled a ton, substituting 3,360 lb, or 30 cwt, as its equivalent. Revised tolls were listed, and the former exemptions continued.

The relative positions of the two companies at amalgamation can be seen from the following combined account for the 18 months from 1 January 1844, when the amalgamation was deemed to have begun, to 20 June 1845:

	£
Total income of canal	21,373
Expenses of canal	7,792
Canal surplus	13,581

	£
Total income of railway	17,335
Expenses of railway	11,649
Railway surplus	5,686
Interest of canal bond debt of £29,450 @ 4 per cent	1,767
Interest of railway bond debt of £69,580 @ 5 per cent	5,218

The accounts for the second half of 1845 show that the canal was getting about an eighth of its revenue from merchandise carrying: coal, £7,200; merchandise £1,118; rents £35: Total £8,353.

By this time, as we have seen, the interests of the Weaver and the Sankey Brook had begun to diverge. No longer was the Weaver far the largest market for Sankey coal, and the first signs of change-over from the Cheshire river's dependence on salt-carrying were beginning to show. (*To continue the history of the St Helens Canal, turn to p.* 393.)

CHAPTER VII

The Leeds & Liverpool Canal

++++++++++++++++++++++++++++++++++++ ✦ ++++++++++++++++++++++++++++++++++++

AT the beginning of 1791 contracts were let for the line from Gargrave to Barrowford, including Foulridge tunnel and locks at Gargrave, Bank Newton and Barrowford. The tunnel proved to be most troublesome. It was to be 1,640 yd long, 17 ft wide with 8 ft headroom above water level, and Whitworth intended some 120 yd to be built on the cut-and-cover system. In September he reported that most of the summit level had been dug except for the tunnel, but that masonry on locks, bridges and the Aire aqueduct near Gargrave was well behind.

Meanwhile some shareholders were saying that the likely effects upon their plans of the current Rochdale Canal (see Chapter X) scheme should have been given greater consideration before work on the summit had been authorized. This proposed to connect the Bridgewater at Manchester with the Calder & Hebble at Sowerby Bridge, and was likely to be a broad waterway. Obviously it would provide a rival cross-Pennine route, shorter from Liverpool to the West Riding though longer to Leeds, but able to tap Manchester traffic at its source. Some felt therefore that the summit section of the Leeds & Liverpool was not entirely necessary, and there were renewed demands for a deviation to serve the East Lancashire towns. Two other factors also emerged: the Lancaster Canal, for which a Bill seeking incorporation was currently being promoted, would cross the Leeds & Liverpool south of Preston; and the proposal to extend the Manchester, Bolton & Bury from Bolton to Red Moss near Horwich (see Chapter IX) if the Leeds & Liverpool would build a branch to meet it. This would, of course, give access to Manchester and in July 1791 Whitworth and Priestley were instructed to survey a route from the Leeds & Liverpool's line at Euxton to Red Moss.

The Rochdale promoters, too, were anxious to connect with the Leeds & Liverpool. They saw the Manchester, Bolton & Bury

link as a means of bringing limestone to Manchester, and a representative attended a general assembly in September to suggest
that the Leeds & Liverpool should construct a branch from Colne
or Burnley to the Rochdale's line near Todmorden, or failing that,
the Rochdale would do it themselves. This proposal received a
cool reception, as a joint committee with the Manchester, Bolton
& Bury was set up at the same meeting to investigate a Red Moss
junction. Meanwhile, the 'deviationists' from Lancashire were
gaining ground among the shareholders. This caused some alarm
among the Lancaster Canal committee, who saw that if the
deviation became reality its lower portion would not only form a
line dangerously parallel with their own but also intercept their
water supplies. They, too, suggested a joint committee to discuss
the matter, which was refused pending a decision by the Leeds &
Liverpool. The meeting then received Whitworth and Priestley's
report, which suggested that the canal line should be completely
changed between Bamber Bridge and Newburgh, to run instead
by Duxbury and east of Blackrod, locking up 215 ft to a summit
at Red Moss where a junction with the Manchester, Bolton &
Bury's extension could conveniently be made, thence falling
through Westhoughton, Hindley and Platt Bridge to the head of
the Upper Douglas Navigation, which would thereby become
part of the main line. There would be obvious difficulties in
supplying the canal with water from the fairly short summit level,
and the report suggested that the rise could be considerably reduced if the entire line from Colne to Newburgh were changed to
take a winding course through Burnley, Accrington and Blackburn on one level, adding 12 miles to the overall distance but
tapping valuable traffic.

Doubts about the tunnel were now voiced in severe criticism
of Whitworth by some proprietors. Would an open level at the
summit not be cheaper, they asked, and in view of the possibility
of a deviation should not the summit level be lengthened to provide water for the twelve extra miles, or at least work on Barrowford locks be suspended until a decision was reached? Whitworth
defended himself stoutly, but criticism was not stifled. His oppo-
nents, not content with the prospect of winning the deviation
battle, were convinced that the tunnel was an unnecessary expense
and produced another deviation line by Longbotham, some 120
ft higher and 11 miles longer than Whitworth's. Though this was
rejected by the committee after Whitworth had strongly criticized
it, the committee felt it prudent to obtain a second opinion on the

Page 151 (*above*) The Springs Branch canal staithes from the foot of the tramroad incline in 1956; (*below*) a steam tug waits at the west end of Foulridge tunnel on the Leeds & Liverpool Canal *c.* 1910

Page 152 Lancaster Canal: (*above*) Four arches of the Lune aqueduct; (*below*) the swift passenger boat *Waterwitch II* in use as an engineer's inspection boat at Lancaster
c. 1900

tunnel from Josiah Clowes.* He considered that a shorter tunnel 300–400 yd long would have been feasible, but as 800 yd had already been cut he thought it would be cheaper to complete rather than to abandon it. Accordingly Whitworth was ordered to engage more men to assist the pilot tunnel contractors.

During this internal crisis, the political interplay between the Leeds & Liverpool, the Rochdale promoters, the Manchester, Bolton & Bury and the Lancaster promoters continued. John Rennie surveyed a branch from the Rochdale's line at Todmorden to the western end of the Leeds & Liverpool's summit above Barrowford locks via Holme Chapel, Ormerod, Burnley Ridge and Colne, with an alternative junction near Burnley if the Leeds & Liverpool decided to deviate their line that way. Deputations met at Burnley in November at which the Rochdale promoters pressed for the Barrowford junction in order that they could avoid 70 ft of lockage down at Burnley and also serve quarries and pits at Worsthorne. In reply the Leeds & Liverpool stated that they would require 6d (2½p) per ton for limestone carried on their canal to the Rochdale's branch. At the same time Whitworth was busy surveying his line through Blackburn and past the proposed Manchester, Bolton & Bury junction at Red Moss, while early in 1792 the latter company came up with a scheme to extend the Bury arm of their canal eastwards to Rochdale and Littleborough, as an alternative to the Rochdale itself and a means of forcing the Leeds & Liverpool's hand.

A month later they offered to drop the scheme if the Leeds & Liverpool would agree to construct the proposed deviation and the junction at Red Moss. A deputation from the Leeds & Liverpool duly reported back to their committee, favouring the Rochdale promoters' branch and frankly admitting that whilst the junction at Red Moss would open up new markets for lime and marl, any eastward extension of the Manchester, Bolton & Bury would be detrimental. Even more frankly, they stated that the value of the east Lancashire deviation necessary to make the junction would more than outweigh the extra cost and mileage. The original concept of linking the east and west seas would be more effectively achieved by the proposed Rochdale Canal, 15 or 16 miles shorter and passing through more populous country, whilst the original Leeds & Liverpool parliamentary line had been

* Clowes had been resident engineer in charge of building Sapperton tunnel on the Thames & Severn Canal and had superintended the construction of Dudley tunnel.

K

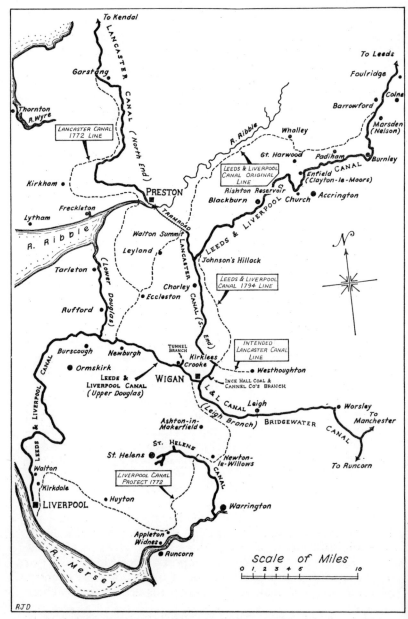

10. The Leeds & Liverpool and Lancaster Canals in south Lancashire, showing completed lines and principal earlier projects

shown by 15 years' experience to be useless. It would therefore be more profitable for the Leeds & Liverpool to concentrate on internal than through traffic. The committee agreed, resolving to ask as many of the distant proprietors as possible to attend a meeting at Newark. It was held in February, when the deviation and the Red Moss junction with the Manchester, Bolton & Bury were approved, and the suggestion made that it might be better if the Lancaster were to join the Leeds & Liverpool south of Preston rather than run parallel. The Manchester, Bolton & Bury agreed to support the deviation and to join in opposing the Lancaster's Bill if the latter would not agree to terminate south of Preston. But the Lancaster had powerful support in the Duke of Bridgewater, who wanted the traffic the Lancaster would bring on to his own canal but had no desire to see a second route from Liverpool to Manchester formed by the Leeds & Liverpool and Manchester, Bolton & Bury alliance. The Lancaster therefore refused to abandon their line south of Preston and pressed ahead with their Bill, which passed on 24 June despite the opposition.

The Rochdale promoters, on the other flank, persisted in pressing for an alternative junction between their somewhat impracticable branch up the Vale of Cliviger from Todmorden, seeking to take advantage of the Leeds & Liverpool's difficulties at Foulridge tunnel by suggesting an even less practicable alternative route near Lothersdale to avoid it, which the Leeds & Liverpool committee brusquely brushed aside.

A Bill was introduced in 1793 for the Blackburn deviation which, near Chorley, would be within 100 yd of the Lancaster. With the support of the Duke, who had agreed to the Lancaster's extension from Westhoughton to Worsley, the latter successfully opposed it and the Leeds & Liverpool were left to appoint a select committee to survey the ruins of their policy. The committee reported that between Holme Bridge (Gargrave) and Burnley 18 miles had been completed, including 350 yd of the tunnel, which would take four years to finish. £70,000 had been spent, with a further £38,000 needed. To add to this gloomy prospect, the committee estimated the cost of the Blackburn deviation at £215,000, with £18,300 more to finish the Holme Bridge–Burnley length. However, income was expected to equal 5 per cent on capital for the Burnley length and 10 per cent for the deviation. Current revenue was running at some £29,000 p.a. and in support of that anticipated from the deviation some interesting figures were quoted of traffic to East Lancashire towns. Some 20,000 tons were shipped from Hull a year via the Aire & Calder and the Leeds & Liverpool as far as Kildwick, between Keighley and Skipton where the road to Colne and Burnley left the Aire valley, continuing thence by road mainly as far as Blackburn, and 10,000 tons by road from the head of the Calder & Hebble at Sowerby Bridge. Eastward, 10,000 tons a year left Liverpool for East Lancashire by the Leeds & Liverpool as far as Wigan, and another 10,000 was despatched via Manchester over the Mersey & Irwell and the Bridgewater. The main committee decided to promote a second deviation Bill for 1794, again with the support of the Manchester, Bolton & Bury, and to negotiate with the Lancaster's supporters and the Duke.

A group of promoters with Manchester, Bolton & Bury backing now produced another scheme to join the Leeds & Liverpool, the Haslingden Canal, from the former at Bury to the latter at Church near Accrington, which, apart from gaining its Act, came to nothing (see p. 259).

The Leeds & Liverpool was by now, the committee admitted, in a critical state. The tunnel was swallowing money so fast that there was unlikely to be any for the various deviations and connections even if they were authorized, a rather unlikely prospect in view of the numerous Lancashire canal schemes then being promoted.

In October the Lancaster tried to turn the tables on the Leeds & Liverpool by suggesting that they should join the Lancaster's line near Heapey where both became parallel. As this would have destroyed the former's level to the Manchester, Bolton & Bury at Red Moss, the Leeds & Liverpool counter-proposed that the Lancaster should abandon their southerly line and strike south-eastwards to join their own canal at Newburgh (on a line close to the one they wished to abandon themselves), and gain the Bridge-water by a branch from the Leeds & Liverpool at Wigan, which would also attract some Liverpool–Manchester traffic. But the Lancaster committee, knowing their own strength and aware that their enemy lacked resources, rejected the Leeds & Liverpool's plan. Work on their south level was proceeding, negotiations were in hand for land for reservoirs, and the company had power-ful support from the Wigan coalowners and the Duke of Bridge-water, while the Leeds & Liverpool, short of funds, was disliked in Liverpool and opposed by the Duke for its support of the Red Moss link. Yet if its badly needed deviation were to be authorized, the support of the Lancaster and the Manchester, Bolton & Bury was essential.

The result was a compromise with the Lancaster in April 1794, whereby the latter undertook to support the deviation and the Manchester, Bolton & Bury extension Bills if the Leeds & Liverpool would support the Lancaster's own Bill for a small deviation at Cabus north of Preston, and the Worsley extension. The agreement recognized that there would be two parallel lines—this ensured that the link with the Manchester, Bolton & Bury could be made and so kept their support—but was subject to a short connecting canal being made at Heapey at the Lancaster's expense —so ensuring that a proportion of the traffic would pass over the Lancaster and on to the Bridgewater. It carried the proviso that should the junction not materialize the Lancaster would pay the Leeds & Liverpool 1d per ton on all Manchester-bound goods which otherwise would have passed through it in order to reach the Manchester, Bolton & Bury at Red Moss and so take the shortest route. The Duke's interest in the Lancaster's Worsley extension was safeguarded (see Chapter VIII) by the Leeds & Liverpool entering into a bond under which they undertook to construct the Heapey–High Charnock section of the deviation last of all. Evidently His Grace anticipated success for the Lancaster's Bill and was making sure that if the Leeds & Liverpool's Bill also succeeded, traffic to Manchester from both canals would pass as far over his own line as possible. On this occasion, however, his judgement failed him, for the Lancaster's Bill was rejected, though the Leeds & Liverpool's passed on 9 May 1794.[1] It authorized the raising of £280,000 in additional shares to pay off loans and help finance the deviation.

In October the general assembly approved the commencement of work westward from Barrowford (to which the canal was complete except for Foulridge tunnel) to Blackburn, at an estimated cost of £100,000 to be raised·by additional shares. At the same time a £4 dividend was declared for the half-year, after a gap of 18 months when none was recorded. To avoid a lengthy detour at Burnley, Whitworth proposed to cross the Calder valley by a long embankment some 46 ft high, for which the deep cutting and short tunnel at Gannow, beyond the southern end, would provide most of the 345,000 cu. yd of spoil required. In autumn 1795 contracts were let between Burnley and Hapton, 4 miles, whilst at Liverpool a new basin was completed. Samuel Fletcher was appointed resident engineer and land was purchased for a large reservoir at Foulridge. Whitworth himself continued as engineer, but in view of his other commitments, at half salary. In

January 1796, a short branch to Rain Hall Rock, a limestone quarry near Barnoldswick, was authorized by the committee.

Work between Barrowford locks and Burnley presented few difficulties and was completed well before Foulridge tunnel, which was at long last opened on 1 May 1796;[2] 1,640 yd long, it had taken five years to complete and the shallow depth and loose ground had in the event necessitated well over half being driven on the 'cut-and-cover' principle. Parts cost as much as £24 per yard.

In December Whitworth reported on a proposed canal from the Lancaster to the Ribble near Lytham, opposite the Douglas outfall. He suggested that the Leeds & Liverpool might improve the navigation of the Douglas up to Sollom lock, at present attainable only on spring tides, by a further artificial cut, so linking the two canals and reducing the cost of coal to Preston. He recommended that the new cut should follow the river from Sollom and join it below Tarleton weir, a length of 2 miles. The Leeds & Liverpool agreed, but the Lancaster, nearing the completion of their canal from Preston to Tewitfield and still struggling with the Wigan–Preston section, was in low financial water and in no mood to encourage competition. They countered with the suggestion of a tramroad on their side of the Ribble, but declined to make active moves until 1798 (see Chapter VIII).

The Tarleton cut was eventually made in 1805, partly as a result of the drainage of Croston Moss which threatened to silt the Douglas below Sollom more than ever, and partly to counter competition in the Preston coal traffic arising from the building of the tramroad connecting the south end of the Lancaster with Preston. Sollom lock was abolished and a new one built at Tarleton; the river was diverted into a new channel, the old one as far as Tarleton bridge being used for part of the canal extension. By 1801 it appears that the upper reaches of the river had become totally superseded by the canal from Wigan.*

The year 1797 saw a national financial crisis. The Leeds & Liverpool treasurer stated in July that he had only £6,630 in hand, nearly all of it owed, and no prospect of raising further loans or capital. It was agreed that, if at all possible, work should be carried on as far as Enfield (Clayton-le-Moors), which would be able to serve Blackburn and Accrington. Elsewhere it was to be suspended or reduced. But to encourage what little investment

---

* Except for a basin on the river at Gathurst, reached by the side lock at Dean, and still shown on the 1845 Ordnance Survey map.

might be obtainable the £4 half-yearly dividend was maintained after a hasty adjournment of the general assembly to examine the accounts.

By the beginning of 1799 more money was needed. Some £19,900 of the allocation for completing the canal to Blackburn had been spent in improvements elsewhere, including a new basin at Liverpool and a dock at Leeds, and £10,000 was still required. Furthermore, considerable sums had been spent in opening up quarries to produce cheap limestone and counter higher prices which would have lowered consumption and reduced canal traffic generally. In particular the Rain Hall Rock branch was being extended, including a short tunnel. So the proprietors were asked for more loans. But response was poor, and £6,000 was borrowed from the company's bankers to enable completion as far as Enfield.

On 30 March Whitworth died and Samuel Fletcher was placed in charge of the Enfield works, with his brother Joseph as assistant. Completion of the 559 yd long Gannow tunnel in early 1801 enabled the Burnley–Enfield section to be opened on 23 April. The cutting of this section in five years, including Burnley embankment and Gannow tunnel, and the maintenance of an 8 per cent dividend at a time of financial stringency was indeed a remarkable achievement. From Gargrave to Enfield had cost £336,753, making a total to date of £564,116.[3]

During the previous two years, much had happened elsewhere on the canal. A new warehouse for the Preston trade at Liverpool was authorized, and the toll on coal from Wigan was raised to 2s 6d (12½p) per ton for coal sold at no more than 10s 6d (52½p) a ton in Liverpool, but subject to a drawback of 50 per cent with a minimum toll of 1s 6d (7½p). Coal selling at more than 10s 6d a ton, however, was surcharged 1d per ton/mile, with a maximum of 33 miles, the object being to promote the sale of inferior coal and so encourage the opening of new pits. The new reservoir at Foulridge (now Foulridge Lower) had been completed about 1798, but in 1800 an enlargement was already necessary and duly authorized. In that year the general assembly received a pathetic petition from John Longbotham, in which he said that he was now in 'the decline of life', without employment and with very slender means of subsistence. He asked for a small annual stipend, in return for any services he could render. Priestley was instructed to see him and agree a figure subject to recovery of certain company papers he still held. Ten months later, in April 1801, Long-

botham was dead. Priestley reported that he had received the
documents in return for which he had from time to time advanced
small sums of money, and also paid the funeral expenses of
£40.

In 1800 and again in 1801 the Duke of Bridgewater was asked
to agree to a connection with his Leigh branch which had been
authorized in 1795 and now just completed. He agreed to a line
from Wigan to Leigh, and Fletcher estimated the cost at £29,826
for a branch with two locks from an extension of the main canal.
This, with two more locks, eventually became the first part of the
Wigan flight. In order to protect the Duke's Manchester–Liverpool trade, the company agreed to a minimum toll of 1d per
ton/mile on goods passing over the branch to Liverpool, and to
accommodate the Lancaster inserted a clause in the Bill allowing
the latter to make a connecting cut or railroad. Unfortunately,
during the successful course of the Bill the death of the Duke
created a setback. R. H. Bradshaw alleged that the Duke had not
been entirely satisfied with the 1d minimum and repudiated the
agreement, whereat the Leeds & Liverpool had no alternative but
to withdraw.

As an alternative, therefore, moves were made once more towards linking up with the Manchester, Bolton & Bury at Red
Moss, and Joseph and James Fletcher (James was the son of
Samuel; they had been appointed joint surveyors in 1804 on his
death) reported in 1805: Enfield to Red Moss (25¾ miles) would,
they estimated, cost £245,275, and Wigan to Red Moss £101,725
(6¼ miles, nearly all locks). The general assembly decided to start
the Wigan–Red Moss works and approached the Bury Canal
proprietors, whom they found were not now ready to make their
connection,* so the decision was revoked; instead, work on the
Enfield–Blackburn section (9 miles) was started. In 1808 agreement was finally reached with the Bridgewater trustees and a Bill
was drawn up to construct the Leigh branch and borrow £500,000
for the Blackburn–Wigan section. The Leeds & Liverpool undertook not to make a junction with the Manchester, Bolton & Bury
or any other canal leading to Manchester, and the 1d minimum
toll was included. Powers were also sought to 'vary the Tonnage
upon Coals according to the value' despite opposition from the
Lancashire coal owners. Both the Rochdale and the Manchester,

---

* This refusal by the Manchester, Bolton & Bury is attested by the Leeds &
Liverpool records, but is not referred to in those of the Bolton company itself. The
truth about the incident awaits further evidence.

Bolton & Bury contested the 'Bridgewater clause', the latter claiming that they had spent £20,000 on widening their canal to take broad boats off the Leeds & Liverpool. The advantages of a junction with the Bridgewater seemed obvious—Wigan to Leigh, 6¾ miles with 2 locks, as opposed to Wigan to Bolton, 13 miles with 49 locks.

The members of the Leeds & Liverpool committee in London promoting the passage of their Bill asked the Bridgewater to relinquish their restraining clause and, when the latter refused, announced that they would withdraw their Bill. This placed the Bridgewater in an embarrassing position and they reluctantly agreed that the clause should not apply to the Manchester, Bolton & Bury. Emboldened by this apparent success, the Bury Canal representatives demanded further concessions, whereupon the Leeds & Liverpool, in the spirit of 'a plague on both your houses', withdrew the Bill entirely rather than surrender their independence. There was a sequel. The Lancaster, who had been waiting in the wings, seized their chance and secured an agreement with the Leeds & Liverpool for a junction between the two canals at Kirklees (near their southern termination, where the line of the Leeds & Liverpool crossed it), to give the Lancaster access to Manchester via the Bridgewater or the Manchester, Bolton & Bury, whichever should win, but of which neither, of course, had knowledge. The Lancaster, in return, undertook not to make any other junction giving access to Manchester (that is, directly with the Manchester, Bolton & Bury) without the consent of the Bridgewater. Seemingly as an afterthought, but indicating the way both canals were thinking, the agreement concluded by stating that a junction near Heapey would be better.

On 21 June 1810 the canal was opened to Blackburn, and three months later the Leeds & Liverpool at last saw common sense and acknowledged that the quickest and cheapest method of completing their line was to use the south end of the Lancaster, by extending their canal from Blackburn to Copthurst, near Heapey, and from Wigan up to Kirklees. To each of these the Lancaster agreed to construct short connecting links, that to Copthurst requiring six locks from their canal at Johnson's Hillock.

It was agreed that the work should be finished within three years, with provision for water supplies for both canals, and for equalizing merchandise tonnage rates on the common section subject to no junction being made with the Manchester, Bolton & Bury. As this represented a concession of ½d per ton/mile on the

11. Eanam wharf, Blackburn, Leeds & Liverpool Canal

part of the Lancaster, the fate of the Red Moss connection seemed
to be finally sealed.

During this period a number of improvements were authorized,
including a reservoir at Anglezark above Wigan,[4] and branches
to Hapton and Altham collieries. The latter do not appear to have
been built, although a cut was made to Peel's works at Church.

Gurney Pearce, a London proprietor, in 1791 started to run
packet boats between Bingley and Skipton on the Yorkshire side.
Shortly afterwards the service was extended to Gargrave, then
from Bingley to Horsforth bridge with a second boat, and in 1793
to Leeds with a third. In Lancashire the company in 1806 took
over Blundell & Hollinshead's licence to ply between Liverpool
and Wigan, and built packet boats which sailed daily from
September 1808. An author wrote of Liverpool in 1835: 'The
canal boat, morning and night, was the only public conveyance
to Bootle and Litherland, and withal, afforded not an unpleasant
journey'.[5]

The Liverpool committee were alarmed at the high prices and
scarcity of coal in 1803 and recommended the main committee to
buy and work collieries of their own. The idea was turned down,
and, worried at the loss on coal tonnage, they increased the dues
from 30 June 1804, which made matters worse. Coal for Preston

and the Fylde was usually landed at Preston quay, at the head of the Ribble Navigation; at Ashton-on-Ribble a little lower down; or at Freckleton, a short distance from the estuary on the little River Dow where tidal restrictions were less and which supported a flourishing shipbuilding and carrying trade in the late eighteenth and early nineteenth centuries. Some was also transhipped to coastal craft off Lytham. Protests revealed that coal carried to Preston on the Lancaster Canal was being sold more cheaply than supplies taken via Tarleton and the Ribble, the newly-opened tramroad from Walton Summit to Preston proving to be less of an inconvenience to traffic, despite transhipment, than the hazards of the estuary and road transport from Freckleton wharf. Discounts of up to 1s 3d (6p) per ton were promptly allowed on coal sold at Freckleton. Orrell coal remained at a disadvantage, however, and in 1809 the probability that this traffic would be entirely lost to the Lancaster's competition forced the Leeds & Liverpool to allow a drawback of 1s (5p) on the 2s 6d (12½p) per ton toll.

Despite these troubles and the continuing difficulty in finding capital to finance the works, a dividend of 8 per cent was maintained and in 1808 there was a surplus of £6,000. The toll revenue was £58,111, of which nearly three-quarters came from Lancashire.[6]

Negotiations for a Leigh branch were reopened with the Bridgewater trustees in 1814, but four years passed before agreement was reached. The Bridgewater's terms were stiff: they demanded a toll of 1s 2d (6p) per ton on all goods entering or leaving their canal at Leigh, in lieu of wharfage, but carrying, in the case of traffic exchanged with the Rochdale, exemption from the Bridgewater's compensation toll imposed at its entrance at Castlefield, and four days' freedom from wharfage and warehousing charges at Manchester. The Leeds & Liverpool were to charge 1½d a ton per mile; were not to increase this without the Bridgewater's consent; and were to spend at least £5,000 on wharves for the Bridgewater's use at Liverpool and elsewhere. The committee objected to the last two items, but eventually agreed to pay a lump sum of £5,000 in lieu. Despite objections from the Manchester, Bolton & Bury, Ashton and Peak Forest companies to the increase in the coal rate to 1½d (which in the event was restricted to merchandise), the Bill passed on 21 June 1819.[7] The branch opened in December 1820,[8] at a cost of £61,419, 5 ft 6 in deep and taking 40-ton barges or 50-ton flats.

Meanwhile work on the connections to the Lancaster had been completed, so that the entire route from Leeds to Liverpool was ready for a grand opening in October 1816. People lined the banks and on the 23rd a flotilla of boats left Leeds, arriving at Liverpool to a tumultuous reception on the 27th. The canal was at last fully open, 127¼ miles long (including 10¾ miles of the Lancaster) with 91 locks.* The progressive opening of the canal helped to give growing local industries a tremendous boost, as the population figures of four sample Lancashire towns show:

	Wigan	Blackburn	Burnley	Colne
1801	10,989	11,980	3,305	3,626
1811	14,060	15,083	6,639	5,336
1821	17,716	21,904	10,068	7,274

In the case of Burnley, it is interesting to note that by the time the East Lancashire Railway reached the town in 1848, the population probably exceeded 20,000; the actual figure for 1851 is 24,745.[9] Increases in Yorkshire, outside Bradford and Leeds, were considerably lower.

Although the proprietors had good reason to feel pleased with themselves, they had a debt of £400,000. In 1814 Priestley suggested that this should be liquidated by asking each proprietor to contribute in proportion to his holding, but instead it was decided to promote a Bill to raise more capital and increase tolls. Great opposition arose from the coal interests at Liverpool and Wigan, Yorkshire ironfounders, farmers, merchants and landowners, and practically all persons of any influence who used the canal, so that after the second reading the company was forced to withdraw it. Rennie was asked to report on the water situation on the summit, which was also causing anxiety; he thought that if the through trade increased, the summit would be short in dry seasons. As merchandise traffic was the most profitable, he suggested it should have prior use of water at the expense of the less profitable limestone. He went on to recommend enforcement of the 'twenty tons rule' whereby, under the 1770 Act, the company could charge a minimum toll for 20 tons on vessels carrying less or empty. Lastly, he considered the full merchandise rates should be charged at the Liverpool end, and rents for yards and staithes increased. His recommendations were put into effect from October

* The single lock at Appley was later duplicated with two locks, and Pagefield lock was added in 1904 to counteract subsidence; then Crooke was removed, making a final total of 92 rises via the Appley pair.

1816 and, perhaps unwisely, the half-yearly dividend was raised in the second half of 1817, making 9 per cent for the year, and 10 per cent in 1818. Simultaneously in 1817, coal tolls between Wigan, Liverpool and the Ribble were increased to 1½d per ton/mile, and merchandise tolls between Newburgh and Wigan to 10½d, which immediately provoked a storm on both sides of the Pennines.

The Leeds '20 tons clause' was condemned and Preston coal dealers demanded restoration of their 1s 6d (7½p) drawback, quoting the following comparative prices:

via Leeds & Liverpool to Preston quay

	per ton		
	s	d	
Orrell coal (best)	17	10	(89p)
Pemberton & Standish coal (lower grade)	14	4	(71½p)
(net cost)			

via Leeds & Liverpool to Freckleton wharf

Orrell coal	16	0	(80p)
Pemberton & Standish coal	12	5	(62p)
(including profit)			

via Lancaster Canal and tramroad to Preston Basin*

Haigh coal (best)	14	2	(71p)
Adlington coal (lower grade)	12	6	(62½p)
(including profit)			

* The Lancaster had the disadvantage of transhipment on the tramroad, but much more convenient wharves near the centre of Preston.

The traders went on to point out that coal brought by coasting craft from Whitehaven and Workington was being sold in Preston as low as 8s 2d (41p) per ton and from Cheshire and Wales at 9s 2d (46p), and blamed the high canal dues for the large difference. Farmers in the Fylde, they said, were now buying coal from merchants on the Lancaster, and merchants at Ulverston bought coal by sea from Cheshire instead of from Freckleton. The committee was instructed to set up an enquiry into the coal trade on other canals before making a decision.

In April 1818 the committee reported. They showed that coal consumption had fallen considerably throughout the north during the depressed years of 1816 and 1817, quoting reduced figures from other navigations roughly in line with the Leeds & Liverpool's experience. The traders' threat to use the Sankey Brook

Navigation as an alternative was an empty gesture, as their tonnage had declined equally, only two pits (near Orrell) could be remotely considered to be served by both canals, and the state of the roads would effectively prevent coal being taken from Wigan to the Sankey at competitive rates. A general reduction of tolls, therefore, was not recommended, except from Newburgh to Tarleton, the high prices of coal being considered due to national economic factors rather than canal toll levels. At the same time a bid was made to attract salt trade from Cheshire by offering a 25 per cent drawback, presumably via the Trent & Mersey, Bridgewater and Leigh branch in competition with the Weaver trade.

The company's policy certainly seems to have been successful. Regularly each half year considerable portions of the debt were paid off and in 1821 the dividend was increased to 12 per cent. The summit water supply continued to give anxiety, however, and enlargements of Foulridge Upper reservoir were authorized in 1812 and 1817. Further relief was gained by replacing the three-rise staircase at Greenberfield by three single locks in 1820. In Lancashire additional water was needed for the long pound from Appley lock to Liverpool, for which once more a reservoir on the moors above Chorley was considered, but nothing was done. Instead, water was taken from the Douglas at Wigan and at Dean lock in 1815. The limestone quarries at Skipton and Rain Hall were progressively extended during these years, and new warehouses built at Leigh and Liverpool. Despite the setback in 1816, toll income continued to rise, as shown by these figures:[10]

Year	Toll Income
	£
1800	47,698
1805	54,005
1810	58,111
1815	67,187
1821	74,811

In 1814 Priestley was presented with a piece of plate worth 100 guineas (£105) inscribed

'From the Company of Proprietors of the Canal Navigation from Leeds to Liverpool, To their Superintendent Joseph Priestley, Esq, In token of his long, able and faithful services and of their individual Esteem & Regard'.[11]

On 14 August 1817 he died, aged 74, having lived to see his canal finally completed. Commencing as book-keeper in 1770, he had assumed more and more duties as the canal extended, and the need for economy grew. In present-day terms he had acted as accountant, secretary, general manager and even as engineer for eighteen years after Whitworth's death in 1799. For the last 21 years his salary had remained unchanged at a mere £170, and although 25 years previously the appointment of an assistant had been authorized, he had insisted on doing the work himself to save expense. The company allotted 500 guineas (£525) to a trust fund in favour of his grandson Joseph at the age of 21, and a tablet to his memory was erected in Bradford parish church (now Bradford cathedral).

No sooner had the Leigh branch been opened than demands were made for its improvement. The locks had been made to accommodate craft 62 ft long, as on the main line of the canal above Wigan, but in 1821 Pickford's asked for them to be lengthened to take their 'long narrow Fly Boats', and early in 1822 the committee resolved to extend them to take 72 ft craft, together with the two locks of the Wigan flight below the junction. The locks below Wigan had been built long enough—a further example of the independence exercised by the Liverpool committee during the early days of construction—in order to accommodate the Douglas coal trade, so that on completion there was a through route for narrow boats from Liverpool to the Midlands and London which avoided the hazardous crossing of the Mersey. At the same time a new lock was built at Dean alongside the old, and a new warehouse erected for Pickfords' use at Liverpool.

Although tolls were higher and the distance 10 miles greater than on the direct routes from Liverpool to Manchester, the uncertainties of the Mersey, less lockage and the use of fly-boats costing £160 instead of flats at £500 to £600 developed a more balanced and economical trade between the two centres than the Bridgewater or the Mersey & Irwell had. The fly-boats operated by John Kenworthy & Sons and, for a short time, Pickfords, took 16 hours, connecting at Liverpool with the Glasgow and Dublin packets. Their reliability gave them a small but increasing share of the cotton trade, and the canal company a total business from Liverpool to Manchester by their means that rose as follows:

Year	Tons
1821	12,693
1822	22,423
1823	26,830
1824	31,437

All the same, the canal's spokesman before the parliamentary committee on the Liverpool & Manchester Railway Bill of 1825 said: 'We have very little trade . . . the overplus trade that comes from the other lines is not sufficient, and for which reason Pickford, who was a carrier on this canal, has given up his establishment'.

The year 1822 saw the first appearance of serious rivalry from railways, in the shape of William James's Liverpool & Manchester scheme, which the Leeds & Liverpool joined the Mersey & Irwell, Bridgewater and Aire & Calder in opposing. In 1825 a Bill was promoted, this time with George Stephenson responsible for the route. But this time the Sankey Brook, Ashton and Peak Forest companies had joined the opposition, and it was defeated together with a Birmingham & Liverpool Railway Bill. But another succeeded in the same session, for the Bolton and Leigh Railway, with a line from the Manchester, Bolton & Bury to the Leeds & Liverpool at Leigh. Clearly the ultimate intention was to join a Liverpool & Manchester line,[12] and the opposition of the Leeds & Liverpool and the Bridgewater was only stilled when the railway company agreed not to cross the canal, to which the waterway interests presumably hoped it would act as a feeder. In 1826 the Liverpool & Manchester finally gained its Act, whereby the Bolton & Leigh was emboldened to come into the open and, with the Liverpool & Manchester, promote a connecting line called the Kenyon & Leigh Junction Railway, incorporated in 1829. To avoid outright opposition from the Leeds & Liverpool, they agreed to pay the canal company £500 compensation, give adequate clearance when bridging the canal and pay £15 per day if navigation was interrupted during construction. The line from Bolton reached the canal at Leigh in October 1829. The expected traffic from the Manchester, Bolton & Bury did not materialize as the railway failed to connect with it.[13] The Kenyon & Leigh Junction was opened in January 1831 (see p. 254).

Other railway schemes followed thick and fast. Hearing that the Wigan Branch Railway (connecting with the Liverpool & Manchester at Newton) was well supported, the Leeds & Liverpool committee decided it would be imprudent to oppose and instead negotiated compensation of £1,475, navigation rights at bridges, and a culvert for the Douglas feeder at Wigan.

The Liverpool & Manchester Railway did not at first offer heavy competition to the canals, although coal owners and canal carriers lost no opportunity to suggest that it did. In 1830 coal was being sold in Liverpool at 8s a ton, they said, from the railway wharf. Unless canal tolls were reduced, they threatened to transfer to the rail, but the Leeds & Liverpool knew that the railway was then unequal to the demand, and refused.

By 1832, in addition to the Liverpool & Manchester, there were lines open from it to Bolton, Wigan and Warrington. That the railways did not immediately have things their own way is illustrated by the deputation received by the Leeds & Liverpool from the Bolton & Leigh, Kenyon & Leigh Junction and Wigan Branch Railways, seeking a rates agreement. They found the present charges too low, and alleged heavy losses. The Bolton & Leigh, among various suggestions, offered on behalf of the three railways £1,000 p.a., or such higher figure of income as the canal company could prove. Alternatively, the canal company could lease the railways. These proposals the Leeds & Liverpool flatly rejected, but they agreed to minimum charges from Liverpool to Leigh of 6s (30p) per ton and to Bolton of 10s (50p) per ton.[14] In 1834 the Bolton & Leigh increased their offer to lease to £2,000 p.a., plus 2s 6d (12½p) for each ton in excess of 100 tons per day, and on refusal raised it to £2,500 plus £1,000 p.a. extra for coal from Bolton to Liverpool, which was again refused on the grounds that it would create a railway monopoly. Dividends had been running at 20 per cent from 1830, so the Leeds & Liverpool could afford to be uncompromising.

In 1835 John Hargreaves & Son, canal and railway carriers, who then leased and operated the Bolton & Leigh Railway and ran their own goods trains on the Liverpool & Manchester, took a hand and obtained a court decree nisi requiring the Leeds & Liverpool to show why a mandamus should not be issued instructing the company to charge equal rates and tolls to all traders. Not only were the canal company circumventing the agreement by deducting 5s (25p) from the 10s (50p) Bolton minimum, and then charging 4s 3d (21p) to 4s 6d (22½p) for cartage to make the total 9s 3d (46p) to 9s 6d (47½p),[15] but apparently they were also discriminating against Hargreaves for their railway activities. Discussions had been going on for several weeks with the Liverpool & Manchester regarding the traffic between Leigh, Wigan and Liverpool, which Hargreaves seems to have feared might turn out detrimental to him, whilst he in turn wanted a branch canal made to his warehouse on the railway at Wigan, to form a transhipment point to the canal for traffic to north-east Lancashire. In September the canal company and the Liverpool & Man-

L

chester, representing Hargreaves and the Bolton & Leigh, reached agreement whereby the last two would lease the canal tolls on Liverpool–Leigh traffic for £1,800 p.a., subject to that in excess of 50 tons a day or 350 tons a week being charged 2s 6d (12½p) per ton. The Hargreaves could make a branch to their Wigan warehouse (they did not), on the understanding that it was only for Preston traffic and not for competition with established Leeds & Liverpool trades to east Lancashire and beyond. The Liverpool & Manchester guaranteed payment of one quarter's rent. That the Hargreaves paid the bulk of the rental is evident from their complaint to the Liverpool & Manchester in 1838 that they had to pay the canal company £1,650 p.a. for carrying 50 tons a day to Leigh, whereas all they could obtain at railway rates was about 23 tons a day. The Liverpool & Manchester agreed to share losses equally on the principle that if less was being carried by canal, more must be going by railway.[16] When the Liverpool & Manchester, Bolton & Leigh and Kenyon & Leigh Junction amalgamated with the Grand Junction Railway in 1845, Hargreaves & Son ceased to carry on the railways and the lease came to an end.

In 1837 protective clauses were successfully included in a Bolton & Preston Railway Act concerning the sale of the Lancaster Canal's tramroad to the railway company, and this year the Leeds & Liverpool's dividend started climbing again. The figures from 1831 to the peak years of 1841–6 are:

Year	Toll revenue £	Dividends per cent
1831	116,336	20
1837	141,922	24
1840	156,875 (peak)	30
1843	128,877	34
1846	150,976	34

In 1843 the company rejected a combined proposal from the Manchester & Leeds and Liverpool & Manchester Railways that in return for a promise to relinquish through trade between Liverpool, Leeds and Bradford, they would not compete for traffic on other parts of the canal. Despite growing railway competition the Leeds & Liverpool were at the height of their power, as their dividend and their refusal to support the Liverpool & Manchester in opposing the projected Bolton, Wigan & Liverpool Railway indicate.

Opposition to the Liverpool & Bury Bill (which proposed to link up with the Manchester & Leeds at Heywood and so provide a second railway route from Liverpool to Leeds) was of no avail and the Act was passed on 31 July. Charles Vignoles, the engineer, was engaged to examine the plans of the railway where it proposed to cross the canal near its Liverpool terminus. A private agreement was then reached under which the canal company agreed to broad arches across the canal and yards, forming a viaduct, in return for £20,500 in compensation and for land, and £500 towards their parliamentary expenses.

The Lancaster Canal's agreement with the Bolton & Preston Railway of 1837 had contained safeguards for the Leeds & Liverpool's traffic on the South End of their canal, and tolls continued to be paid to the Lancaster company (see Chapter VIII). In 1845 the Lancaster offered to 'sell' the South End outright to the Lancaster & Carlisle Railway or the Leeds & Liverpool. Subsequently it was offered to the Leeds & Liverpool alone, including Johnson's Hillock locks and land at Anglezark, for £7,000 per annum for three years and £6,300 per annum in perpetuity afterwards. The agreement with the railway (now the North Union) was excluded. The Leeds & Liverpool declined.

Railway expansion spurred the company towards another attempt at connecting with Liverpool docks, and negotiations were reopened with the trustees in 1844. These agreed to buy land and construct a 2 furlongs cut with 4 locks falling 20 ft from the canal into what is now Collingwood dock. To the west side of Regent Road the new cut was vested in the Leeds & Liverpool, who contributed £50,000 towards the cost, and vessels entering the docks were charged 1½d per ton, excluding outwards traffic and flats returning inwards light or in ballast after unloading. The docks trustees retained the right to re-purchase and develop the land between Great Howard Street and Regent Road at its existing value—this subsequently became Stanley dock. Provisions were incorporated in the Liverpool Docks Act of 1844, and the branch was opened in 1846.

Improvements took place at the Leeds end too. Across the River Aire above the canal junction was a ford and weir giving access to the canal wharves from Neville Street, and as early as 1823 a suggestion was made that a lock should be constructed from the canal into the river above the weir in order to give access to new industrial premises extending upstream. It was repeated in 1837, and in July John Leather of George Leather & Son,

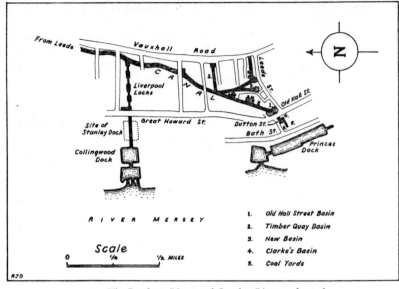

12. The Leeds & Liverpool Canal at Liverpool, 1846

Leeds engineers, reported in favour of the lock but the committee considered it would be prejudicial to their interests. Leather, together with John Atkinson, a Leeds solicitor, thereupon interested themselves in a proposed Leeds & Armley Navigation Company seeking to make the river navigable from Leeds Bridge up to Armley Mills, with a capital of £20,000. In April 1839 the new company proposed to connect the two sections of river above and below Queens Mills upper weir by a cut and a lock, with a wharf on the south side for the Leeds & Liverpool's free use. The road from the ford would cross the lock by a swing bridge, and the navigation be capable of taking craft up to 7 ft draught—the river under Leeds & Liverpool control could only take 5-ft craft. The promoters proposed to claim freedom from Leeds & Liverpool charges between Leeds bridge and the canal junction, but would, of course, levy their own tolls on a tonnage basis.

Robert Nicholson, the law clerk, and James Fletcher and Walmsley Stanley, joint engineers, reported that although there were practical difficulties the scheme would be unlikely to affect the canal company's income, as the 8 miles toll chargeable for the use of River lock at Leeds already encouraged the carriage of

most goods from the Aire & Calder to Armley by road, and
merely recommended the committee to demand free use of the
new lock.

The scheme evidently foundered, and it was the incorporation
of the Leeds & Bradford Railway in 1844 which finally precipi-
tated matters. In September it was

'Resolved that a Lock and Cut be made at Leeds to form a
connection with the River Aire and the Basin of the Canal upon
the Space reserved for the purpose by the Act for making a
Railway from Leeds to Bradford'.[17]

This Act gave the Leeds & Bradford powers to purchase Leeds &
Liverpool land at Leeds between the canal and the river above the
ford to construct their station, and the lock would increase its
value. After a wrangle, an arbitrator awarded £5,734 to the canal
company, and Arches lock, as it was later called from its situation
beneath the arches under the railway station, was opened in
September 1845.[18] The river upstream was used by craft for a
little over half a mile.

At the peak period, roughly 35 per cent of toll revenue came from
traffic on the Yorkshire side, 45 per cent from the Lancashire side,

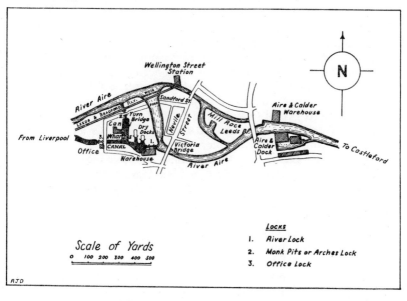

13. The Leeds & Liverpool Canal at Leeds, 1850

15 per cent from the Lower Douglas to Tarleton and 5 per cent from the Leigh branch, the last figure continuing to increase to 7 per cent in 1845 when, like the others, it began to drop, although a rapid fall-off did not occur until 1849–50. In Yorkshire, merchandise traffic provided the predominant income, and coal in Lancashire, as shown by this table:[19]

	Merchandise Tolls		Coal Tolls	
Year	Yorkshire	Lancashire	Yorkshire	Lancashire
	£	£	£	£
1824	20,321	23,865	4,937	32,938
1834	28,861	27,179	5,176	35,981
1845	31,205	26,921	10,199	64,414

The Ribble coal traders made another effort to reduce their tolls in 1822, alleging that Orrell, Pemberton and Standish coal could not be sold at less than 17s (85p) a ton at the wharves compared with King coal carried on the Lancaster Canal to Preston sold (delivered) at 14s 2d (71p). Moreover, coal for Ireland was going from west Cumberland via Preston at 7s 6d (37½p) a ton, they said, instead of from Wigan at 12s 9d (64p) for the poorest quality. Finally, the Lancaster Canal's proposed branch to Glasson Dock was felt likely to be a further impediment.

The canal company asked George Leather of Bradford to investigate, and in 1823 he reported that 41 vessels were regularly carrying coal to the Ribble, 30 for export and 11 for sale at Preston. Tonnages at Tarleton lock had been irregular since 1800, and since 1815 had dropped by 25 per cent, while coal prices generally had risen, Liverpool's, for example, from 11s 3d (56p) a ton in 1800 to 15s 6d (77½p) in 1817. Best Orrell coal carried by the Leeds & Liverpool was sold in Preston at 16s 8d (83½p) a ton; Best King coal carried over the Lancaster Canal sold at 15s (73p). Leather blamed the coal owners' varying pit-head prices for the decreasing trade which gave advantages to the coal owners on the Lancaster who were opening up new pits and now supplied nearly all Preston. Many of them acted as carriers and merchants too, whereas the Leeds & Liverpool trade involved coal owner, canal carrier and merchant—each making a profit—which, in Leather's opinion, was where the trouble lay. As he pointed out, coal by the Leeds & Liverpool incurred no transhipment and tramroad charges and ought to be cheaper than that by the Lancaster by at least 1s 8d (8½p) a ton.

He demolished the contention that coal traffic to Freckleton and Lytham was declining. These places were wholly supplied via the Leeds & Liverpool and trade was actually increasing rapidly, mainly for forward shipment to Ireland with return cargoes of corn and cattle, and to Ulverston. No Lancaster Canal coal was, in fact, exported, and only one Preston merchant was taking coal from west Cumberland. However, a customs duty of 4s (20p) a ton levied on sea-borne Cumberland coal landed outside the county (i.e., south of the Duddon) was likely to put a stop to this traffic—although, as an aside, he mentioned that some traders were landing coal on the north side of the Duddon sands in Cumberland and carting it across at low tide to the Lancashire shore. For the future, he admitted that there was cause for concern from the Lancaster's Glasson branch as the dock would form a better and safer anchorage than the Ribble, and he advocated a rival dock at Lytham. The canal company therefore compromised and reduced the canal dues from 2s (10p) to 1s 6d (7½p) per ton for coal sold at 6s (30p) (instead of 9s (45p)) at the pithead. Coal at higher prices would retain the old 2s toll.

The forecast effect of the Glasson branch was correct, for in 1826 the Ribble Navigation proprietors* complained that trade from the Leeds & Liverpool was dropping owing to the drawbacks being allowed by the Lancaster on coal shipped through Glasson dock, and again in 1828 the Preston merchants did the same. The Leeds & Liverpool agreed to approach the Lancaster, who in turn proposed reduced charges during the winter for coal vessels ascending Wigan locks, reflecting their concern at the loss of water on their South End. The Preston traders replied that this would react only on them, and not the Lancaster traders, going on to urge the Leeds & Liverpool either to reduce the Lower Douglas tolls or to make a new cut from Tarleton to the Ribble opposite Preston.

Accordingly, Fletcher and Stanley reported on two schemes for the Douglas: one, improvements to the river below Tarleton at an estimated cost of £27,740; two, a new canal extending the navigation from Tarleton, parallel with the river, to Hutton Grange Deeps, at £17,425. As, however, there would be only marginal benefit to the company, the committee decided to take no action.

Next the coal owners themselves tried to influence the canal company, using the newly-opened Liverpool & Manchester Rail-

* The first Ribble Navigation Company, incorporated 1806 (see also p. 202).

way as a lever, but as the railway did not seriously affect the canal for a number of years, this attempt also failed.

At this time the Leeds & Liverpool had by far the lion's share of the coal trade to Liverpool, as the figures for 1833 show:

		tons
Total consumption in Liverpool (domestic, steam shipping and export):		584,950
	tons	
Supplied by Leeds & Liverpool	270,753	
Supplied by Railway	56,858	
Road from Prescot, etc.	120,000	
Sankey Brook Navigation	123,928	
From Welsh pits	3,411	

Costs of conveyance were:

By Leeds & Liverpool Canal	5s 6½d (27½p) per ton of 22 cwt
By rail from Swarbrick	5s 6d (27½p) per ton of 20 cwt (commenced 1833)
By rail from Bolton	6s 5d (32p) per ton of 20 cwt

Ten years' peace ensued until 1840, when traders and coal owners once more pressed for reductions and improvements below Tarleton, arguing that their trade to Preston had been all but lost to the North Union Railway and the Lancaster Canal, while vessels from Preston bound for Ireland preferred to sail in ballast to west Cumberland and pick up coal cargoes there. Earl Balcarres was delivering his Haigh coal direct to Preston mills via the Lancaster at 9s (45p) per ton, including cartage, and Burgh collieries were selling even cheaper by using the railway; the best the Leeds & Liverpool collieries could do was to sell at 10s 10d (54p) per ton at Preston wharf. The Ribble Navigation Company contemplated dredging off Lytham to accommodate larger vessels, which would help to regain the Irish trade, and in conjunction with Preston corporation threatened to promote a rail branch from the North Union Railway to the quay if coal could not be loaded aboard vessels more cheaply at Lytham. The coal traders feared that coal traffic would be forced on to this line, or the Preston & Wyre Railway to Fleetwood, by lack of action on the part of the Leeds & Liverpool. Yet the figures showed that Leeds & Liverpool coal tonnages through Tarleton were still rising,[20] so it is not surprising that the petition was rejected.

The growth of coal traffic between 1821 and 1846 was matched by other goods, particularly at Liverpool. In 1823, about 40 vessels were on the Leeds–Liverpool through run, fly-boats taking 4 days for the trip.[21]

In 1840 the Leeds Union Company asked for reduced terms for through traffic, Leeds to Liverpool, because of rate-cutting by the Manchester & Leeds Railway. Although a reduction to match the railway's was refused, an allowance of 3s (15p) a ton was made on all goods shipped at Leeds for Liverpool, ostensibly to offset the cost of collection and cartage.

Regular passenger boat services had operated on the canal from the beginning, and now grew in popularity. In 1814 the company was operating services daily in each direction between Liverpool and Wigan, and in April that year a 'suburban' service was instituted, running twice a day in each direction from Old Roan (Aintree), with an extra market boat on Saturdays and an evening service on Sundays.[22] In 1821 a service from Manchester to Scarisbrick commenced, for the growing resort of Southport; a time-sheet of May 1827 advertized a daily summer service from Liverpool to Manchester serving Crosby, Southport (via Scarisbrick) and Wigan. The local service to Crosby by this time was quite intense, with seven daily sailings, and six on Saturdays and Sundays. Season ticket rates were quoted for periods up to 4 years, and 'family' tickets from 4 to 20 weeks during the summer season. The Manchester service, it was stressed, was 'without the risk of the Tideway, or the frequent accidents attendant on Steam Boats'.[23] In 1824 the daily summer swift packet left Liverpool for Manchester at 06.15, arriving at Manchester at 20.00 hrs, but in winter through passengers had to take two days on the journey, spending the night at Wigan. There were numerous private fly-boats operated by carriers, those of the Liverpool Union, Leeds & Liverpool Union and Leeds Union companies operating daily. Wigan, for example, in 1824 was served by an overnight fly-boat service to and from Liverpool, daily departures for Leigh, Chorley, Blackburn, Burnley and Yorkshire, and thrice weekly for Manchester. The Union companies served Blackburn and Burnley daily, and in addition the Leeds & Liverpool ran a packet service between the two towns on Wednesdays and Saturdays. Chorley had a fly-boat service to Blackburn and to Manchester six days a week from Knowley wharf.[24] But in 1833 a report to the general assembly on the Lancaster's swift packet boat *Waterwitch* was unable to recommend the design for the company's Liverpool–Manchester service. Its only claim was speed, there being no comfort or economy to recommend it. The operation of boats on Sundays did not pass without protest, and in 1847 the committee ordered that passengers were not to be landed from the packets at Blackburn on Sundays.

In 1842 Thomas Batho of the Manchester Police was appointed Superintendent of Police on the canal at £150 p.a. and travelling expenses, with command of a company of constables, in an effort to prevent robberies, pilferage and disorderly behaviour along its line.

The autumn of 1824 brought trouble in Foulridge tunnel. On 11 October *The Leeds Mercury* reported:

'A singular occurrence has, during the last week, taken place at Foulridge, near Colne: the tunnel of the Leeds and Liverpool canal, which there passes under a high hill, has so far been contracted in depth, by the rising of the bottom (which has been forced up by some cause not yet ascertained), as to prevent all vessels passing which draw more than three feet four inches of water. Several stones have also fallen from the top of the arch: some apprehensions have of course been entertained for the safety of this stupendous work, which cost immense sums of money; but the persons most likely to form a correct judgement on the subject do not anticipate any further mischief. Preparations are making for the immediate and effectual repair of it, and the water will be drawn off in the course of next week. We are informed that the repair will occasion no material interruption to the trade by the canal, as arrangements will be made for carting the goods over the tunnel.'

The collapse was near the west end, and a temporary road was made across the top. Substantial restoration work was necessary for a long time. For his work in supervizing, Fletcher was granted an increase in salary and a present of 100 gns 'in consideration of his extraordinary exertions in repairing the Tunnel'.[25] In 1840 he unsuccessfully suggested the tunnel should be opened out to ease congestion, at an estimated cost of £23,000. Then in March 1843 there was a further collapse and the tunnel was again closed for two months. But still the heavy capital cost deterred the committee and the tunnel remained. Railway competition was looming despite the canal's prosperity, and all resources were directed towards maintaining high dividends and liquidating the debt of £53,983, which was finally discharged in 1847.

Improvements did, of course, take place during this period of greatest prosperity, although the Liverpool plans generally were frustrated. Additional warehouse space was provided at Wigan and Leigh in 1835, a covered basin for Leeds was approved in 1841, and Barrowford warehouse in 1846, but anything large was generally frowned on. In 1844 a provisional committee was formed to promote a branch canal to Ormskirk, but the company declared that they 'do not entertain any idea . . . of a junction canal',[26] which in view of the successful promotion of the Liverpool, Ormskirk & Preston Railway in 1846 was probably wise.

The company's quarrying operations progressively extended, not only at Skipton (see Springs Branch Canal), but at the Rain Hall Rock at Barnoldswick where more land was leased in 1828. The quarry took the form of a deep, narrow rock cutting with a short tunnel, the bottom forming the canal so that stone could be loaded direct into boats from the working faces. As quarrying extended, a second short tunnel became necessary beneath a road, and later still, probably in 1862, a lofty, three-arched stone viaduct to carry an occupation road, forming a remarkable sight in such an unusual location.

The problem of keeping full the summit level and, to a lesser degree, the two long pounds from Barrowford to Johnson's Hillock, continued to cause anxiety in dry summers. In 1824 and 1826 the summit was closed for lack of water, the *Leeds Patriot* reporting in November 1826:

'The part of the Leeds and the Liverpool canal between Kilnwick (sic), near Skipton, and the vicinity of Burnley, in Lancashire, has not been navigable for several months, and all goods are obliged to be carried over-land at great expense to parties and loss to the company'.[27]

In 1832 Foulridge Lower reservoir was deepened by 3ft, and in 1840 Whitemoor reservoir was completed. The same year it was resolved to construct a fourth summit reservoir nearby at Slipper Hill. The Burnley pound was fed from a new reservoir at Rishton, near Blackburn, opened about 1830, which was deepened by raising the banks in 1836. Further conservation measures included, rather unfairly, the reduction of lock-keepers' and bank-rangers' wages to half-pay in times of low water to 'stimulate a sufficient vigilance and care of the water'.[28]

James Fletcher, the engineer, died in 1844 and was succeeded by Walmsley Stanley who since 1827 had been resident engineer at Liverpool following the brief reign of Abinus Martin. Thomas Fletcher, who had been resident engineer on the Yorkshire side from 1844, became his assistant.

It was during this period that the number of tramroads feeding the canal reached its maximum. Except for the one at Skipton they were all on the Lancashire side, three in the Burnley area at Marsden, Habergham, and Altham, seven between Kirklees and Wigan wharf, and no less than 13 between there and Appley locks. Hustler's Tramroad from Billinge to Gathurst dated from 1788 and seems to have been connected with a colliery enterprise of Huslter's. Most of them closed during 1840–60, or were converted into standard-gauge railways. Two tramroads ran down to the Leigh branch.[29] The Ince Hall Coal & Cannel Company had several basins between locks 17 and 19 at Wigan, with connecting tramroads, and a branch canal over $\frac{1}{2}$-mile long to Ince Hall colliery.[30] A curious canal branch which tunnelled 1,100 yd into the hillside at Crooke, below Wigan, was constructed at the end of the eighteenth century in the fashion of the Duke of Bridgewater's at Worsley. Coal was discharged from baskets at an underground wharf into 7-ft boats which were legged out.[31] It was still busy in 1835[32] and existed until recent times.[33] (*To continue the history of the Leeds & Liverpool Canal, turn to Chapter XVI.*)

The Springs Branch or Lord Thanet's Canal

In 1792 the Leeds & Liverpool again approached Lord Thanet, this time for leave to take the proposed Haw Bank tramroad through the castle yard. Apparently it was refused, for instead in 1794 an extension of Lord Thanet's Canal was authorized by the committee, with a tramroad to Haw Bank from the new terminus. Work commenced that summer and was completed in 1797 by the company after the task of cutting through the rock at the back of the castle had overcome the two contractors. The tramroad ended at lofty staithes close on 100 ft above the head of the canal, with a short tunnel close to the castle wall. At first it had wooden rails, which after 1808 were replaced by iron.

The company adopted the practice of subletting the quarry to contractors, with the prices of limestone and preferential tonnage rates already laid down, except when trade slumped. Then they would extract the stone themselves rather than let the traffic decline. They retained responsibility for maintaining the tramroad but let the contractors work it. In 1833, when the company's lease expired, Lord Thanet offered reduced terms if they would extend the tramroad to the Leeds & Liverpool main line and so avoid the branch canal—he doubtless objected to the clangour at the staithes behind his castle—but the company refused and a new 21 years' lease was negotiated on the old conditions. (*To continue the history of the Springs Branch, turn to p. 411.*)

Bradford Canal

The opening of the Bradford Canal gave great impetus to stone quarrying in the district, and a heavy traffic in limestone from Skipton to kilns alongside the canal quickly grew up. Coal pits on the south side of the town expanded rapidly and ironworks at Bowling and Low Moor built a network of tramroads. Two lines ran down to Bradford but were unable to reach the canal basin owing to the close-packed town intervening, the nearer being ¼ mile away.[34] But they enabled easier transport of cast-iron from the works for shipment by canal. A chemical works was also established on the canal bank. From the 1820s, Australian wool formed an important traffic. In 1828–9, packets sailed daily to Leeds and Selby in connection with sailings to Hull and London, and by 1845 to Goole for Hull, London and Newcastle, 'also with boats from Leicester'. The twice weekly service to Liverpool of 1828 by this time had become daily.[35] (*To continue the history of the Bradford Canal, turn to p. 412.*)

CHAPTER VIII

The Lancaster Canal

THE promotion of the Lancaster Canal largely came from the city of Lancaster itself. Ever since Robert Lawson began in 1680 to develop Sunderland Point as a port on the north side of the Lune estuary, Lancaster merchants had been preoccupied with improving communications. Despite its location in the tidal Lune, constantly shifting sands made Lancaster a tricky port to enter. An Act of 1749 appointed Port Commissioners to improve the estuary and construct St George's Quay below the town, which superseded Sunderland Point, followed by the completion of Glasson Dock some five miles to the seaward of Lancaster in 1787, where a fully-equipped wet dock was capable of holding 25 large merchantmen. But still the sandbanks of the outer estuary had to be negotiated, and in 1799 it was decided at a public meeting that improvement of the river and port could only be fully served by 'a Wet Dock at Thornbush* and a navigable Canal for large ships from thence to Lancaster, there to form a commodious Basin, with Graving Docks and other conveniences'. A committee was appointed, but the West India trade, on which the port primarily relied, declined rapidly and the scheme was abandoned.[1]

Coal for Lancaster and its hinterland came by sea from the Douglas, which also supplied Kendal and the surrounding country through Milnthorpe, a small port on the River Beela close to the Kent estuary. The high price of coal and difficulty of land carriage as an alternative led to parallel ideas of a canal from Kendal through Lancaster and Preston to join the newly-successful Leeds & Liverpool Canal near Walton-le-Dale, south of the Ribble. The canal mania was beginning and there was the additional prospect of a return traffic of limestone from north Lancashire and Westmorland to be burnt into lime for agricultural use in the arable country to the south. A scheme was put forward in

* About a mile further out from Glasson.

the late 1760s, which it was urged should be continued beyond
Walton to join the Bridgewater at Worsley.[2] Matters progressed
further when at a meeting at Lancaster Town Hall on 13 November 1771 it was decided to make a survey.[3] Brindley was
approached,[4] but Robert Whitworth carried it out, and in 1772
he put forward a plan for a canal from the Leeds & Liverpool
near Eccleston to Kendal, crossing the Ribble below Penwortham
Bridge and thence out into the Fylde almost to Kirkham before
swinging back eastward to near Barton, where a northerly course
was resumed. The Lune was to be crossed just below Skerton
Bridge at Lancaster and the long level of 54½ miles terminated
with a rise of 86 ft at Tewitfield, north of Carnforth, the remaining
18 miles to Kendal being again level. The committee asked Whitworth to try to find an easier crossing of the Lune, and he replied
with a higher line locking up 24 ft from the Ribble, a shorter loop
westward but a second loop up the Lune to Halton Scars where a
shorter aqueduct was possible, and a second rise of 62 ft at
Tewitfield.[5] This line was only about ½ mile longer. During the
next few years other opinions were sought upon easier ways to
cross the Ribble and the Lune, and upon shorter routes, but none
were better.[6] Meanwhile, in 1781 a survey was made for a canal
from Ingleton and Burton-in-Lonsdale to the Lune at Lancaster,
possibly a sequel to the abortive scheme of 1773 for a branch to
the Leeds & Liverpool from Settle (see p. 74). It came to nothing.[7]

Six years later a quite different scheme emerged, when John
Wilkinson, the ironmaster, of Castle Head near Lindale on the
west side of the Kent estuary, promoted a scheme that seems to
have originated with John Jenkinson of Yealand. This was to
enclose and drain 38,710 acres of sands and mosses on the north
and east fringes of Morecambe Bay at a cost of £150,000, towards
which the enthusiastic Wilkinson offered £50,000.[8] John Longbotham had been engaged to survey, primarily, it seems, for a
coastal canal until Wilkinson had pointed out the prospects for
land reclamation. Longbotham then proposed to enclose the
sands and build an artificial channel from the River Winster where
it entered the Kent estuary near Castle Head across Foulshaw
Moss to Nether Levens, where it would join the Kent which in
turn would be diverted along the coast to Arnside, there cut
across the isthmus to the coast again below Warton Crag, and
then follow the coastline once more to enter the sea at Heysham
Head where there was deep water. By this means large areas of

sands would be drained, and Longbotham suggested that the channel could be navigable from the Kent to Bare, where a short canal could be cut across the intervening neck of land to lock down into the Lune almost opposite Lancaster. Writing to Lord George Cavendish of Holker Hall in 1787, John Jenkinson declared:

'The whole will then make a Noble Water for the use of Navigation from Lancaster to two Miles above Milnthrop* . . . The space for the river he (Longbotham) lays down at 60 yards wide the land side or East side to be the Canal part or part for Navigation.

My Lord beside the great Scheme for recovering the Sands it will lay a foundation for extending the Navigation up to Kendal by a Canal to bring down the Westmorland Slate, and also of carrying another to the Southward from Lancaster to the Coal, which with Limestone at Warton, Silverdale and Arnside and the slate from the North will very probably make it one of the most useful Navigations in the Kingdom'.[9]

As soon as £15,000 had been raised it was intended to start work; presumably there was insufficient support, for nothing came of the idea.[10]

By 1791 patience was running short.

'With Respect to Kendal, Lancaster, and perhaps Preston, it is now no longer a Question of Choice, but Necessity:—either they must put themselves on a Footing with their Southern Neighbours, or submit to a Decline of their Trade and Population, and a Decrease in the Value of their Land, as a natural and inevitable Consequence: In short, a Canal is now become as necessary an Appendage to a Manufacturing or Commercial Town as a Turnpike Road'.[11]

On 8 June a meeting in Lancaster town hall convened by the mayor at the request of 29 prominent townsmen resolved to promote a canal, and a subscription list was opened. The next day Samuel Gregson, of Lancaster, was appointed clerk, and Robert Dickinson of Gargrave, Richard Beck and Longbotham during the next few months were asked to resurvey Whitworth's line and extend it southward to Worsley. They were unable to find a better alternative, and in October John Rennie was asked to try. The committee was undecided whether to make for the Manchester, Bolton & Bury Canal at Bolton or the Duke's canal. Rennie, working fast during December and January, produced a

* i.e. Milnthorpe; one of many variations.

plan which was accepted.[12] He recommended a broad canal commencing at Westhoughton, conveniently situated in the coalfield
midway between Wigan and Bolton, and striking north for $15\frac{1}{2}$
level miles to Clayton Green where the Ribble crossing would be
commenced by descending 222 ft through 32 locks to an embankment across the valley and an aqueduct over the river to Preston.
Beyond, he followed Whitworth's upper line as far as Tewitfield,
but with a short-cut at Ashton south of Lancaster and a Lune
crossing further downstream, $42\frac{1}{2}$ miles on the level. Beyond, he
proposed a more direct line to Hincaster, rising 65 ft by 5 locks at
Tewitfield and 4 near Milton, where he rejoined Whitworth's line
to tunnel through Hincaster hill in order to serve Wakefield's
gunpowder mills at Sedgwick.[13] Another five miles took it to
Kendal, a total length of $75\frac{1}{2}$ miles. Rennie added branches from
near Chorley to Duxbury (3 miles), and Tewitfield to Warton
Crag ($2\frac{1}{2}$ miles) neither of which was built.

Speed in obtaining an Act was now essential, for the Leeds &
Liverpool were proposing to alter their line to a new course
roughly parallel to Rennie's route between Whittle-le-Woods and
Wigan. The negotiations between the Lancaster committee, the
Leeds & Liverpool and the Manchester, Bolton & Bury, and the
opposition to the Lancaster's Bill, have been described in Chapter
VII. They failed, and the Lancaster obtained their Act in June
1792,[14] authorizing Rennie's line, the Duxbury and Warton Crag
branches, and junctions with possible future canals from Hornby
and Ingleton, Kirkby Lonsdale and the Fylde. Water could be
taken from the River Mint at Kendal but was severely restricted
elsewhere. From the authorized capital of £414,100 in £100
shares, £60,000 was to be set aside for the Westmorland portion.
An additional £200,000 could be raised by mortgage or additional
shares if needed. Duty on coal was fixed at a maximum of 2s 3d
(11p) per ton passing down the locks to the Ribble and not proceeding more than 18 miles north of Chorley, and $1\frac{1}{2}$d per ton/
mile elsewhere. The petitioners included the Earl of Balcarres, a
prominent coalowner, John Brockbank shipbuilder of Lancaster,
John Dilworth (the first chairman) and Thomas Worswick,
Lancaster bankers (the latter was treasurer), John Wakefield and
Thomas Crewdson of Kendal, and other prominent Lancaster
and Kendal people. Also mentioned were two of the powerful
Hesketh family—Robert and Bold Fleetwood—and Edmund
Rigby of Liverpool.

A committee was formed of Lancaster men, with one each from

M

Preston and Kendal, and in July Rennie was appointed engineer at £600 p.a. in return for five months residence per year at Lancaster and attendance at other times as requested. William Crosley of Brighouse was appointed assistant surveyor, and in 1793 Archibald Millar of Dublin joined him as resident engineer & superintendent. Although the battle with the Leeds & Liverpool and the Manchester, Bolton & Bury and over the former's deviation south of the Ribble occupied much of the committee's attention for the first two years, they lost no time in pressing on with construction. At the end of 1792 John Pinkerton, a well-known canal contractor, and John Murray of Colne were awarded the first contract, between Tewitfield and Ellel, followed in 1793 by Ellel to Ray Lane, near Catterall, in all some 27 miles; much too long a length, as experience was to show. Speed was essential also in starting work south of Preston in order to outflank the Leeds & Liverpool, and the Bark Hill (above Wigan) to Nightingales (near Chorley) length was let to Paul Vickers of Thorne in July.

At the first annual shareholders' meeting in January 1793 it was decided that communication with the sea was desirable. Rennie's proposed Glasson branch was approved, and a second Act to authorize it was secured in May.[15] This also imposed further restrictions on taking water from the Rivers Lune and Wyre, and from mines adjacent to the Leeds & Liverpool's parliamentary line near Heapey. Elsewhere mines within 2,000 yd of the canal were to supply it free if required, provided it did not need pumping from the pithead. Successful negotiations were concluded with the Duke of Bridgewater for extending from Westhoughton to his canal at Worsley, which Rennie estimated would cost £63,544. A Bill to authorize the connection was promoted in 1794 but lost, mainly through the opposition of Miss Henrietta Atherton of Atherton Hall. It was not revived as the Duke had decided to build his Leigh branch, which the Lancaster felt might be more advantageous for a junction. Meanwhile agreement had finally been reached with the Leeds & Liverpool (see Chapter VII).

In 1795 recurrent troubles with Pinkerton & Murray came to a head. Millar had constantly complained of bad workmanship and inattention to his instructions, and Robert Whitworth was called in to arbitrate. The company took over the disputed works in September and re-let them in single lots under Millar's supervision, but a year's delay had been caused.[16] Henry Eastburn was appointed resident engineer south of the Ribble in 1794, assisted by Thomas Fletcher, and by July 1796 enough work had been done to allow a little coal traffic to commence earning revenue, which by this time was badly needed. The pressure of the French Wars restricted the flow of capital and share calls were being ignored by some shareholders. An appeal was made for further subscriptions in advance, without much success, and the company was heavily indebted to the treasurer's bank. A second appeal in 1797 was more fruitful, but money had to be spent in obtaining a third Act in May 1796[17] to authorize the purchase of Duchy of Lancaster lands for a small deviation at Myerscough near Garstang.

To add to the committee's troubles, the Westmorland proprietors were becoming restive, mainly because of an ill-judged proposal to appropriate the statutory £60,000 reserve in order to finance current work.

The Preston–Tewitfield section was by this time all but complete except for the Lune aqueduct. Rennie's design incorporated a structure 600 ft long and 60 ft high, with five 70-ft semi-circular arches topped by a massive cornice and a partly balustraded parapet. He seems to have favoured brick construction but the committee preferred stone. Commenting on masonry tenders, he compared the aqueduct with brick structures on Midland canals, writing to Gregson '. . . I still wish the Committee had tried brick it would have saved many thousand pounds'.[18] Alexander Stevens & Son of Edinburgh were appointed contractors for the superstructure, the company undertaking to build the foundations for the piers themselves. Millar started pile-driving in January 1794 within 20 ft coffer dams sunk in the river bed, which were kept dry by steam pumps. William Cartwright was appointed assistant resident engineer that month, with special responsibility for the foundations, and in July 150 men were at work, day and night. Troubles were encountered from sudden rises in the river level flooding the coffer dams, recalcitrant workmen, drunken engine attendants, and bad weather, but, remarkably, the piers were completed by July 1795 after only 18 months' work. The committee patted themselves on the back—'Altho the Cost has been considerable the Committee trust that succeeding ages will give credit and have reason to boast of the permanency of that Work'[19] —and presented Cartwright with a silver cup 'as a reward for his extra care and attention in superintending the Foundations of the Lune Aqueduct'.[20]

The Stevens' proceeded with the upperworks with all speed, although Rennie's advice was not entirely followed, as for instance when Alexander Stevens considered his modifications to give added strength unnecessary, and was backed by the committee.[21] Stevens was evidently a man of strong principle, yet of friendly disposition; when he died during the work, on 29 January 1796, both Rennie and Millar were prompted to write movingly of his loss. The aqueduct was completed by his son in the autumn at a cost of £48,321,[22] and on 22 November 1797 a cavalcade of six boats formally opened the canal from Tewitfield to Spital Moss, just out of Preston. The actual voyage was from Lancaster to the aqueduct and back, followed by a procession to the King's Arms for dinner. The total cost so far was £269,406.[23] Other notable aqueducts crossed the Rivers Keer and Wyre by single spans, the latter of 34 ft, and ingenious means were found to cross streams which were almost level with the canal. The River Brock was dug out below the canal and a weir built above it to drop the water down under the aqueduct; the River Calder and a stream near Ashton Hall (where there was also a deep cutting) were carried beneath the canal by syphons.

By February 1798 the South End, as it came to be officially called, was open from Bark Hill to Knowley wharf, near Chorley, and £382,565 had been spent. In July 1799 Cartwright, who was now resident engineer for the whole canal, Millar's and Eastburn's contracts not having been renewed, reported that it was open to Johnson's Hillock (12 miles) and almost ready to Clayton Green except for Whittle Hills tunnel. Considering the financial difficulties of the last few years, this was good going, for response from the proprietors had been poor and in July 1798, for instance, the committee had had only £6,500 in hand. But traffic was growing, and two packet boats were started by the company in October on the North End between Preston and Lancaster, so that in the second half of 1799 the committee was able to report a total revenue of £2,022. Limekilns were being built, including some at Preston by Gregson and three other committeemen trading as Samuel Gregson & Co, and the company opened up quarries to encourage traffic. From this time until the railway era of the 1840s canalside industry grew. New pits were opened between Bark Hill and Chorley, limekilns appeared at numerous places at both ends, and cinder ovens were erected in the Tewitfield area to provide a fluxing agent for the charcoal iron smelting in Lonsdale and probably Furness. Coal came not only from the south but from small local pits in the Farleton district.[24] Later, coke ovens were established near Carnforth.[25]

The overwhelming problem at this period was to decide how best to cross the Ribble and connect the canal's two sections. Already coal from collieries opened close to the South End near Wigan was being carted down to the Douglas and so taken that way to Preston; there it had to be laboriously carted again up to the North End, mainly because the roads at Johnson's Hillock were so bad. In 1796 and 1797, various proposals were considered for a short branch canal from Salwick on the North End to Savock followed by an inclined plane down to the Ribble, or alternatively a tramroad from the canal at Tulketh, the idea being to exchange traffic with the Douglas. The Leeds & Liverpool agreed to improve the Douglas, but the Lancaster was unable to finance their work (see Chapter VII). Then in 1799 the committee asked Cartwright's opinion, and he advised building a tramroad from the South End at Clayton Green, to take the traffic 5 miles to Preston, to where the North End would require a short extension from Spital Moss.[26] To finance it, an Act was obtained in 1800 to raise £200,000 additional capital in £30 shares.[27]

A Mr Monk now stepped in with a fresh proposal to join the Leeds & Liverpool, in which he suggested that the Douglas Navigation should be extended along the south side of the Ribble to Penwortham, there to lock down into the river. From a basin in the opposite bank, an inclined plane could be built up to the Lancaster. A connection between the Lancaster and the Leeds & Liverpool would be necessary from Haigh to Wigan by locks. Monk estimated that the extra time required to take coal from Chorley to Preston by this circuitous route, compared with Cartwright's tramroad, would be only four hours, to compensate for which he advocated a 6d (2½p) per ton reduction in the Leeds & Liverpool's tolls.

It seems likely that 'Mr Monk' was James Monk, a Leeds & Liverpool committeeman. A number of Lancaster proprietors owned collieries between Chorley and Wigan; one of them, Alexander Haliburton of Haigh, writing to George Clayton, derided the scheme as a bait to the Lancaster's coal owners, estimating that by it the company would lose £54,100 in the first instance and £10,750 a year thereafter. In his opinion Cartwright's plan was much to be preferred. 'Was this part of the canal cut up to Clayton Green', he concluded, 'the north end would be from thence supplied with a much greater proportion of the trade than has been calculated upon; and should it never go further, the views of the company would be more amply fulfilled than by falling in with the *insidious* proposals of their Leeds & Liverpool Rivals'.[28]

So much talk of tramroads so alarmed some of the proprietors that the committee asked Rennie and William Jessop[29] to pass an opinion on the two schemes, and also to advise on the best site and mode of taking the canal directly across the Ribble, whether partly on an embankment and partly over a stone or iron aqueduct or wholly on an aqueduct. In May 1801, the two engineers reported that an 'Embankment to the full height of the Lancaster Level (about 40 ft) and a Stone Aqueduct will be most advisable', together with locks up to Clayton Green. The work could be done in five years, they thought, or three if the company was prepared to go to 'extraordinary expense'.[30] A design for an aqueduct was attached to their report, 640 ft long with three 116-ft elliptical arches, 57 ft high from low water mark to towing path. Cartwright also submitted a design, slightly shorter but with three 120-ft spans, incorporating Corinthian pilasters. A third drawing was made by Thomas Gibson for a continuous aqueduct on pointed arches, three spanning the river, with cross arches between the main spans and an immense pediment.[31]

Rennie and Jessop went on to approve Cartwright's tramroad estimated at £21,600, as an immediate but temporary means of crossing the valley, and condemned the Douglas scheme not on practical grounds but because of the great advantage it would give to the Leeds & Liverpool.[32] The tramroad was immediately authorized, Jessop being retained to survey the line at the Preston end. For this and his work on the report he was paid £70, and Rennie's account was credited with £112 5s 4d (£112·26½). Work commenced without delay, together with a 259-yd long tunnel at Whittle Hills which was necessary to complete the canal to Clayton Green and on a further mile to Walton Summit where the tramroad began. The tunnel was far more difficult to cut than Cartwright anticipated, taking two years instead of one, and it was not until 1 June 1803 that the first boat passed through and transhipped its cargo of coal into the tramroad waggons at the Summit. The tramroad was finished as far as Bamber Bridge only, and was not completed to Preston (where the canal had been brought in to a basin north of Fishergate) until the end of 1803. It was double track, with three inclined planes worked by stationary engines and endless chains, one rising directly from the end of the wooden trestle bridge over the Ribble.[33]

Cartwright only just lived to see it completed for he died, probably of overwork, on 19 January 1804.[34] He had been a zealous and ingenious engineer. His other works included a scheme for taking water from the River Keer at Capernwray which incorporated a series of reservoirs upstream on Dalton Moor, feeders to the canal, and the use of the wheel at Capernwray Mill to pump the water into it[35]. The reservoir and pump were not built due to opposition from riparian owners, but a feeder from the river was cut, compensation water from the mill being let out through a pipe in the canal bank directly on to the overshot wheel.* Cartwright also designed and supervized the cutting of a tunnel from the canal at Preston down through the rock into the Ribble, through which water was pumped by a Boulton & Watt steam engine. Pumping commenced in July 1806, after the work had been completed by William Miller of Preston, who had been an assistant engineer for some years after 1794. One of Cartwright's last designs was for a tramroad from Tewitfield to quarries at Kellet Seeds, about 2,200 yd long, which was never built.[36]

The effect of the tramroad on revenue was immediate. Gross income for 1803 was £4,853; after it had opened, the income for 1804 was £8,490, and in the first six months of 1805 had risen to £5,241. A first dividend of ½ per cent was paid in 1803, then there was a gap until 1805 when 1 per cent was declared. This rate continued unchanged until 1825. Revenue from tolls between 1803 and 1811 was:

	North End	South End and Tramroad	Total
	£	£	£
1803	3,062	1,270	4,332
1807	6,053	6,409	12,467
1811	8,243	7,307	15,550

As the distance on the South End and the tramroad was only 19 miles compared with 57 miles on the North End, obviously the greater part of the traffic was being discharged at Preston, which now began to assume greater importance in the canal's affairs than Lancaster. But Lancaster men still controlled matters, as is shown by the continued deferment of completion of the line to Kendal despite frequent and justified protests by the Westmorland proprietors. In 1805 Miller made surveys for a continuation of the canal by two routes, one through Hincaster with a 340-yd tunnel and the other, shorter, but with a 670-yd tunnel at Rains

* It still (1969) exists, though ruinous.

Hall. Alternatively, he suggested a 13-mile tramroad from Tewit-field with three inclined planes. The cheaper canal estimate was £71,755 and that for the tramroad £38,575. The committee decided to adopt the Hincaster line, in deference to the Wake-fields' gunpowder interests at Sedgwick, and an Act was obtained in 1807[37] empowering the company to vary Rennie's original line between Tewitfield and Hincaster, and to construct tramroads to Farleton Knott, Kellet Seeds and within the line of the canal—so giving retrospective authorization of the Preston tramroad. The Act also permitted the abstraction of surplus water from Farleton, Stainton and Crooklands (Peasey) becks to feed the Kendal level, and repealed the River Mint provisions of the original Act.

In 1810 the committee agreed terms with the Leeds & Liverpool for their use of the South End, involving construction by the Lancaster of seven locks rising 64 ft from Johnson's Hillock, and ½ mile of canal towards Wigan from Bark Hill already under construction. They also bought 86 acres of land on Killington Common, under the fells between Kendal and Sedbergh, for a reservoir for the Kendal level, but this left no money for the canal extension itself, which was temporarily forgotten when a serious dispute arose in 1811 in which twelve Liverpool shareholders alleged favouritism in the placing of a number of contracts. In particular, several committeemen and Gregson were accused of receiving favoured treatment in connection with their private trading activities on the canal and with their colliery interests. A committee of investigation was appointed which concluded that the accusations were unfounded. Their report ended by praising Gregson and several committee members for setting up as canal carriers in 1797, in order to promote trade which had proved beneficial to the company, and pointed out that Gregson for many years had gratuitously carried out numerous duties far beyond his office of clerk.

> 'To his enterprize on the opening of the Canal, and to his subsequent indefatigable exertions, united with those of the Committee, may be attributed the progressive increase of the Tonnage Duties'.[38]

The committee also came in for praise for raising money on their own securities when no further calls on shareholders could be made.

In 1812 Thomas Fletcher was appointed engineer and instructed to prepare detailed estimates for the Kendal extension. His figure was £98,095, in return for which he anticipated an annual revenue of £7,589. Finally, a resolution to begin work was approved in 1813. At the same time Fletcher was asked to advise on a scheme put up by a Preston proprietor called Shuttleworth, and several others, for crossing the Ribble on the level, which he dismissed as impracticable, followed by another for a lower level aqueduct which would involve more lockage, and on both sides. This, Fletcher agreed, could be done, but it would endanger water supplies and there was obviously no money available for an expenditure of £160,537, which was his estimate. Shuttleworth demanded a special general meeting in 1817 and advocated applying for a loan from the Exchequer Bill Loan Commissioners, but was defeated.

Work started on Tewitfield locks and Hincaster tunnel, and in May 1817 William Crosley was appointed to complete the work north of the locks, including Killington reservoir, independently of Fletcher. The tunnel was completed on Christmas Day, 1817. It had been lined with brick above water-level, not without misgivings by the committee on the use of a new and, to them, inferior material to stone. Two more years passed before the locks were complete, by which time Killington reservoir was full. On 18 June 1819 a grand opening ceremony was held with the usual flotilla of boats, procession through Kendal, and dinner and ball at the Town Hall. The extension was some 14½ miles long, rising 76 ft by eight locks at Tewitfield. Hincaster tunnel was 378 yd long, and there were aqueducts over three roads and three sizeable streams in addition to smaller works. Killington reservoir covers 153 acres, having had its embankment raised several times.

The effect of the canal on Kendal was immediate. Whilst the extension was in progress in 1818 the corporation undertook to construct a basin, wharves and warehouses at the head of the canal, and a new bridge across the river Kent to give better access. In return, the canal company agreed to take the canal a few yards further at the Aynam, but not to extend beyond without corporation consent.[99] The work was completed in time for the opening, the basin being set back at an acute angle from the end of the canal. It cost the corporation £7,004, including the bridge, (later called Miller bridge), and the income from the warehouses and wharves was about £550 per annum.[40] Development in the areas between the canal and the river, and between the river and the old town, followed rapidly. 'In a very short time, the town assumed a new and modern appearance—so very different that any

TO BE LET,

FOR A TERM OF YEARS,

At the CANAL OFFICE, in Lancaster,

On Friday the 29th December next,

At ELEVEN o'Clock in the Forenoon:

Two Wharfs,

Adjoining the *Canal* at

CROOKLANDS,

In one of which, the Canal Company will erect OVENS, for the burning of Cinders, if required by the Taker. *Crooklands* Wharf is the most convenient, and the best communication from the Canal to MILNTHROP, and only Six miles from KIRKBY-LONS-DALE, and is well situated for the sale of Coal and Cinders, to a large neighbourhood requiring a considerable consumption of both articles.

For any information inquire at the Canal Office, in Lancaster, or of Mr. CROSLEY, Engineer to the Canal Company.

Canal Office, Lancaster, 5th December, 1820.

G. CLARK, PRINTER, MARKET-PLACE, LANCASTER.

14. A Lancaster Canal handbill advertizing wharfs to let, 1820

person having been absent a few years, could scarcely have identified it'.[41]

The Lancaster proprietors now wanted to make the Glasson Dock branch which had been authorized in the 1792 Act, in an endeavour to improve the fortunes of the Port of Lancaster, and a Bill was drafted seeking powers to raise more capital. There was immediate opposition from Preston, where a canal crossing of the Ribble was considered the more important, in order to eliminate the cost of carrying coal over the tramroad. The company, they said, had wasted money in 'ornamenting the town of Lancaster, with a grand aqueduct over the Lune, upon which the water had laid stagnant for over 20 years', and now proposed a branch to Glasson Dock in the hope of reviving 'the decayed port of Lancaster'.[42] However, Lancaster again got its way and an Act was passed in 1819[43] authorizing (again retrospectively) the construction of Killington reservoir and the connection with the Leeds & Liverpool at Johnson's Hillock to which the 2s 3d (11p) toll under the 1792 Act was to apply, together with powers to raise £270,000 on mortgage of the tolls, in order to finance the work on the branch and repay debts.

Crosley, who had been appointed superintendent of the entire canal in 1820, estimated the cost of the Glasson branch at £34,608, and a decision to commence work was made in 1823. Lancaster Port Commissioners agreed to reduce their dues from as much as 1s 3d (6p) to 4d per ton when the branch was made, by which means it was hoped to divert trade from Preston and to export coal from Glasson. In return the company paid the Port Commissioners £500 and guaranteed an income of £200 p.a. from ships from Ireland, the Isle of Man, and beyond Holyhead and Galloway. But the decision to start was not made before consideration had been given to a connection with the sea at Hest Bank, a village between Lancaster and Carnforth, where the canal was within ¼ mile of the foreshore; Crosley estimated the cost at £69,591 including a dock. Doubtless the Hest Bank Shipping Co. was behind this scheme. Since the opening to Kendal they had transhipped regularly from coastal vessels at Hest Bank, where a stone pier was built in 1820,[44] for forwarding by canal to Kendal and thence by road carriers to as far afield as Hawes, Kirkby Stephen and Penrith. In 1820 four vessels sailed from Liverpool every four or five days,[45] and perhaps to placate the shippers the company, at the same time as the Glasson decision was made, resolved to allow a drawback of 1s 8d (8½p) a ton on all merchandise transhipped at Hest Bank for Kendal. Crosley reported the branch, which fell 52 ft by 6 locks in 2½ miles from Galgate, to be ready in December 1825, but shortage of money for constructing wharves and warehouses led to a slow initial growth in trade. Still, the company managed to raise the dividend to 1½ per cent, despite the failure of Dilworth, Arthington & Birkett's bank which lost the canal £4,500, but in 1828 it dropped back to 1 per cent. Mortgages of £134,550[46] had been raised under the 1819 Act, and interest rates were rising—4 per cent in 1825 was 5 per cent in 1826.

With the branch open, in June 1826 Crosley announced his resignation in order to become engineer to the Macclesfield Canal, and was succeeded by Bryan Padgett Gregson, Samuel's son, who from about 1813 had been assisting his father and by now was in charge of the day-to-day management of the canal. He was much involved in the development of packet boat services on the North End. These had run between Preston and Lancaster from the beginning and were extended to Kendal in 1820, competition with the turnpike coaches at times being intense. With some encouragement, trade through Glasson increased, and it has been computed that in 1830 16,036 tons passed through the dock, the bulk of it on to the canal.[47] Trade to Lancaster quays remained relatively static, as indeed did the growth of the town for a time, but Hest Bank finished as a port in 1831 when the Hest Bank Company transferred to Glasson.[48] Milnthorpe rapidly declined as a port for Kendal, to revive at Sandside on the Kent estuary until the Ulverston & Lancaster Railway finally killed it in 1857.[49] The town of Preston, on the other hand, flourished after the canal and tramroad reached it; in 1804 the population was about 10,000, in 1825 over 30,000.[50] The opening of the Glasson branch accentuated this process; in 1829 the Ribble Navigation Company complained that 'Scotch and Foreign trade vessels had left the port for the superior advantages of Glasson'. The cost of importing a ton of merchandise to Preston via Glasson and the canal was 13s 9d (69p), discharged into lighters off Lytham and landed at Preston quay, it was 14s 10d (74p).[51] For smaller craft there was no need to tranship at Glasson, either. The first seagoing vessel to use the canal was the sloop *Sprightly* in May 1826, taking a cargo of slate from the Duddon to Preston; in August of the next year, the 60-ton schooner *Seaforth* was the first to sail to Kendal, with salt from Northwich.[52] In 1830 the number of ships whose cargoes passed over the canal from

Glasson, from within the territorial limits of the £200 guarantee, was 64 (4,633 tons), and in 1840, 185 (12,128 tons). One can fairly assume that a good proportion sailed directly up the canal.[53] Trade comprised principally grain, timber, potatoes, and slate inwards; and outwards coal to Ulverston, Ireland and North Wales.

Taking stock of the canal's progress by the early 1820s, therefore, we find that by 1823, £600,000 had been spent on capital projects, excluding the Glasson branch. Tonnages increased as follows:[54]

	South End & Tramroad Coal tons	Total tons	North End tons	Total tons
1813	90,000	109,000	113,000	222,000
1820	121,000	179,000	115,000	294,000
1825	215,000	303,000	156,000	459,000 (Now open to Kendal)

Gross income was:[55]

	South End & Tramroad £	North End £	Packet Boat Profit £	Rent, Interest etc. £	Total £
1810	7,615	7,758	602	740	16,715
1815	8,568	8,264	477	1,005	18,314
1820	12,486	12,803	43	1,344	26,676
1823	12,870	14,199	247	1,558	28,874

A last scheme to unite the Lancaster and the Leeds & Liverpool via the Douglas was published by Twyford & Wilson, surveyors and civil engineers of Manchester, in 1827. They proposed lines of wooden booms moored across the Ribble from the Douglas mouth to Freckleton to form a floating towpath. Two navigation channels would be left in the middle, but on the important question of how these were to be crossed the authors are strangely silent. From Freckleton a new canal would rise 79 ft 4 in. by 10 locks to join the Lancaster near Salwick, and another from it across the Fylde, passing Kirkham and Poulton-le-Fylde, to enter the Wyre estuary at Thornton, where a new harbour would be made, the proposal thus pre-dating Fleetwood by some twenty years. The Lancaster's tramroad would no longer be a hindrance to canal traffic, and valuable grain cargoes would be carried from the Fylde. The 11¼ miles of new canal were estimated at under £80,000.[56] Neither the Lancaster nor the Leeds & Liverpool took any notice.

With the early thirties came the first threat of railway competition. The Wigan & Preston Railway was authorized in 1831, and during its promotion B. P. Gregson, realizing the danger of a line running parallel with the canal, put four alternative suggestions to the committee:

1. Convert the tramroad into a railway, to speed up tranship-ment.
2. The same, but in addition make suitable deviations to permit locomotive working.
3. Seek amalgamation with the railway and abolish the tram-road.
4. Abolish the tramroad independently and leave the South End solely for the use of the Leeds & Liverpool, so forcing the railway to make branches to the pits at Arley, Haigh and elsewhere on the canal.

He pointed out that railways were now undoubtedly here to stay and, if the canal company successfully opposed the Wigan & Preston another scheme would soon take its place. The established pattern of trade would inevitably be disrupted, and this the company must face. If the committee insisted on opposing the railway, he felt the most effective method would be to promote one of their own instead.[57]

George Stephenson was appointed to report on the tramroad conversion possibility, and recommended two diversions and four self-acting inclines, retaining the existing engine-worked incline from the Ribble bridge. Gregson was not impressed. 'I cannot but consider Mr. Stephenson's plan attended with many difficulties and inconveniences, not only in execution, but even in operation'. He estimated the cost would be £11,895.[58] Meanwhile, other lines were being promoted from Manchester to Bolton and Bolton to Preston via Chorley.

The Lancaster's policy was to compete where it could with advantage, but to co-operate where it could not. The North Union Railway, of which the Wigan & Preston had become part, in 1834 opened its main line to Preston and a branch from Wigan to New Springs. The latter crossed the parliamentary line of the canal to Westhoughton just beyond the junction with the Leeds & Liverpool at Wigan Top Lock and to force the railway to build a bridge the company hastily extended their canal in 1836 a few hundred yards towards Westhoughton. It was useless, of course, as the canal company by this time must have abandoned all thought of completing their line, but it made the North Union, who had refused to agree to a protective clause in their Bill, realize that they could not ride roughshod.

With the Bolton & Preston the company adopted different tactics. This company wanted to use the tramroad course in order to gain entry to Preston and in January 1837 agreement was reached whereby the canal company leased the tramroad to the railway in perpetuity, together with land near Preston basin for a station and all tolls received off the South End except income from Leeds & Liverpool traffic. In return the railway promoters agreed to pay the Lancaster £8,000 p.a., construct a short transfer siding from their terminus to Preston basin, and reserve a loco-motive solely for the use of the canal company's transhipment traffic between the North and South Ends. They obtained their Act in July, and then a year later a second one authorizing them to enter Preston over the North Union from Euxton. So they were saddled with the tramroad which they no longer needed, but which the canal company had no desire to take back. Eventually they agreed to maintain it for the canal company's use at a reduced rental of £7,400 to allow for the expense of upkeep, later reduced by the Lancaster to £7,000 rather than allow the railway company preferential coal rates for traffic transferred to the North End at Preston.

Ridding themselves of the tramroad was a sagacious move by the committee. Gregson foresaw that coal traffic would gradually shift to the railways as branches were made to the collieries, so he advised shedding the tramroad when the chance came, concen-trating instead on the old-established trade of the North End through the new transfer sidings at Preston. After 1840, as he forecast, tramroad traffic declined (helped by the Bolton & Preston's increased tolls). Net profit from the South End tolls and tramroad in 1839 was about £1,000 out of the gross income of £10,000, after paying for heavy repairs, maintenance and the rent (180,000 tons passed over them)[59] but in 1850 the North Union Railway (which had acquired the Bolton & Preston) was losing £5,600, the revenue being only £1,780.[60]

In 1843 the Bolton & Preston opened to Euxton. Calculating that it would not be long before moves would be made to extend the railway northward from Preston, the Lancaster decided to step in first and institute swift packet boats on the canal. Having inspected those used on the Glasgow, Paisley & Ardrossan Canal,

Canal Packet Boats

BETWEEN

Kendal, Lancaster, & Preston.

THE NEW

SWIFT BOAT,

CALLED

" The WATER WITCH "

WILL be employed between LANCASTER and PRESTON, for the present, and perform the distance of 30 Miles in about three hours.

THE BOATS WILL SAIL

On MONDAY the 1st April,

From Kendal to Preston, and from Preston to Kendal, on alternate days, (Sundays excepted.)

The Packet will leave KENDAL at SIX o'Clock in the Morning, and LANCASTER at ONE o'Clock, every *MONDAY, WEDNESDAY,* and *FRIDAY,* and arrive at PRESTON soon after FOUR o'Clock,

And will leave PRESTON *at half after* NINE o'Clock, and LANCASTER at ONE o'Clock, every *TUESDAY, THURSDAY,* and *SATURDAY,* and arrive at KENDAL, at half-past SEVEN o'Clock.

FARES.

FIRST CABIN.—The whole length — — — — — Six Shillings;
            Between *Kendal* and *Lancaster,*⎱ Three Shillings;
            or *Lancaster* and *Preston,*⎰
            shorter distances, *three half-pence* per Mile;
            but no Fare less than Nine Pence.

SECOND CABIN.—The whole length — — — — — Four Shillings;
            Between *Kendal* and *Lancaster,*⎱ Two Shillings;
            or *Lancaster* and *Preston,*⎰
            shorter distances, *one penny* per Mile;
            but no Fare less than Six Pence.

☞ *The Boat will sail from Kendal an hour earlier than heretofore, and both boats will leave Lancaster at ONE o'clock.*

*** Small Parcels between *Lancaster* and *Preston,* or *Lancaster* and *Kendal,* Six Pence each, the whole length between *Preston* and *Kendal,* One Shilling each, delivered free of Porterage,

Lancaster, March 28th, 1833.

15. Lancaster Canal swift boat timesheet, 1833

the committee ordered a similar one called *Waterwitch* and a new daily service was begun between Preston and Lancaster in March 1833, extended to Kendal in July. A second boat with an iron hull, named *Swiftsure*, joined *Waterwitch* in March 1834, and a daily service from Kendal and twice daily from Lancaster (summer months only) began. They were joined by *Swallow* in August 1835. The old packet boats had taken ten hours for the through journey, the new ones did it in eight. The Lancaster run, on which there were no locks, was done in three hours, at a speed of 10 m.p.h. Eleven stables were built at the horse-changing points, boat-houses at Kendal, Lancaster and Preston, and a passenger shed at Preston.

During this time, other developments took place. In 1836 the Ribble pumping engine and land were sold, as Killington reservoir now proved to be adequate to supply the canal. Then, in 1838, 150 yd of Whittle Hills tunnel was opened out in the middle to form two separate short tunnels, following two collapses in 1827 and a third in 1836. The Glasson trade continued to increase, reaching a peak of 185 vessels, with cargo for the canal (12,128 tons) from within the £200 area in 1840. This represented the peak year for the canal as a whole, the figures being:

	South End & Tramroad		North End	Total	Revenue
	Coal tons	Total tons	tons	tons	£
1836	251,000	377,000	173,000	550,000	33,000
1840	291,000	424,000	193,000	617,000	34,200

In 1837 the dividend rose to $1\frac{1}{4}$ per cent and in 1840 £$1\frac{7}{20}$, while steady repayment of the mortgages continued. There had been much talk of connecting Preston basin with a proposed Preston & Lytham Ship Canal (see p. 202), where only 600 yd separated the respective locations, but no more came of this than of Twyford & Wilson's scheme of 1827 for Ribble–Fylde canals.

The anticipated railway north of Preston materialized in 1836 as the Lancaster & Preston Junction.[61] The Lancaster obligingly sold it some land at Dock Street, Preston, and at the same time ordered a fourth swift boat, *Crewdson*, named after the chairman. This arrived in time to start additional sailings in May 1839, connecting with North Union trains at Preston. There were three daily summer and winter services to Lancaster and two to Kendal, improved accommodation was prepared for passengers in Preston

N

boat-house, and an omnibus was run between the canal basin and the stations. When the Lancaster railway opened in June 1840 the canal company promptly halved their fares—they had previously been 3s (15p) in the fore-cabin and 2s (10p) in the after-cabin. The swift boats were heated in the winter, and refreshments were served on board; travelling was smooth, comfortable and efficient, and the company lost no passengers despite a cut-rate combined rail and coach fare of 4s (20p) to Kendal.[62] Next year the dividend crept back to 1½ per cent.

The Lancaster & Preston Junction Railway, meanwhile, were having an unhappy time with their neighbours the North Union and the Bolton & Preston over the use of Preston station, added to which they had a second competitor to the canal in the Preston & Wyre Railway, opened to Fleetwood in July 1840, which was a strong contender for the Scottish traffic via a steamer service to Ardrossan. Finding themselves in financial difficulties, panic-stricken, they sought a bidder. Neither the North Union nor the Bolton & Preston were interested in their terms, so, again seizing their chance, the Lancaster Canal Company stepped in and, reversing the now customary procedure, on 1 September 1842 took a 21-years lease of the railway. (*To continue the history of the Lancaster Canal, turn to Chapter XVII.*)

Preston Ship Canal Schemes

The Ribble Navigation Company was incorporated by an Act of 1803 to improve the tidal channel of the river up to Preston, where there was an existing quay at the foot of Fishergate Lane. The capital of £2,000 was only sufficient to buoy the channel and effect a few minor improvements,[63] after which work languished until 1834 when a group of promoters resolved to explore the possibility of constructing a ship canal from Lytham Pool to Marsh Lane, Preston, on the north bank of the estuary. Thomas Fletcher, engineer with the Lancaster from 1812 to 1819, and who had also had experience on the Gloucester & Berkeley Canal, surveyed and reported.[64] He advocated a canal just over 9 miles long, mainly through flat marshy country but requiring a cutting 3,555 yd long through a 46-ft rise in the land near Freckleton. His canal would take vessels of 200 tons, drawing up to 14 ft 6 in., as on the Gloucester & Berkeley, and would be 24 ft deep at the bottom (20 ft in the cutting) and between 78 and 82 ft wide at the top. An entrance lock 110 ft long by 27 ft was proposed, available at all states of the tide, and a large basin at Preston. His estimate, including land, was £101,078. Water could be taken from streams, but if a reservoir were made in the Savock valley, a further £3,200 would be needed.

The provisional directors were headed by Sir Henry Philip Hoghton and Sir Thomas Dalrymple Hesketh, and included Thomas Clifton, a local and powerful landowner, and the Mayor and Recorder of Preston among eighteen others.[65] It was proposed to seek an Act in 1835, but the scheme was undersubscribed and dropped,[66] probably because the contemporary Preston & Wyre Railway project and its associated scheme for a port on the Wyre was more attractive.

In 1838 a new Navigation Company was incorporated, by which time Preston had several quays, and a new channel was then cut. But this, too, was only a temporary palliative, as the size of vessels increased, and in 1842 a dock was opened at Lytham, with a branch railway in 1846. Vessels unable to reach Preston could then discharge in the shelter of the dock instead of overside into lighters as hitherto. A third company was formed in 1853, followed by the Ribble Navigation and Dock Act of 1883 by which the navigation company was sold to Preston Corporation.

Construction of Preston Dock commenced, to be opened in 1892, and about 1888 G. Henry Roberts proposed a ship canal to the dock along the southern shore from Southport. In 1893 he published a pamphlet advocating his scheme, which involved opening up the old Ribble channel which had just been diverted to allow space for the dock works, a suggestion which was unlikely to endear him to the corporation. The Douglas channel would be diverted for 5 miles alongside the canal, to enter the sea below Southport, and a new 5-mile branch of the Leeds & Liverpool canal would likewise be necessary to Tarleton. Roberts' estimate of £1½ millions was considered to be ludicrous, and not surprisingly nothing more was heard except at the election of each new mayor of Preston. During the rest of his lifetime Roberts made this an opportunity to issue a reminder of his scheme, accompanied by an offer to build the canal himself.[67]

Ulverston and The Lakes

In 1727 Defoe recorded of his journey through Cumberland: 'Cockermouth stands upon the river Derwent, about twelve

miles from the sea, but more by the windings of the river, yet
vessels of good burthen may come up it.'[68]
But by 1746 navigation seems to have ceased when an anonymous
writer said:

'The river Darwent is the second for magnitude in Cumberland; it might be made navigable to Cockermouth by cutting
through some grounds, and erecting locks; for it admits ships
of tolerable burthen for coasters to Workington',[69]

which still represents the state of the river today. The same author
also noted that ships used the Esk 'even a great way above Mon-
caster Hall, Sir Joseph Pennington's seat, quite to the mountains,
for vessels of tolerable burden',[70] probably to above Eskdale
Green for cargoes of the rich haematite iron ore of Furness.

This ore has been worked since Roman times, and charcoal
smelting continued into the nineteenth century long after coke
smelting had been introduced elsewhere. Both Coniston Water
and Windermere were busy waterways for the carriage of charcoal
from the surrounding wooded slopes throughout the eighteenth
century. Backbarrow furnace, on the River Leven between
Greenodd and Newby Bridge, was supplied with large quantities
by the Backbarrow Company's own boats on Windermere and
Coniston, which were transported overland from one lake to the
other as required. The cost of boating from Coniston Waterhead
to Nibthwaite, at the foot of the lake, was 1s (5p) per dozen sacks,
whence they were carted by road to Backbarrow; on Windermere
it was 1s 4d (6½p) per dozen for the 'Long Voyage' from
above Rawlinson Nab and 11d for the 'Short Voyage' from
below. Charcoal from the north end of the lake was loaded
at Brathay and Bowness, and on both voyages discharge was
at Newby Bridge for road transit to Backbarrow.[71] Backbarrow
furnace is thought to have been established in 1711, and to
feed the second blast completed in 1715, about 500 boatloads
of charcoal were brought down Windermere.[72] Other furnaces
owned by the company and supplied by boat were at Coniston
and Cunsey. The latter was close to Windermere and was
leased by the Backbarrow partners in 1750 'together with the
Liberty of free passing and re-passing with boats for the carriage
of any material whatsoever to and from the said premises in and
upon the water or meer commonly called Windermere'.[73] Disputes
over boating rights arose from time to time: in 1750 the Backbarrow Company ordered boaters on Coniston Water 'to take no
stop from any person or persons whatsoever' and undertook to

indemnify them, concluding 'let this then be your sailing and fighting orders'.[74]

At this time, ferrying on Windermere was in private hands, and in 1726 the Backbarrow Company complained about George Braithwaite's 'bustle about the boats', and later that his boats were so overloaded that they had to be lightened by partly discharging on a deep-water shore in order to reach the landing stage in shallower water at Newby Bridge. Boating of charcoal on both lakes finished in 1783, when the boats were sold,[75] but other materials continued to be carried: in 1834 copper ore and slate were waterborne on Coniston for carting to Penny Bridge and Greenodd,[76] and probably continued until the Coniston Railway was opened in 1859; and gunpowder from the Lowwood works near Haverthwaite (established on the site of a former iron furnace in 1799) on both lakes for the mines and quarries in the central Lake District.[77]

Coastal shipping extensively used the shallow shores of Morecambe Bay and the Duddon and Leven estuaries, landings being made at high water at numerous points, often wherever happened to be most convenient. The first quay in the district was built in 1781 at Greenodd, where the little River Crake entered the Leven estuary, by the Newland Company, who became the principal mine and furnace owners in Furness. Greenodd grew into a flourishing small port until 1868 when the Lakeside branch railway killed it, but some coastal craft ventured further inland. About 1793 Thomas Rigge of Hawkshead had several sloops regularly engaged in carrying slate from his mines from Penny Bridge, about ½ mile up the Crake, and there may have been a shipbuilding yard there.[78] Greenodd and Penny Bridge served as ports for two furnaces on the Crake, and in 1737 ships moored at Haverthwaite on the Leven about a mile below Backbarrow.[79] The Leven was used for boating ore and iron to and from Backbarrow and for the Cunsey furnaces; in 1747 65 tons of iron shot were boated down the Leven from Backbarrow to Hammerside (near Ulverston) for shipment to the navy at Portsmouth.[80] At Lowwood, 'Bigland Dock' was in existence before 1729, serving the forge and later furnace there.[81] The Crake and the Leven were used, therefore, by seagoing craft as far as Penny Bridge and Haverthwaite respectively, which probably represented the then tidal limits, and the Leven by river craft as far as Backbarrow but not, apparently, between that place and Windermere at Newby Bridge, at both of which there were weirs.

With navigable water reaching well inland there was little need for artificial cuts, only two being recorded. The first appears to have been associated with John Wilkinson, the famous Shropshire and North Wales iron master who lived in his later years near Lindale at Castle Head, then a promontory on the coast, where he projected land reclamation schemes (see p. 183). He spent his youth at Backbarrow under his father Isaac and then at Wilson House, also near Lindale. Here Isaac unsuccessfully attempted to smelt iron with peat fuel, and is said to have cut a canal into the nearby peat moss in order to transport it to his furnace. If the canal existed it probably led from the River Winster, which appears to have been used to bring in Lindale ore for the Wilkinsons; the remains of a wharf near Wilson House were stated to be visible in 1914.[82]

John Wilkinson went on to found his famous ironworks in Staffordshire and Shropshire and in 1787 he launched an iron boat into the Severn near Broseley. James Stockdale, the historian of Cartmel, suggests, however, that this was not the first iron boat. Writing of the Wilson House canal in 1872 he said:

'The first operation . . . was to cut a canal into the midst of the turbary (peat) sufficiently wide for the passage of a small boat, intended to be used in conveying the peat moss to the iron furnace; which boat, tradition says, was actually constructed, not of wood, but of *Iron*! and there are people still living . . . who remember having seen it seventy years ago.'[83]

Dr H. W. Dickinson, commenting on Stockdale in 1914, noted that if an iron boat was made at Wilson House it must have been the work of Isaac, for John left home about 1744; alternatively John could have made it after he settled at Castle Head in 1799, which seems unlikely. According to Dickinson, the boat Stockdale said existed about 1800 was on Helton Tarn, some four miles upstream from Wilson House, 'but how much earlier than this the boat was built there is no evidence to show'. After remarking that experiments would more likely have taken place at Broseley he went on: 'It is quite possible that he placed the boat on the Winster about the time that he built his other iron boat. Attempts have been made recently to recover the remains of this boat, up to the time of writing without success; possibly it has rusted away entirely'.[84]

More recently attempts have been made to locate the site of Wilkinson's canal, unsuccessfully,[85] yet the fascinating fact remains that Stockdale, although an old man when he wrote, was not retelling mere village hearsay. His grandfather had a close business and personal friendship with the Wilkinsons and with Boulton & Watt, and a cousin had married John Wilkinson's young brother William,[86] so it was much more of a family matter.

In the mid-eighteenth century there began a rapid growth in the export of Furness ore to other parts of the country for the newly introduced coke-smelting process, and in 1780 the Newland Company built a quay at the hamlet of Barrow, to which ore was carted from their mines at Dalton and on Lindal Moor.[87] Despite being over a mile inland, the market town of Ulverston had been declared a port in 1774 when seventy ships were registered there, craft of 150 tons being able to come up to the neighbouring shores at high water.[88] Consequently the town did not take kindly to the prospect of a rival. The export trade in ore and slate was expanding and the promotion of the Lancaster Canal on the other side of the sands gave local emphasis to the canal mania sweeping the rest of the country. These three factors[89] probably led to William Burnthwaite, an Ulverston solicitor, being asked to call a meeting in July 1791:

'Several Gentlemen having proposed a Canal to be made from Hammerside Hill to the Weint end as an advantage to the town of Ulverstone,* and the Country adjacent, and desired me to make a survey of the same, and to call a meeting of the Gentlemen, to take the same into consideration.'[90]

His estimate was £2,000, which took ten months to raise to May 1792, by which time John Rennie had been asked to survey and produced a plan for a ship canal 1 mile 3 furlongs long from the coast at Hammerside Point to the town. Rennie's estimate was £3,084 including a sea lock, so it was decided to increase the subscription to £4,000. In October £3,800 had been raised, £1,200 of it from Liverpool, small sums from London, Manchester, Lancaster and Kendal, and the remainder locally.[91] An Act was obtained in May 1793[92] empowering the Proprietors of the Ulverstone Canal Navigation from 1 June to construct a canal 15 ft deep and 66 ft wide at top, with a capital of £4,000 in £50 shares and powers to raise £3,000 more if necessary.

The Lancaster Canal Company supported the Bill and agreed that coal should be conveyed from one canal to the other free of duty other than ordinary canal tolls.[93] The Ulverston promoters had informed the Lancaster committee that 'they proposed in the

* Eighteenth-century spelling, which died out in the nineteenth century except in legal documents.

Act they were going to obtain a provision should be made for connection with the Lancaster Canal'[94] and the Act appears to recognize that this might be made, but then continues to give specific freedom from sea duty on 'coals, culm and cinders'. Whether a physical connection between the two canals was intended is not clear.

Pinkerton and Murray were awarded the contract for cutting and John Lancaster and James Duckworth that for the lock masonry.[95] The first sod was cut by the chairman, Lt Col Thomas Sunderland of Ulverston, on 23 August 1793, and the second, it is said, by a labourer, Edward Banks, who later became the great contractor.[96] Pinkerton and Murray were at the same time working on the North End of the Lancaster and probably overreached themselves in taking the Ulverston contract, for in August 1795 they abandoned the works owing to shortage of cash to pay wages; at the same time they were discharged by the Lancaster for bad workmanship. Delay ensued, and instead of the contractual date of September 1794 the canal was not finished by H. Baird until October 1796.[97] To open it on 18 November, an enthusiastic crowd hauled three brigs up to the canal head followed by a sloop which, being smaller, enabled its hauliers to overtake the larger vessels, and so arrive, triumphant, first in the basin.[98] The lock took craft 100 ft long by 27 ft beam drawing 12 ft 6 in. at spring tides and 7 ft 6 in. at neaps. There was a swing bridge alongside the lock, and water was taken from Newland Beck.

The cost of building appears to be over £9,200[99] but the opening took place during a slump in the ore trade and development was slow. It was June 1797 before Burnthwaite was appointed clerk and the decision made to build a warehouse at the canal head and a toll office. Calls of £5 had to be made to finance them as a separate venture from the canal, so that proprietors not participating would not share in the proceeds. Slate and coal wharves were laid out at the same time. To promote slate traffic the company decided in 1798 to build a road from Kirkby quarries across the moor to Netherhouses, whence existing roads led to Ulverston, but in 1801 the treasurer was instructed to take arbitration proceedings against the contractors and the following year Fisher and Lowry, the quarry operators, agreed to finish the road and keep it in repair. On condition that the canal company paid them £21 15s (£21·75) on completion, and charged other users until their respective expenses were defrayed, they undertook to ship three-quarters of their output by the canal. Meanwhile the company had to mortgage their tolls for £370 to repay their debts.

In 1798 94 vessels (4,704 tons) entered the canal and from 1802 to 1814 the annual average was 132 (6,600 tons).[100] Canalside land was let for iron ore floors (dumping grounds) in 1798 and 1799 but administration of the company was very casual between 1806 and 1815, with irregular meetings frequently lacking a quorum, until an attempt was made to improve matters. Share transfers had not been registered, accounts had not been properly balanced and presented, taxes and charges for which the company were not liable had been unquestioningly paid, and the Local Board of Health had helped themselves to gravel from canal land. Furthermore, no one seemed sure which shareholders had invested in the warehouse, which had made enough profit to enable £220 to be transferred to the canal account, and in the end the two accounts were consolidated in 1823 although precisely who owned it was still unsettled. A new pier was built at the canal foot in 1815–20, designed by a local wine and spirit merchant, James Butcher,[101] costing £688, and a new wall around the basin for £342.[102]

The constantly shifting sands of Morecambe Bay moved the Ulverston Channel towards the Cartmel side of the estuary from about 1805, and continued to move it back and forth so that larger vessels could enter the canal only intermittently, but it was 1824 before a survey of the channel was made, with another the following year, although nothing was done until 1835. In 1821 the tolls were leased to William Town and T. B. Tolming until 1828, by which time trade was improving. Receipts for the five years 1815–20 were £1,528, thus averaging some £300 p.a., against £860 expenses, or about £170 p.a. net. After the lease from 1828 to 1833 receipts were £2,472 (say £500 p.a.) against £708 expenses (£140 p.a.). But in the latter period £1,337 capital expenditure was incurred in major repairs and building a new warehouse, so the actual surplus was only £428.[103] In 1821 259 vessels (13,960 tons) used the canal;[104] by 1828 the number had reached 695 (37,431 tons)[105] when there were three regular sailings to London, six to Liverpool, three to Scotland and several to Preston.[106] A period of mild prosperity commenced in 1829, when a wide variety of goods entered and left the canal, so that when in 1834 the powerful Newland Company asked for reduced iron ore tolls if they used the canal exclusively and ceased shipping from Conishead Bank, the committee felt emboldened to refuse. The Newland Company went to the growing port of Barrow instead.[107] One of the Ulverston shipbuilding firms transferred their yard to the canal side, where vessels were launched broadside, and several other yards were at work at various periods until at least the 1850s.[108] In 1835, 2,000 tons of copper were exported down the canal from Furness mines.[109]

Passenger services commenced in 1835 when the steam packet *Windermere* sailed from the canal foot pier for Liverpool, provoking a drawn-out argument about charges. The canal company demanded the incredible sum of £10 p.a. for each passenger landed, allowing up to 5 lb of luggage, and after threatening to stop passengers landing (but not goods), even more incredibly had their way. The packet called at Blackpool, but a few years later the service from Liverpool went to Bardsea via Fleetwood.

The first half-yearly dividend was paid in June 1836, when £295 6s 10d (£295.34) was divided among the proprietors, and continued until December 1846. The sum is stated to represent 5 per cent on the invested capital.[110] The first chairman of the company was Thomas Sunderland, who rented the first iron ore floor, followed by Colonel Thomas Richard Gale Bradyll of Conishead Priory, a wealthy coalowner in Cumberland and Durham. After the lease ended in 1828 the Rev. John Sunderland was in the chair for many years, possibly until 1850, perhaps longer.[111]

James Butcher tried his hand at civil engineering again in 1835 when his plan for a breakwater was approved. It stretched out from the Cartmel shore, intending to divert the channel back towards the canal foot.[112] Evidently work of some kind had started by 1840 when 'Geo. Smith had let off Water from the Canal, and that his doing so injured the works going on on the Sand',[113] but it was probably not taken very seriously until 1848 when the tonnage dropped by nearly half. By this time, too, railways were on the scene. The Furness Railway Act of 1844 authorized lines from Kirkby and Dalton to Barrow and Piel to carry ore to the coast, and an Ulverston extension was promoted in 1845. The Whitehaven & Furness Junction Railway also proposed to build an extension from their line at Dalton through Ulverston to the Lancaster & Carlisle Railway at Carnforth, and a third scheme projected a line from Ulverston through Greenodd to join the Kendal & Windermere Railway.[114] On another front fear of railway competition produced a scheme to improve the approaches to the flourishing port of Greenodd by cutting a canal to the coast at Salthouse Point to by-pass the Leven estuary. It would intersect the Ulverston Canal. A Greenodd Navigation Company was formed, 'being a company for continuing and improving the navigation of Ulverston and Greenodd', which offered to buy the Ulverston Canal for £12,000. The Ulverston proprietors declined to consider it until the new company was provisionally registered. All these schemes foundered, but they spurred the Ulverston to do something about the channel and in 1848 Admiralty consent was obtained to a stone breakwater from Parkhead to Black Scar, about one-third of the distance out from the Cartmel side. George Collins' tender of £1,150 was accepted, and the work was completed for £1,658 in 1849.[115] (*To continue the history of the Ulverston Canal, turn to p. 428.*)

NOTES

Notes to Chapter I

1. T. C. Barker, 'The Beginnings of the Canal Age in the British Isles', *Studies in the Industrial Revolution*, 1960; A. W. Skempton, 'The Engineers of the English River Navigations, 1620–1760, *Trans. Newcomen Soc.*, 1953.
2. See Skempton, op. cit. For Sorocold and the Derwent (Derbyshire) Navigation, see Charles Hadfield, *The Canals of the East Midlands*, 2nd ed., 1970, p. 32.
3. T. S. Willan, *River Navigation in England, 1660–1750*, 1933, quo. JHC, xi, p. 444.
4. For fish-weirs, see Charles Hadfield, *British Canals*, 4th ed., 1969, p. 15.
5. Letter from Thomas Patten to Richard Norris, 8 January 1697(8), *Chetham Society 9 (OS)*, 1846, Norris Papers, pp. 37–9.
6. JHC, 15 February 1721.
7. Letter from Thomas Patten, op. cit.
8. Thos. Steers, *A Map of the Rivers Mercy and Irwell from Bank-Key to Manchester*, 1712. (Manchester Central Library).
9. See the analysis of these men in Willan, op. cit., pp. 59–61.
10. 7 Geo I *c*. 15.
11. Patten deeds, Box Warrington No. 1, Parcel 1 (Warrington Public Library). They were appointed on 17 February after a meeting on the 3rd. A surviving share certificate is dated 10 June 1724, and is signed by the seven. (Manchester Ship Canal Co's museum.)
12. V. I. Tomlinson, 'Early Warehouses on Manchester Waterways', *Trans. Lancs & Cheshire Antiq. Soc.*, Vol. 71, 1961, quoting S. & N. Buck, *The South-West Prospect of Manchester*, 1728.
13. V. I. Tomlinson, 'Salford Activities connected with the Bridgewater Navigation', *Trans. Lancs & Cheshire Antiq. Soc.*, Vol. 66, 1956, quoting R. Whitworth, *Prospect of Manchester and Salford*, 1734.
14. On 7 August 1736 Thomas Patten rented to himself and seven Manchester merchants, all Mersey & Irwell shareholders, half of Bank Quay, with warehouses, buildings and a house for £30 p.a. (Patten deeds, Box Warrington No. 1, Parcel I (Warrington Public Library). See other deeds of the same date for Atherton's Quay and Great Sankey Quay.
15. Another Patten deed of the same date, loc. cit.
16. W. H. Thomson, *History of Manchester to 1852*, 1967, quoting from the Burton MSS, vii, 39. A Mersey & Irwell petition of 9 March 1753 against a roads Bill also says that the navigation had been perfected 'about Sixteen Years'. JHC, 9 March 1753.
17. Herbert Clegg, 'The Third Duke of Bridgewater's Canal Works in Manchester', *Trans. Lancs & Cheshire Antiq. Soc.*, Vol. 65, 1955, p. 92. The agreement is an undated draft, but is likely to have been earlier than the subsequent Act.
18. 10 Geo II *c*. 9.
19. See V. I. Tomlinson, 'Salford Activities', op. cit., and JHC, xxviii, 335.
20. Mersey & Irwell Navigation Minute Book, 4 June 1783.
21. Manchester Central Library.
22. See S. 4 of the Duke's Act of 1760.

23. When opposing the Duke of Bridgewater's Bill of 1762.
24. 26 Geo II *c*. 63.
25. *Manchester Mercury*, 17 April 1753.
26. Quoted by V. I. Tomlinson, 'Salford Activities', op. cit., from *Bradshaw's Manchester Journal*, No. 2, May 1841, 25–6. Similar rates were advertized in the *Manchester Mercury*, 13 August 1754.
27. JHC, 18 January 1754.
28. Clowes Deeds 698 (Rylands Library, Manchester).
29. See Charles Hadfield, *The Canals of the West Midlands*, 2nd ed., 1969, p. 19.
30. For the Duke's background, see Bernard Falk, *The Bridgewater Millions*, 1942.
31. *Observations upon a proposed Navigation between Manchester and Liverpool*, *c.* 1761. Manchester Central Library, M/CR f. 1706/1.
32. Anon., *The History of Inland Navigations*, 2nd ed., 1769, p. 21.
33. Clowes Deeds, 110 (Rylands Library, Manchester).
34. Christopher Byron to Edward Chetham, 27 January 1759; the same, 4 February, Clowes Deeds, 110 (Rylands Library, Manchester).
35. Clowes Deeds 696 (Rylands Library, Manchester).
36. 32 Geo II *c*. 2.
37. E. Mally, *The financial administration of the Bridgewater Estate, 1780–1800*, unpublished thesis, 1929. (Eccles Public Library.)
38. 'Salford Activities', to which we are much indebted.
39. JHC, xxviii, 724.
40. *History of Inland Navigations*, op. cit.
41. 33 Geo II *c*. 2.
42. 'Salford Activities', op. cit.
43. XI and XII.
44. *Annual Register*, 1760, p. 160.
45. *Manchester Mercury*, 21 July 1761.
46. James Ogden, *A Description of Manchester*, 1783.
47. For these, see Clegg, 'Canal Works in Manchester', op. cit.
48. See Tomlinson, 'Early Warehouses', op. cit.
49. *Derby Mercury*, 24 October 1766.
50. Clegg, 'Canal Works in Manchester', op. cit. See also Tomlinson, 'Early Warehouses', op. cit.
51. See Charles Hadfield, *The Canals of the West Midlands*, 2nd ed., 1969, p. 41.
52. See Charles Hadfield, *The Canals of the West Midlands*, 2nd ed., 1969, p. 157.
53. This account is based on Frank Mullineux, 'The Duke of Bridgewater's Underground Canals at Worsley', *Trans. Lancs & Cheshire Antiq. Soc.*, Vol. 71, 1961.
54. *Bridgewater's Canal*, from the Northern Tour. MS. 1777. (Manchester Ship Canal Museum.)
55. *Observations upon the proposed Navigation between Manchester and Liverpool*, *c.* 1761, op. cit.
56. *Observations*, op. cit. The contrary statement in F. H. Egerton, *The First Part of a Letter, to the Parisians, and the French Nation, upon Inland Navigation*, that the navigation had been offered to the Duke for £13,000, and refused, is likely to be a later justification for the Duke's misjudgement of the future competitive ability of the Mersey & Irwell.
57. *Williamson's Liverpool Advertiser*, 23 April 1762.
58. *Manchester Mercury*, 11 May 1762.
59. The Bridgewater Estate accounts (Lancashire Record Office) for 1766 show that he subscribed some £12 a share. He held 138 out of 200 shares in 1768.
60. 2 Geo III *c*. 11.
61. Lords Committee Book, 11 March 1762.
62. For a fuller account of the relations between the Duke and the canal promoters, see Chapter I of Charles Hadfield, *The Canals of the West Midlands*, 2nd ed., 1969. For the Weaver, see Chapter II of this book.

63. For the Trent & Mersey Canal generally, see Charles Hadfield, *The Canals of the West Midlands*, 2nd ed., 1969.
64. A copper and brass manufacturer with works at Eaton and Bosley between Congleton and Macclesfield. See W. H. Chaloner, 'Charles Roe of Macclesfield (1715–81): An Eighteenth Century Industrialist', in *Trans. Lancs & Cheshire Antiq. Soc.*, Vols. 62 and 63.
65. H.M.C., *Kenyon MSS*, 1894. George Kenyon to Thomas Banks, 3 December 1765.
66. 6 Geo III *c.* 17.
67. See Charles Hadfield, *The Canals of the West Midlands*, 2nd ed., 1969, p. 27.
68. *Prescott's Manchester Journal*, 13 June 1772.
69. *Derby Mercury*, 4 October 1776.
70. For much detailed information upon construction generally, see Samuel Smiles, *Lives of the Engineers*, 1861, Vol. I, under James Brindley; Hugh Malet, *The Canal Duke*, 1961; and Mally, 'Bridgewater Estate', op. cit.
71. S. R. Harris, 'Liverpool Canal Controversies, 1769–1772', *Journal of Transport History*, May 1956, and see Chapter II.
72. *Prescott's Manchester Journal*, 13 June 1772.
73. *Derby Mercury*, 12 June 1772.
74. *Annual Register*, 1773, p. 65.
75. Ibid., 1774, p. 145.
76. Ibid., 1776, p. 127.
77. *Derby Mercury*, 29 March 1776.
78. *Gore's General Advertiser*, Liverpool, 29 March 1776.
79. 24,000 in 1774 in the township of Manchester, 76,000 in 1801. Owen Ashmore, *The Industrial Archaeology of Lancashire*, 1969, p. 22.
80. Smiles, *Engineers*, op. cit., Vol. I, pp. 395 et seq.
81. John Phillips, *A General History of Inland Navigation*, 2nd ed., 1795, p. 77.
82. For some figures of construction costs, see Charles Hadfield, *The Canal Age*, 1968, Appendix III.
83. Bridgewater Estate Account Books, Lancashire Record Office.
84. *Manchester Historical Recorder*, 20 April 1789. I am indebted to Mr. F. C. Mather for this quotation.
85. James Ogden, *A Description of Manchester*, 1783.
86. F. C. Mather, *After the Canal Duke*, 1970. See this book for further information about the cut.
87. Bridgewater Estate accounts for 1791 (Lancashire Record Office).
88. *Derby Mercury*, 4 October 1776.
89. Mally, *Bridgewater Estate*, op. cit.
90. *Williamson's Liverpool Advertiser*, 14 January 1774.
91. Bridgewater Estate accounts (Lancashire Record Office) show receipts from passenger carrying from 3 October 1767.
92. *Derby Mercury*, 9 September 1774.
93. Ibid., 8 July 1784.
94. Lewis's *Directory for Manchester and Salford*, 1788.
95. Bridgewater Estate accounts, Lancashire Record Office.
96. *Prescott's Manchester Journal*, 23 January 1779.
97. Ibid.
98. Ibid., 10 April 1779.
99. Mersey & Irwell Navigation Minute Book, 2 June 1784.
100. Liverpool Town Books, 2 December 1789.
101. (Holme, Edmond) *A Directory of the Towns of Manchester and Salford* (1788).
102. The Duke of Bridgewater paid £185 for five shares in 1790.

Notes to Chapter II

1. For the history of the Weaver to 1800, the reader cannot do better than refer to T. S. Willan, *The Navigation of the River Weaver in the Eighteenth Century*, Chetham Society, 1951. Our account is based upon it.
2. 7 Geo I *c.* 10.
3. *Liverpool Chronicle*, 7 October 1757.
4. JHC, 16 December 1754.
5. F. A. Bailey, 'The Minutes of the Trustees of the Turnpike Roads from Liverpool to Prescot, St Helens, Warrington and Ashton-in-Makerfield, 1726–89', *Trans. Lancs & Cheshire Antiq. Soc.*, Vol. 88, 1937. The purpose behind the 1753 Act was to make it easier to bring coal to Liverpool. We may note that one of the new toll-gates it authorized was at Sankey Bridges.
6. This account of the early history of the Sankey Brook Navigation is based on Professor T. C. Barker's paper, 'The Sankey Navigation' in *Trans. Lancs & Cheshire Antiq. Soc.*, 1948, and Professor Barker's and Dr J. R. Harris's book, *A Merseyside Town in the Industrial Revolution: St Helens 1750–1900*, 1954.
7. The will of John Woodcock of Warrington, merchant, dated 15 June 1745, and proved 25 May 1751, mentions 'my share in the Navigation at Sankey Bridges' (Barker & Harris, op. cit., p. 19, n3). An advertisement in *Williamson's Liverpool Advertiser* for 17 September 1756 offers for sale: 'the Sankey Quay . . . with all the warehouses &c. thereto belonging . . . there is a Public House and coal yard not let at the yearly price of £28'; on 26 May 1758 a similar advertisement appeared, this time including: 'the *Resolution* sloop, belonging to the said Quay, burthen 60 tons or there abouts'.
8. Liverpool Town Books, 25 October 1754.
9. Willan, *Weaver*, op. cit.
10. 28 Geo II *c.* 8.
11. See Charles Hadfield, *The Canals of South and South East England*, 1969.
12. *Williamson's Liverpool Advertiser*, 4 November 1757.
13. Ibid., 23 December 1757.
14. See the plan of 1763 by John Eyes, from a survey of April and May 1759 by Eyes and Thomas Gaskell. BTHR SAN 3/1.
15. JHC, 10 February 1772; the Sankey company say they have completed their canal and its three branches.
16. Inf. from Dr J. R. Harris.
17. *Gore's General Advertiser*, 5 February 1784, advertisement for the sale of Stanley mill.
18. *Williamson's Liverpool Advertiser*, 17 February 1758.
19. Ibid., 21 April 1758.
20. Ibid., 1 May 1761.
21. *Williamson's Liverpool Advertiser*, 11 January 1760.
22. 2 Geo III *c.* 56.
23. J. Aikin, *Description of the Country from Twenty to Thirty Miles round Manchester*, 1795.
24. Ibid.
25. *Gore's General Advertiser*, 1 November 1771.
26. Liverpool Town Books, 7 September 1757.
27. 33 Geo II *c.* 49.
28. *Billings's Liverpool Advertiser*, 9 November 1801.
29. *Liverpool General Advertiser*, 21 February 1772.
30. Barker & Harris, *A Merseyside Town*, op. cit., pp. 29–30.
31. *Williamson's Liverpool Advertiser*, 29 January 1762.
32. The account of the next few years relies upon J. R. Harris's article, 'Liverpool Canal Controversies, 1769–72' in *Journal of Transport History*, May 1956.

33. See Charles Hadfield, *The Canals of the West Midlands*, pp. 19ff., and J. R. Harris's article just quoted.
34. *Williamson's Liverpool Advertiser*, 14 January 1774.
35. Ibid., 9 December 1774.
36. Barker, 'The Sankey Navigation', p. 146.
37. Ibid., p. 147, n.2.
38. Mersey & Irwell Navigation Minute Book, 4 June 1788.

Notes to Chapter III

1. *A Mapp of ye River Douglas and Rible with ye Level of Douglas in order to make it navigable from Rible to the Towne of Wigan, survey'd by Thomas Steers. 1712.* (Moore Papers, Lancs C.R.O.)
2. JHC, 12 January 1719/20.
3. T. S. Willan, *River Navigation in England, 1600–1750*, 1936.
4. JHC, various dates April and May 1713, and JHL, various dates, May and June 1713.
5. Notes on Douglas Navigation in Kenyon papers, probably 1712–13. (Lancs C.R.O.)
6. JHL, 6 June 1713.
7. JHC, 5, 12, 13 February 1719/20. An effort to delay the third reading in the Commons was defeated 48 to 44, and eight days later another by 69 to 39, after which the third reading was carried by 73 to 27.
8. 6 Geo I *c.* 28.
9. *Reasons against the Bill for Making the River Douglas Navigable*, ND (1719). (Lancs C.R.O.) See also *Answers to the Reasons for making the River Douglas Navigable*, ND (1719). (Lancs C.R.O.)
10. This account is based on A. P. Wadsworth & J. de L. Mann, *The Cotton Trade and Industrial Lancashire, 1600–1780*.
11. Ibid.
12. Douglas Navigation, Commissioners' Minute Book, 12 March 1739/40. (Wigan Central Library.)
13. Willan, *River Navigation*, op. cit.
14. Three bills issued by Alexander Leigh, 1770. (Wigan Central Library.)
15. J. Barron, *A History of the Ribble Navigation*, 1938.
16. MS agreements, 13 April 1754. (Lancs C.R.O.)
17. Tripartite agreement re land, 28 September 1761, Hesketh papers. (Lancs C.R.O.)
18. Ed. E. Baines, *Lancashire*, 1868 ed.
19. Commissioners' Minute Book, Douglas Navigation, 30 April 1753, empanelling a jury to settle the purchase price of land, the first since the navigation was completed. Also P. P. Burdett & R. Beck, *A Plan of an Intended Canal from Coln to Liverpool*, 1769. (Westmorland C.R.O.) shows 'Leigh's Cut' from about Gathurst bridge to the line of the Leeds & Liverpool Canal north of the aqueduct over the Douglas at Newburgh. *Appendix to A Cursory View of a proposed Canal from Kendal, to the Duke of Bridgewater's Canal, &c.* ... (*c.* 1771) to which this map is sometimes attached, refers to the advantages which would accrue to 'Mr Lee's Canal' from the Liverpool Canal Scheme of 1770–72. (Moore Papers, Lancs C.R.O.)
20. Broadsheet, 4 May 1753. (Lancs C.R.O.)
21. Douglas Navigation, Commissioners' Minute Book, 15 July 1767.
22. Holt Leigh's *Diaries* (Lancashire C.R.O.) refer to land registrations and navigation works still going on in 1770–3; see also Leeds & Liverpool Canal Minute Book, 1772.
23. Plan of the Leeds & Liverpool Canal by Joseph Priestley, ND. (Manchester Cen Lib.) The 1845 6-in OS also shows Ell Meadow on a lock cut.

24. J. Aikin, *A Description of the Country Thirty to Forty Miles round Manchester*, 1795.
25. J. Houseman, *A Topographical Description of Cumberland, Westmorland and Lancashire*, 1800.
26. Holt Leigh's *Diaries*. (Lancs C.R.O.)
27. For the Lagan Navigation, see W. A. McCutcheon, *The Canals of the North of Ireland*, 1965.
28. For the Forth & Clyde Canal, see Jean Lindsay, *The Canals of Scotland*, 1968.
29. For the Trent & Mersey and Staffordshire & Worcestershire Canals, see Charles Hadfield, *The Canals of the West Midlands*, 2nd ed., 1969.
30. J. Priestley, *Historical Account of the Navigable Rivers, Canals, etc.*, 1831.
31. H. F. Killick, 'Notes on the Early History of the Leeds and Liverpool Canal', *The Bradford Antiquary*, N.S., Vol. 3, 1896–1900.
32. Leeds & Liverpool Canal, Yorkshire Committee, Minute Book, 2 July 1766.
33. Anon, *The History of Inland Navigation*, 2nd ed., 1769.
34. Killick, op. cit.
35. *Williamson's Liverpool Advertiser*.
36. Leeds & Liverpool Canal, Yorkshire Committee Minute Book, 14 June 1769.
37. Ibid., 3 July 1769.
38. Killick, op. cit.
39. Killick, op. cit.
40. Harris, 'Liverpool Canal Controversies', op. cit.
41. Burdett & Beck's *Plan* of 1769, op. cit., showing Leigh's Cut ending in the Leeds & Liverpool, supports this view.
42. 10 Geo III *c.* 114.
43. Killick, op. cit.
44. 23 Geo III *c.* 47.
45. Harris, 'Liverpool Canal Controveries', op. cit.
46. Harris, 'Liverpool Canal Controversies', op. cit.
47. Killick, op. cit.
48. *Leeds Intelligencer*, 13 April 1773.
49. Ibid., 26 October 1773, 22 February 1774.
50. Ibid., 22 March 1774.
51. Ibid., 28 June 1774.
52. *Case in favour of the Settle Canal*, 1774, Petre of Dunkenhalgh papers. (Lancashire C.R.O.)
53. *York Chronicle*, 8 October 1774.
54. MS 'Statistical History of the Leeds & Liverpool Canal', compiled by Law Clerk, *c.* 1898 (BTHR).
55. Killick, op. cit.
56. Ibid.
57. *Plan of the Intended Leeds & Liverpool Canal*, Priestley, op. cit.
58. *Manchester Mercury*, 1 May 1781.
59. 'Statistical History', op. cit.
60. Ibid.
61. Son of Robert and grandson of Alexander Leigh (*Victoria Country History of Lancashire*, Vol. IV).
62. 23 Geo III *c.* 47.
63. Leeds & Liverpool Canal, General Assembly Minute Book, 24 January 1783.
64. *Report*, in circular to proprietors following General Assembly, 9 & 10 October 1789 (Moore Papers, Lancs C.R.O.).
65. 30 Geo III *c.* 65.
66. 'Statistical History', op. cit.
67. JHC, 1 February 1744.
68. Turnpike Act of 1815, 'Historical Links between Bradford & Shipley', W. Robertshaw, *The Bradford Antiquary*, N.S. Pt. XXXV, 1951.
69. JHC, loc. cit. A draft MS of the petition exists in Bradford Central Reference Library.

O

70. 11 Geo III *c.* 89.
71. Abraham Balme's Day Book, 1771–6, (Bradford Central Library) details instructions and disbursements, but on 3 July 1776 a Commissioners' award was witnessed by Priestley (Bradford Canal Minute Book) and in 1815 he was referred to as agent (ibid., 11 May 1815).
72. Balme's Day Book, op. cit.
73. *Leeds Intelligencer*, 26 October 1773.
74. 8 Geo III *c.* 47.
75. Ibid.
76. Leeds & Liverpool Canal, Yorkshire Committee, Minute Book, 27 January 1786.

Notes to Chapter IV

1. For these, see Charles Hadfield, *The Canals of the West Midlands*, 2nd ed., 1969, and *The Canals of the East Midlands*, 2nd ed., 1970.
2. For the Ellesmere Canal, see Charles Hadfield, *The Canals of West Midlands* 2nd ed, 1969.
3. Mersey & Irwell Navigation Minute Book, 2 June 1790.
4. Ibid., 7 August 1793.
5. 34 Geo III *c.* 37. This substituted a new Company of Proprietors of the Mersey & Irwell Navigation for the undertakers of the 1721 Act, and made the shares personal estate. The company had tried also to get powers to charge a mileage toll and make other changes, but had been defeated by the Duke of Bridgewater's influence in the sessions of 1791 and 1792. He allowed their 1794 Bill through on the understanding that it contained nothing but incorporation matter.
6. *A Plan of the present and intended Canals in the Counties of Lancaster and York*, 1793, (Lancashire Record Office). On the other hand, Cary's map of 1795 in *Inland Navigation* does not show the Butchersfield cut. This may have been built later, or the map may have been drawn earlier, in spite of its publication date. The old Woolston cut, with a new lock at Powder Mill, had been made by the old company. It is shown on a map of the Mersey & Irwell in the 1770s in Anon, *The History of Inland Navigations*, 3rd ed., 1779.
7. Mersey & Irwell Navigation Minute Book, 4 September 1799.
8. *Billings's Liverpool Advertiser*, 25 July 1804.
9. Proceedings of the House of Commons committee on the Liverpool & Manchester Railway Bill, 1825.
10. *Dean's Manchester & Salford Directory for 1808 and 1809*.
11. Mersey & Irwell Navigation Minute Book, 2 June 1813.
12. Ibid., 6 August 1806.
13. Pigot's *Manchester & Salford Directory*, 1813.
14. 35 Geo III *c.* 44.
15. Thomas Moore Papers (Lancashire C.R.O., DP 175).
16. Scholes, *Directory of Manchester*, 1794, 1797 eds.
17. H. Philip Spratt, *The Birth of the Steamboat*, 1958.
18. Mersey & Irwell Navigation Minute Book, 5 November 1794.
19. Tomlinson, 'Salford Activities', op. cit.
20. Spratt, *Steamboat*, op. cit.
21. Dean's *Manchester & Salford Directory for 1808 and 1809*.
22. Sir George Head, *A Home Tour through the Manufacturing Districts of England in the Summer of 1835*, 1836 (rpt. 1968) Chapter I.
23. *Gore's Liverpool Advertiser*, 18 January 1816.
24. *Manchester & Salford Directory*, 1802.
25. *Pigot & Dean's Manchester Directory*, 1824–5.
26. Mersey & Irwell Navigation Minute Book, 22 September 1815.

27. Ibid., 25 September 1815.
28. F. C. Mather, 'The Duke of Bridgewater's Trustees and the Coming of the Railways', *Trans. Royal Historical Soc.*, 1964.
29. *Derby Mercury*, 26 January 1809.
30. Mersey & Irwell Navigation Minute Book, 2 November 1808.
31. *Manchester Mercury*, 4 September 1810.
32. Mersey & Irwell Navigation Minute Book, 25 August 1813.
33. Ibid., 29 October 1823.
34. For a description of the Bridgewater and Mersey & Irwell establishments at Runcorn in 1835, see Head, *A Home Tour*, Chapter I, op. cit.
35. Stockport P.L., PDC/38 and 39.
36. For the Macclesfield Canal, see Charles Hadfield, *The Canals of the West Midlands*, 2nd ed., 1969.
37. All are taken from the Proceedings of the House of Commons Committee on the Liverpool & Manchester Railway Bill, 1825.

Notes to Chapter V

1. Mersey & Irwell Navigation Minute Book, 6 November 1822.
2. Ibid., 4 August, 6 October 1824.
3. *Proceedings* of the House of Commons Committee on the Liverpool & Manchester Railway Bill, 1825.
4. For instance, when the Chester Canal Bill was in Parliament in 1771, Northwich merchants suggested a canal from the Dee to the Mersey & Irwell below Ince. Again, a line from below Chester to Frodsham on the Weaver is shown on a Rochdale Canal map of *c.* 1792.
5. Plans, National Library of Scotland, MSS 5876/8–13.
6. *John Bull*, 6 February 1825.
7. There are many newspaper references during February 1825.
8. *Manchester & Dee Ship Canal. Report of William Chapman Esq.*, 1825 (Institution of Civil Engineers Library).
9. *Manchester Ship Canal. Mr Dumbell's Observations relative to making Manchester and Warrington into Sea Ports*, 2nd ed., 1826. (I.C.E. Library.)
10. For this scheme, see E. Cuthbert Woods, 'The Intended Ship Canal', *Transactions of the Liverpool Nautical Research Society*, Vol. IX, 1955–61, p. 74.
11. *Derby Mercury*, 30 August 1837, quoting the *Manchester Times*.
12. MS *Reports* of the Rennies (I.C.E. Library).
13. *Manchester Ship Canal*, op. cit.
14. *Proceedings* of the House of Commons Committee on the Liverpool & Manchester Railway Bill, 1825.
15. Op. cit.
16. Much has been written on the line, A short account is G. O. Holt's *A Short History of the Liverpool and Manchester Railway*, Railway & Canal Historical Society, 1965. Its early years are described in Robert E. Carlson, *The Liverpool & Manchester Railway Project, 1821–31*, 1969.
17. J. Sandars, *A Letter on the Subject of the projected Rail Road between Liverpool and Manchester*, 3rd ed., 1825.
18. Owen Ashmore, *The Industrial Archaeology of Lancashire*, 1969, p. 23.
19. See also F. C. Mather, *After the Canal Duke*, 1970, Chapter I.
20. Ibid.
21. Mersey & Irwell Navigation Minute Book, 7 January 1825.
22. Ibid., 1 June 1825.
23. See Charles Hadfield, *The Canals of the West Midlands*, 2nd ed., 1969.
24. We are indebted to F. C. Mather's, 'The Duke of Bridgewater's Trustees and the Coming of the Railways', *Trans. Royal Historical Society*, 1964, for our

O*

material about Lord Stafford. For a fuller account, see Mather, *After the Canal Duke*, Chapter II.

25. Mather, *After the Canal Duke*, Chapter III.
26. Mersey & Irwell Navigation Minute Book, 28 December 1825.
27. Ibid., 4 January 1826.
28. Ibid., 13 September 1826.
29. Thomas Jevons, *An Attempt to investigate the Cause of the late extraordinary changes in the bed of the River Mersey*, 1828, (I.C.E. Library).
30. Mersey & Irwell Navigation Minute Book, 3 October 1831.
31. Mather, *After the Canal Duke*, Chapter III.
32. Mersey & Irwell Navigation Minute Book, 13 October 1813.
33. Ibid., Liverpool Committee, 17 February 1831.
34. Mersey & Irwell Navigation Minute Book, 4 May 1831.
35. Ibid.
36. For much material in the following account, we are indebted to Mather, 'The Duke of Bridgewater's Trustees', op. cit.
37. Mather, *After the Canal Duke*, Chapter III.
38. Mersey & Irwell Navigation Minute Book, 3 October 1832.
39. Ibid., 4 February 1835.
40. Passenger and tonnage figures are from Mather, *After the Canal Duke*, Chapter III.
41. Mersey & Irwell Navigation Minute Book, 4 November 1835.
42. Ibid., 5 September 1836.
43. Pigot & Slater's *Manchester Directory*, 1841.
44. Slater's *Manchester Directory*, 1845.
45. J. Corbett, *The River Irwell*, 1907.
46. Many details of Mersey & Irwell and Bridgewater packet services can be learned from local directories. For descriptions of journeys by both, and also by the Leeds & Liverpool's Manchester–Liverpool service, see Sir George Head. *A Home Tour through the Manufacturing Districts of England in the Summer of 1835*, 1836 (rept. 1968), Chapter I.
47. For more information about Fereday Smith, see Mather, *After the Canal Duke*.
48. B. W. Clapp, *John Owens, Manchester Merchant*, 1965, pp. 155ff.
49. *The Herald of Improvement, or Manchester as it ought to be*, No 1, April 1841, (Manchester Central Library, M/CR, f.1841/5).
50. Report of conversazione, 28 January 1841, at Manchester, 'On the Improvement of the Mersey and Irwell Navigation'.
51. See Charles Hadfield, *The Canals of the West Midlands*, pp. 212–13.
52. Mather, *After the Canal Duke*, Chapter VII.
53. Mersey & Irwell Navigation Minute Book, 5 February 1840.
54. Manchester & Leeds Railway Minute Book, 26 October 1840.
55. Mersey & Irwell Navigation Minute Book, 3 June 1840.
56. Manchester & Leeds Railway Minute Book, 17 May 1841.
57. Mather, *After the Canal Duke*, Chapter VII.
58. Mersey & Irwell Navigation Minute Book, 8 February 1842.
59. Ibid., 18 December 1843.
60. Information Mr F. C. Mather has given from the Loch-Egerton papers.
61. Statement on the part of the Bridgewater Trustees, ND (*c*. 1850), Manchester Ship Canal (Bridgewater Dept) Records.
62. Mather, *After the Canal Duke*, 1970, Chapter VI.
63. Manchester, Bolton & Bury Canal Minute Book, 26 November 1801.
64. Ibid., 28 July 1825.
65. Mersey & Irwell Navigation Minute Book, 16 June 1835 and preamble to the 1836 Act.
66. Ibid., 12 August 1841.
67. 6 & 7 Will IV *c*. 115.
68. For details of the canal's course and the position of the locks and pumping plant, see the O.S. plan of 1850.

69. 3 & 4 Vic *c.* 15.
70. Manchester & Salford Junction Canal, report of 30 April 1840, Mersey & Irwell Navigation Minute Book.
71. Mersey & Irwell Navigation Minute Book, 17 April 1841.
72. Ibid., 12 August 1841.

Notes to Chapter VI

1. *Gore's General Advertiser*, Liverpool, 3 May 1792.
2. Weaver Navigation Minute Book, 6 November 1788.
3. See Charles Hadfield, *The Canals of the West Midlands*, 2nd ed., 1969, p. 154.
4. 47 Geo III *c.* 83.
5. Weaver Navigation Minute Book, 24 August 1807.
6. See *The Canals of the West Midlands*, p. 181.
7. Weaver Navigation Minute Book, 29–30 June 1842.
8. 6 Geo IV *c.* 29.
9. F. C. Mather, *After the Canal Duke*, 1970, Chapter III.
10. 3 & 4 Vic *c.* 124.
11. Weaver Navigation Minute Book, 6 November 1848.
12. H. Philip Spratt, *The Birth of the Steamboat*, 1958, p. 57.
13. T. C. Barker, 'The Sankey Navigation', *Trans. Lancs & Cheshire Antiq. Soc.*, 1948.
14. Proceedings of the House of Commons Committee on the Liverpool & Manchester Railway Bill, 1825.
15. 11 Geo IV *c.* 61.
16. JHC, 8 December 1819, 11, 16, 19 May 1820.
17. Mersey & Irwell Navigation Minute Book, 2 March 1831 (recording Liverpool sub-committee minutes of 17 February).
18. Quoted by Barker and Harris, *A Merseyside Town*, op. cit., pp. 195–6. See the whole Chapter XV, 'The Merseyside Coal Trade, 1830–1845'.
19. 11 Geo IV & 1 Will IV *c.* 50.
20. St Helens & Runcorn Gap Railway Minute Book, 25 July 1834.
21. *Railway Times*, 24 February 1838.
22. Ibid., 15 January 1842.
23. *Plan and Section of an intended Branch from the Sankey Canal to the River Mersey near Warrington Bridge, 1844.* (Warrington P.L.)
24. St Helens & Runcorn Gap Railway Minute Book, 11 January 1844.
25. 8 & 9 Vic *c.* 117, 21 July 1845.

Notes to Chapter VII

1. 34 Geo III *c.* 94.
2. J. Phillips, *A General History of Inland Navigation*, 1805, 5th ed., p. 587.
3. MS, 'Statistical History of the Leeds & Liverpool Canal', compiled by Law Clerk *c.* 1898 (BTHR).
4. Land was actually purchased, but the agreement with the Lancaster removed the immediate need.
5. Benj. Blower, *The Mersey, Ancient & Modern*, 1878.
6. 'Statistical History', op. cit.
7. 59 Geo III *c.* 105.
8. Leeds & Liverpool Canal Committee Minute Book, 20 December 1820, authorizes the branch to open 'immediately'.
9. The figures are from E. Baines, *Lancashire*, 1824 ed., except for Burnley 1811–51 which are from W. Bennett, *History of Burnley*, 1948.

10. 'Statistical History', op. cit.
11. Leeds & Liverpool Canal General Assembly Minute Book, 16 September 1814.
12. See L. Basnett, 'The First Public Railway in Lancashire', *Trans. Lancs & Cheshire Antiq. Soc.*, Vol. LXII, 1950–1.
13. Basnett, op. cit.
14. Copies of Liverpool & Manchester Railway Minutes, 30 September 1833 (BTHR).
15. Ibid., 17 February 1834.
16. Ibid., 12 November 1838.
17. Leeds & Liverpool Canal Committee Minute Book, 20 September 1844.
18. Fletcher reported that the lock would be ready before 1 October. Ibid., 18 September 1845.
19. 'Statistical History', op. cit.
20. Ibid.
21. Thomas Baines, *Yorkshire Past & Present*, 1873.
22. Leeds & Liverpool Canal timetable, 28 March 1814, Moore papers (Lancashire C.R.O.).
23. Ibid., May 1827, Moore papers (loc. cit.).
24. Baines, *Lancashire*, op. cit.
25. Leeds & Liverpool Canal Committee Minute Book, 16 September 1826.
26. Ibid., 12 April 1844.
27. Reprinted in *The Times*, 7 November 1826.
28. Leeds & Liverpool Canal Committee Minute Book, 12 April 1832.
29. For details see B. Baxter, *Stone Blocks & Iron Rails*, 1966, and Owen Ashmore, *The Industrial Archaeology of Lancashire*, 1969.
30. Ordanance Survey 6 in plan, 1845 (Lancashire C.R.O.).
31. Ashmore, *Lancashire*, op. cit.
32. Leeds & Liverpool Canal Committee Minute Book, 19 September 1835, refers to the widening of the entrance of the tunnel.
33. It is shown on the 1952 1-inch and 1953 2½-inch Ordnance Survey maps.
34. Baxter, op. cit.
35. T. R. Roberts, 'Bradford Waterways' Rise & Fall', *Journal*, Bradford Textile Society, 1962–3.

Notes to Chapter VIII

1. These and following details of the Port of Lancaster are taken from M. M. Schofield, *Outlines of an Economic History of Lancaster, 1680 to 1860*, 1951.
2. Anon., *A Cursory View of the proposed Canal from Kendal, to the Duke of Bridgewater's Canal*, N.D. but probably *c.* 1769.
3. Broadsheet, October 1771 (Lancaster Library).
4. J. F. Curwen, 'The Lancaster Canal', *Trans. Cumberland & Westmorland Antiq. & Arch. Soc.*, XVII (NS), 1917.
5. See Curwen, op. cit., and Whitworth's plan of 1772 (BTHR).
6. Report to Lancaster Canal Committee by Samuel Gregson, 20 January 1792 (Lancaster Library).
7. Receipt for subscription of 1 guinea 'towards a survey &c. for an Intended Canal from Ingleton and Burton to the River Lune at or near Lancaster' (Lancaster Library).
8. J. Holt, *General View of the Agriculture of the County Palatine of Lancaster*, 1794 ed.
9. Letter, John Jenkinson to Lord George Cavendish, 2 December 1787 (Cavendish papers, Lancs C.R.O.).
10. Holt, *Agriculture of Lancaster*, op. cit.

11. Anon., *Thoughts on the present design of making a Navigable Canal from the vicinity of Kendal to join some of the Canals in the South Parts of Lancashire, by way of Lancaster*, 1791 (Levens MSS, Westmorland C.R.O.).

12. *Plan of the proposed Lancaster Canal from Kirkby Kendal in the County of Westmorland to West Houghton in the County Palatine of Lancaster; surveyed in the years 1791 and 1792 by John Rennie, Engineer* (BTHR).

13. Opened 1764; Paul N. Wilson, 'The Gunpowder Mills of Westmorland and Furness', *Trans. Newcomen Society*, XXXVI, 1963–4.

14. 32 Geo III *c.* 101.

15. 33 Geo III *c.* 107.

16. Lancaster Canal Committee Report to General Meeting, 20 July 1793.

17. 36 Geo III *c.* 97.

18. Letter from J. Rennie to S. Gregson, 13 November 1795 (BTHR).

19. Lancaster Canal Committee Report to General Meeting, 7 July 1795.

20. Lancaster Canal Committee Minute Book, 6 October 1795.

21. Ibid., 3 March 1795.

22. Balance Sheet December 1798, in Curwen, op. cit.

23. Ibid.

24. *Thoughts on the present Design*, op. cit.

25. Owen Ashmore, *The Industrial Archaeology of Lancashire*, 1969.

26. Printed report and plan, 1 November 1799 (BTHR).

27. 40 Geo III *c.* 57.

28. *Mr. Monk's Plan for a Junction of the Lancaster with the Leeds and Liverpool Canals*, printed with copy of Haliburton's letter, 25 February 1800 (Crewdson papers, Westmorland C.R.O.).

29. Jessop was an experienced engineer who had built a number of canals, particularly in the Midlands and the North East, and was at this time completing the Rochdale Canal. He was partner in Butterley Ironworks with Benjamin Outram, and had practical experience of building tramroads. See Charles Hadfield, *The Canals of the East Midlands*, 2nd ed., 1970, *The Canals of the West Midlands*, 2nd ed., 1969.

30. Report of Lancaster Canal Committee to General Meeting, 7 July 1801.

31. The coloured originals are at BTHR, and photocopies of the first two also at Lancs C.R.O.

32. Committee Report, 7 July 1801, op. cit.

33. For a detailed account of the tramroad, see Gordon Biddle, 'The Lancaster Canal Tramroad', *Journal* of the Railway & Canal Hist. Soc., Vol. IX, No 5, p. 88.

34. Lancaster Canal Letter Book, Gregson to Committee, 19 January 1904 (BTHR).

35. *A Plan of the Intended Reservoirs and Leaders for supplying the Lancaster Canal Navigation with Water from the River Keer, by William Cartwright, Engineer, 1800* (Crewdson papers, Westmorland C.R.O.) and a drawing of the pumping arrangements, 1797 (Miscellaneous Plans, BTHR).

36. Miscellaneous Plans, 11 December 1802 (BTHR).

37. 47 Geo III *c.* 113.

38. Lancaster Canal Meetings Minute Book, Report of Special Committee, 7 August 1812.

39. Lancaster Canal Committee Minute Book, 27 March 1818. See also Paul N. Wilson, 'Canal Head, Kendal', *Trans. Cumberland and Westmorland Antiq. & Arch. Soc.*, LXVIII (N.S.), 1968, for a full account of the history of the canal head.

40. Wilson, 'Canal Head, Kendal', op. cit.

41. C. Nicholson, *The Annals of Kendal*, 2nd ed., 1861.

42. Broadsheet reprinted from *Preston Chronicle*, 13 March 1819 (BTHR).

43. 59 Geo III *c.* 64.

44. Schofield, *Economic History of Lancaster*, op. cit.

45. Handbill, 1 May 1820 (Westmorland C.R.O.).

46. *A Historiette of the Lancaster Canal,* believed to be written by R. C. Harker ((LNWR Canal Agent at Lancaster, 1875–1906) or T. Kittson, or both (Lancaster Library).
47. Schofield, *Economic History of Lancaster,* op. cit.
48. Report by B. P. Gregson to Committee, 27 October 1831.
49. T. W. T. McIntyre, 'The Port of Milnthorpe', *Trans. Cumberland & Westmorland Antiq. Soc.,* NS, XXXVI, 1936.
50. Baines' *Lancashire,* 1824.
51. J. Barron, *History of the Ribble Navigation,* 1938.
52. Schofield, op. cit., quoting *The Lancaster Gazette,* 27 May 1826, and *Lancaster Records, 1801–1850,* (entry dated 13 August 1827) respectively. B. P. Gregson's Report to the canal committee, 30 August 1827, also mentions the latter event.
53. Schofield, *Economic History of Lancaster,* op. cit.
54. *Historiette,* op. cit.
55. Baines, *Lancashire,* op. cit.
56. Printed pamphlet, 25 October 1827 (Lancs C.R.O.).
57. Report by B. P. Gregson to Lancaster Canal Committee, 20 July 1830.
58. Ibid., 25 November 1830.
59. Bolton & Preston Railway Minute Book, 31 January 1839.
60. Ibid., 3 January 1850.
61. For a full history see M. D. Greville & G. O. Holt, *The Lancaster & Preston Junction Railway,* 1961, from which part of this account is taken.
62. Ibid.
63. J. Barron, *History of the Ribble Navigation,* 1938.
64. Report to the committee by Thomas Fletcher, Engineer, 29 August 1834 (Crewdson Papers, Westmorland C.R.O.).
65. *Preston Chronicle,* 1 November 1834.
66. Barron, *Ribble Navigation,* op. cit.
67. From 1838, this account is based on Barron, *Ribble Navigation,* op. cit.
68. Daniel Defoe, *A Tour through England and Wales,* 1724–7 (Everyman ed.), Vol. II, p. 274.
69. 'Survey of the North West Coast of England, in August 1746', *The Gentlemen's Magazine,* January 1748.
70. 'Description of the Cumberland Coast, a new Survey', ibid., July 1748.
71. A. Fell, *The Iron Industry of Furness & District,* 1908.
72. J. D. Marshall, *Furness & the Industrial Revolution,* 1958.
73. Fell, *Iron Industry,* op. cit., quoting the lease to the Backbarrow Co.
74' Ibid., quoting letter from Backbarrow.
75. Ibid.
76. Ibid., also Baines' *Lancashire,* 1824.
77. Paul N. Wilson, 'The Gunpowder Mills of Westmorland & Furness', *Trans. Newcomen Society,* XXXVI, 1963–4.
78. Marshall, *Furness,* op. cit.
79. Fell, *Iron Industry,* op. cit.
80. Ibid.
81. Ibid., quoting a lease of 1729.
82. H. W. Dickinson, *John Wilkinson, Ironmaster,* 1914, quoting Stockdale, below.
83. J. Stockdale, *Annales Caermoelenses, or Annals of Cartmel,* 1872.
84. Dickinson, *John Wilkinson,* op. cit.
85. By Dr J. D. Marshall of Lancaster University.
86. Stockdale, *Cartmel,* op. cit.
87. Marshall, *Furness,* op. cit.
88. H. F. Birkett, *The Story of Ulverston,* 1949.
89. Marshall, *Furness,* op. cit., suggests that they led to the promotion of the Ulverston Canal; the early history can only be deduced at present, owing to lack of known records.
90. J. Park, *Some Ulverston Records,* 1932: MSS William Burnthwaite.
91. Ibid.

92. 33 Geo III *c.* 105.
93. Lancaster Canal Committee Minute Book, 21 September 1792 (BTHR).
94. Ibid.
95. Park, *Ulverston Records*, op. cit.
96. Baines, *Lancashire*, op. cit.
97. Park, *Ulverston Records*, op. cit.
98. *Jackson's Ulverston Almanac*, 1852.
99. *Ulverston Canal Sundry Disbursements Book*, June 1793–April 1796, (BTHR) abstracts of figures which appear to be directly attributable amount to £9,218 8s 5d (£9,218·42).
100. Marshall, *Furness*, op. cit.
101. *Jackson's Almanac*, op. cit.
102. Park, *Ulverston Records*, op. cit.
103. Ibid.
104. *Jackson's Almanac*, op. cit.
105. Marshall, *Furness*, op. cit.
106. W. White, *Furness Folk and Fact*, 1930.
107. Marshall, *Furness*, op. cit.
108. *Jackson's Almanac*, op. cit.
109. White, *Furness Folk*, op. cit.
110. Park, *Ulverston Records*, op. cit. The final subscribed capital is not stated and does not appear to have been noted in other records.
111. Ulverston Canal Minute Book. In later years committee members are not always given, and the minutes end abruptly in September 1850.
112. *Jackson's Almanac*, op. cit.
113. Ulverston Canal Minute Book, 22 June 1840.
114. M. Andrews, 'The Origins of the Furness Railway', *Journal* of the Railway & Canal Hist. Soc., XI, 4, October 1965.
115. White, *Furness Folk*, op. cit.

INDEX TO VOLUME I

The principal references to canals and river navigations are indicated in bold type